NEW BEDFORD MANSIONS

NEW BEDFORD MANSIONS

Historic Tales of County Street

PEGGI MEDEIROS

THE History PRESS

Published by The History Press
Charleston, SC 29403
www.historypress.net

Front bottom cover: The Rotch Jones Duff House at night. Photographer Tim Sylvia. Courtesy of the Rotch Jones, Duff House & Garden Museum. *Back cover*: Portrait of James Arnold. Courtesy the Trustees of the New Bedford Free Public Library.

First published 2015

Manufactured in the United States

ISBN 978.1.62619.791.6

Library of Congress Control Number: 2015934348

Notice: The information in this book is true and complete to the best of our knowledge. It is offered without guarantee on the part of the author or The History Press. The author and The History Press disclaim all liability in connection with the use of this book.

For Alayna Marie Pavao,
my great-niece and the future.

Contents

Acknowledgements

New Bedford Mansions: Historic Tales of County Street would not have been possible without the photographs taken for the Historic American Buildings Survey at the Library of Congress and the Library of Congress Prints & Photographs Division. It truly is a national treasure. I offer many thanks to and for the following.

The city of New Bedford's greatest treasures, including the New Bedford Free Public Library; the New Bedford Whaling Museum (Old Dartmouth Historical Society); Rachel Howland's Association for the Relief of Aged Women, still caring for the lost and desperate; the Rotch Jones Duff House and Garden Museum; and the Wamsutta Club in the James Arnold Mansion.

My fellow scholars who have shared their love of New Bedford unreservedly. Their special genius gave me encouragement, friendship and support. Joan Barney, Joe Booth, Sally Bullard, P.J. Carroll, Michael Dyer, Carole Foster, Chuck Hauck, David Harrington, Llewellyn Howland III, Richard C. Kugler, Judith Lund, Bob Maker, Philip Marshall, Dan Perry and Elsie and Tony Souza.

The late, forever-to-be-missed David B. Boyce, an awe-inspiring critic, and Christopher Gillespie, a truly great preservation architect. I wish they had seen this book.

My friends Kate Corkum, Diane Gilbert, Janice Hodgson and Arthur Motta Jr. They contributed photographs, cheered me up and pushed me through the book. I cherish your friendship.

My friends and editors at the *New Bedford Standard Times*: Dave Cuddy, Susan Pawlak Seaman, Jack Spillane, Andy Tomolonis and Steve Urbon. All of you helped give me a voice.

My first true friends, Virginia Christensen, Amy Meyer and Bonny Saulnier—a long way from Dartmouth High School and still together.

Most of all, my family: Nancy and Denis Souliere, Melissa and Sue Callis, Melissa and Ryan Brynes, Gabby and Elliott Brynes, Louis and Dinorah Martin, Mary Ann and Larry Nobrega, Fran Ferro and finally Naomi, my small spoiled cat.

Introduction

The City of Light

On January 3, 1841, Herman Melville sailed out on the *Acushnet* on the whaling trip that would, ten years later, yield him the material for *Moby Dick*. In 1841, New Bedford's "brave houses and flowery gardens" described in his opening chapters were flourishing.

Lady Emmeline Stuart-Wortley, in her 1851 best-selling *Travels in the United States*, mentions "a kind invitation from Mrs. Joseph Grinnell to visit them at New Bedford. That is called the City of Palaces from the beautiful buildings it contains. It is also the great whaling metropolis of the North."

President John Quincy Adams was at home in New Bedford and visited in 1841 and 1843. His son, Charles Francis Adams, wrote in 1843 of the Arnold Mansion, "Their house was then graceful and comfortable, and furnished with elegance and at great cost. It is now embellished with many articles of exquisite luxury from Italy, so that it is like a second princely palace."

What made New Bedford this city of palaces? The answer is fortunes made from whaling. New Bedford, Massachusetts, is a city built by the owners of its great whaling houses. Ships from the Houses of Rotch, Morgan and Howland conducted a vastly lucrative trade that took them from the Arctic to the Antarctic and from the Sea of Japan to the coasts of Patagonia.

By 1841, New Bedford had long overtaken Nantucket as the whaling capital of the world. The Rotch, Rodman, Morgan and Howland families had built multinational companies that were operating across the world. From the Arctic to New Zealand, New Bedford ships were there. The great wealth from oil, bone and ambergris made New Bedford at one point the richest city per capita in the world. Sperm whales, right whales and bowhead whales provided the riches that raised granite and brick mansions along County Street.

New Bedford whaling magnates found the nation's finest architects—Russell Warren, Alexander Jackson Davis, Robert Sterns Peabody and Robert Mills—to design their mansions that are now National Historic Landmarks. Commercial buildings constructed in the early nineteenth century close to the waterfront ships, candle factories and counting houses created what in 1996 became the New Bedford Whaling National Historical Park. Riches from creating light gave New Bedford great gardens that were considered horticultural masterpieces and, in two cases, city parks: Hazelwood and Brooklawn.

Members of the Society of Friends, "Children of the Light," founded the whaling houses. Their strong principles made New Bedford a city of abolitionists. It was a safe place where William Lloyd Garrison and Wendell Phillips were trusted and welcome. Frederick Douglass came out of slavery to New Bedford and began his work here. Harriet Tubman received shelter here.

Iconic American writers found like minds in New Bedford. Ralph Waldo Emerson stayed with James and Sarah Arnold. Mary Rotch was a close and influential friend of both Emerson and Margaret Fuller, who called her "Aunt Mary." Henry David Thoreau stayed with Daniel Ricketson in his shanty and had an iconic daguerreotype taken at Bierstadt Brothers. Together, Thoreau and Ricketson hatched a plot to turn Louisa May Alcott's eccentric father, Bronson, into a lecturer. Alcott lectured at the Arnold and Robeson Mansions, launching a career that finally fed his family.

John James Audubon, desperate for financial support, turned to New Bedford. His diary brings the city alive. James Arnold was the seventy-fourth of eighty-one American subscribers to Audubon's *Birds of America*, often known as the "Double Elephant Folio." His copy was left to the New Bedford Free Public Library.

Albert Bierstadt and his family came to New Bedford. The career of one of America's great nineteenth-century painters began here. New Bedford families financed his apprenticeship in Germany and Italy. They hung his paintings in their drawing rooms. His sister, Eliza, was perhaps the first female art dealer. His brothers, Charles and Edward, began their careers as photographers with magical images of then new public buildings. New Bedford's other nineteenth-century artists include William Bradford, Charles Henry Gifford, Robert Swan Gifford and Albert Pinkham Ryder. Although their paintings are centerpieces at New York's Metropolitan Museum of Art, their best work is in the New Bedford Whaling Museum and the New Bedford Free Public Library.

While still a Congressman, an unknown young Abraham Lincoln was a guest at Joseph Grinnell's home. He spoke to crowds, who received their first glimpse of the man who would save the country. Herman Melville immortalized New Bedford in *Moby Dick*. His sister and brother-in-law lived on Madison Street.

Nineteenth-century New Bedford was a place of now unimaginable wealth, intellectual ferment and artistic treasures. It was a city of secrets that often became very public scandals that destroyed lives and broke families. This is a biography of that New Bedford.

Chapter 1

The Houses of Rotch

Seeking to Own the World

It is ironic that William Rotch Jr. has become the best known of the Rotches. He spent his life in the shadow of his far more famous father, William Rotch Sr., and his grandfather Joseph, who founded the House of Rotch. Joseph was the first to reach New Bedford. Through the vision and hard business sense of Joseph and William Rotch Sr., they became an international family as comfortable in Paris and London as in the New Bedford they largely built.

Thinking far ahead, Joseph Rotch left Nantucket in 1765 and made a ten-acre purchase of prime land in New Bedford. In 1767, he built the first ship in what was then Bedford and named it the *Dartmouth*. The ship was one of the three Boston Tea Party ships and drew the family into American history, like it or not.

On Nantucket, Joseph Rotch and William Sr. established what became an international whaling empire. The Nantucket Rotches did business with Aaron Lopez of Newport, a Portuguese Jew who established his own massive firm that whaled, processed oil and bone and traded slaves. The Rotches learned Lopez's secrets for producing spermaceti candles and established a monopoly on them that even the great John Hancock couldn't break.

During the Revolution, Nantucket attempted to stay neutral. William Rotch Sr. continued his profitable whale fishery, often with Aaron Lopez sending whaling ships to the Falklands Islands. He opened diplomatic relations for the island with both the British and the Continental Congress. This brought him dislike, suspicion and two trials for treason from the

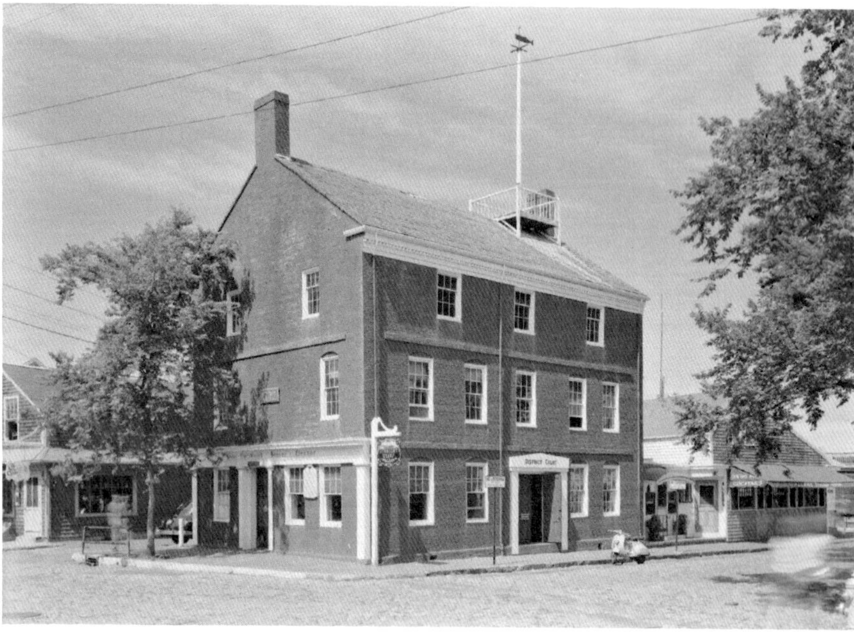

The Rotches begin. William Rotch Sr.'s warehouse on Nantucket Island. *Library of Congress, Historic American Buildings Survey.*

American side. As his descendant John Morgan Bullard explained in *The Rotches*, "Though he thought of himself as a man of peace, he went out of his way to stir up trouble if his conscience so demanded, and it all too often did. He was a strong man, and strong men usually make enemies."

When the war ended, William Sr. left Nantucket. William Rotch Jr. stayed to administer the House of Rotch. British ports were closed to American ships, and Europe seemed a good place for his whale fishery. He took the family firm to Dunkirk, France, and then to England. He faced down the French Assembly and brought his wife and daughter safely out of France during their far more dangerous and bloody revolution. The family left France two days before Louis IV went to the guillotine in 1793. William Rotch Sr. was the legend.

William Rotch Jr. became the head of family and marked his adopted city forever. He was the builder of two New Bedford mansions—the first in the New Bedford Whaling National Historical Park and a second on a full city block on County Street. Both houses are open to the public.

By 1791, the Rotches and their large extended family had relocated to New Bedford. In a few decades, they made New Bedford the whaling center

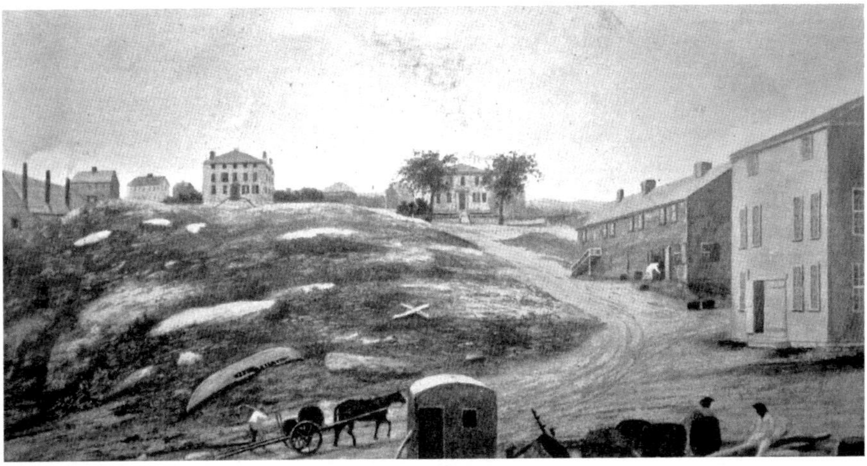

After the Revolution, the Rotch and Rodman families moved to New Bedford. The town of Bedford, 1790. *Collection of author. Courtesy of Arthur P. Motta.*

of the world. William Rotch Jr. was twenty-eight when he left Nantucket. In 1782, he had married Elizabeth Rodman, the wise and beautiful sister of his closest friend and business partner, Samuel Rodman. In a neat family exchange, Samuel married Elizabeth Rotch, William's older sister, and his brother, Thomas, married Charity Rodman. The Rotch Rodman marriages created a dynasty of hyphenated children, grandchildren and great-grandchildren. Affection proved very good for business.

Rotch immediately built a classic Federal home on North Water Street over the exact spot where Joseph Rotch's home had stood until being burned by the British in 1789. On January 15, 1791, William Rotch Jr. wrote from New Bedford a letter to his uncle, Francis, who remained in England:

> *I have also a House covered and now finishing upon the spot my grandfather's stood 15 feet back from the street, 46 Feet front & 40 feet back that in a few years I hope the desolation occasioned by the fire will be no more traced.*
>
> *The Town grows very fast, but being entirely dependent upon the spermaceti fishery, it is precarious. But I hope it will always find a support…We have three promising children Sarah 4½ years old, William 2, & Joseph the Infant.*

On May 22, 1790, he wrote, "I shall want a platform & steps, also two sets jambs Mantel Pieces & Hearths, which request thou would have made

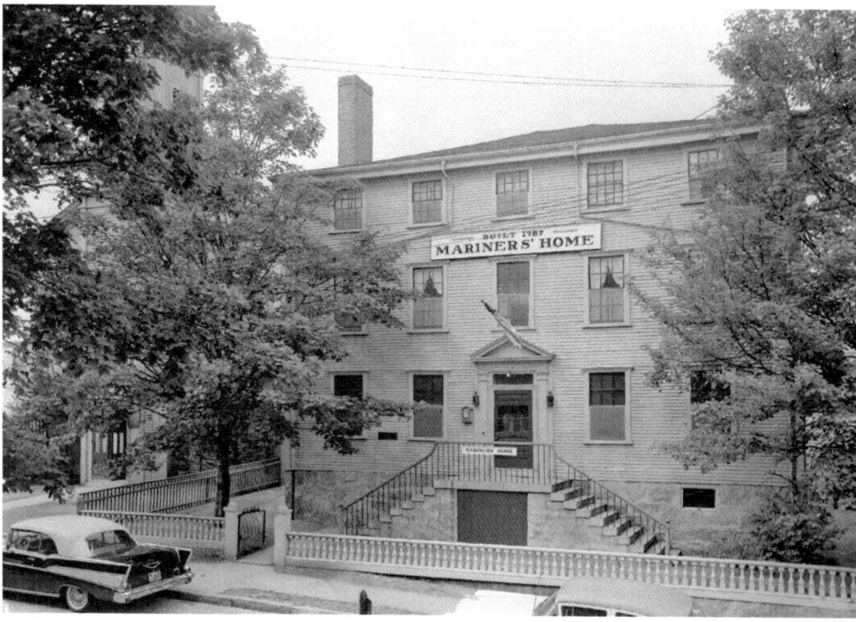

William Rotch Jr.'s first house, originally on North Water and William Streets. *Library of Congress, Historic American Buildings Survey. Ned Goode, photographer.*

in the best...I will either send thee the Candles or Cash—My Candles are of the best quality & of the best kind for the West India market." Rotch knew exactly what he wanted: "The steps to descend in front & on each end & connected all round those three sides." Visitors can still find those steps and platform. Inside he specified exact dimensions and style: "Mantle pieces—Fit them 40 inches long exclusive thickness of Jambs the Jambs to flare so as to agree with the front of 40 inches & the back 28 Inches."

A careful ledger keeper, he added a bit unhappily, "The prices thou sent me of the foregoing articles are higher than I expected or than I was informed of from Nantucket." By May 14, 1790, Rotch had turned to Joshua Eddy for a detail that would finally mark the house as his: "I herewith send thee a mold for a Chimney back, & request thou would have me Cast two backs as soon as may be. If thou has a neat Roman Alphabet I shall like to have this Motto put on them in a neat manner in one line viz: Nobilitas est unica virtus...But if it cannot be done well I had rather it was omitted."

Rotch specified that his marble be imported from Pennsylvania and arrive properly polished. He requested either white or chocolate marble and ring-handled closet fasteners. Finally, on November 24, 1791, he sent shipbuilder

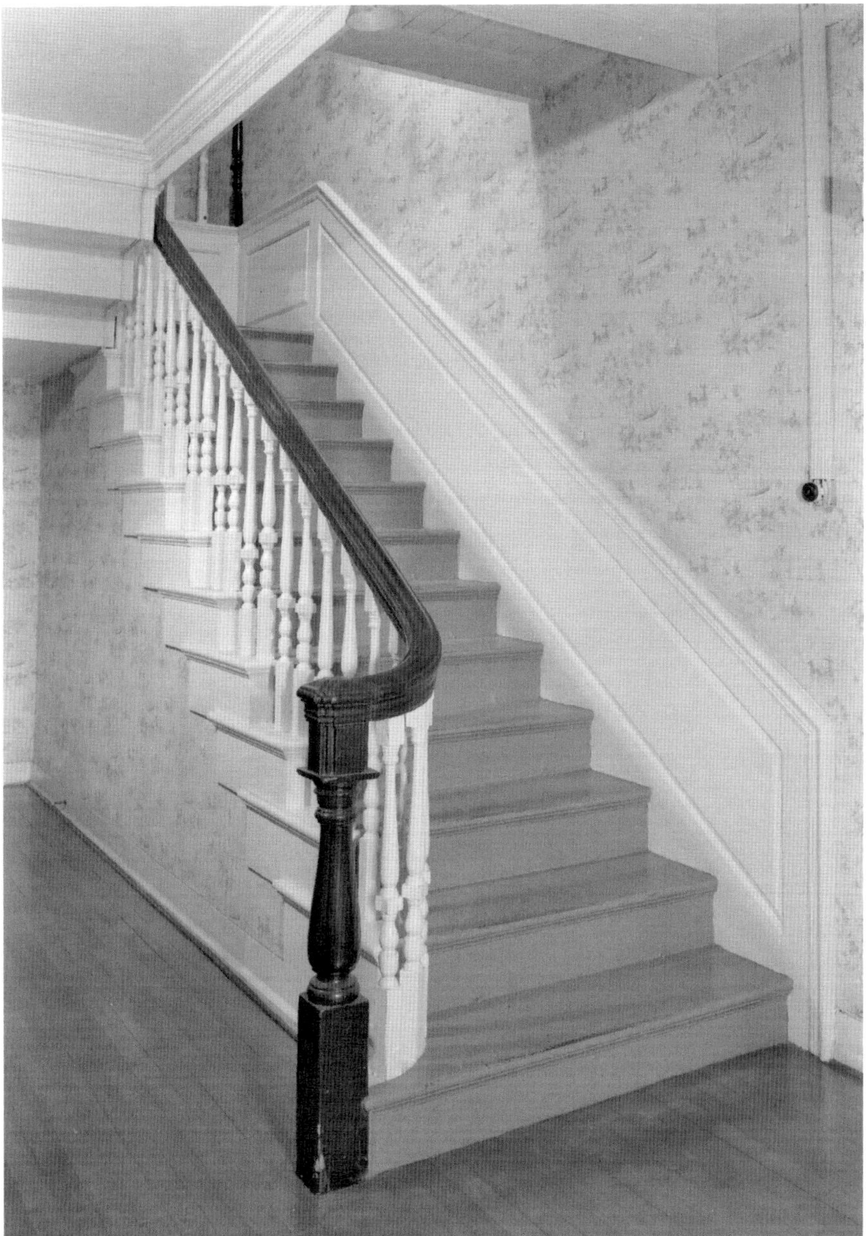

Front staircase, William Rotch Jr. House. The house is now the Mariner's Home. *Library of Congress Historic American Buildings Survey. Ned Goode, photographer.*

Zachariah Hillman to North Carolina for ship timber and a few last items for the house: "[A]lso Garden posts of Cedar & Joists for Sills & rails of my walk—also Cedar timber of large for 80 ps. 6 feet & 80—41/4 for window frames. Should any accident happen to thee send for Beetle if Cushing is not sufficient. If more help is want'g thou must hire it."

The finished house was an elegant compromise with Quaker doctrine, which stated in no uncertain terms that homes built by members of the Society should not be ostentatious or display wealth too openly. That ruling was further enforced by a tax on brick houses.

William Rotch Jr. cleverly circumvented both tax and doctrine by clapboarding the front façade of the house and using brick on the three other facades. It was originally painted a straw color. The house had four rooms on the ground floor, window seats in the formal parlor and very fine paneling that is still intact. With three stories, a central entrance with formal stairs and a balustrade at the roofline, it was the first of the great Rotch houses. It proved large enough for the growing family. Sarah, William and Joseph were joined in 1792 by Thomas and in 1793 by Mary. All of the children grew up in this house.

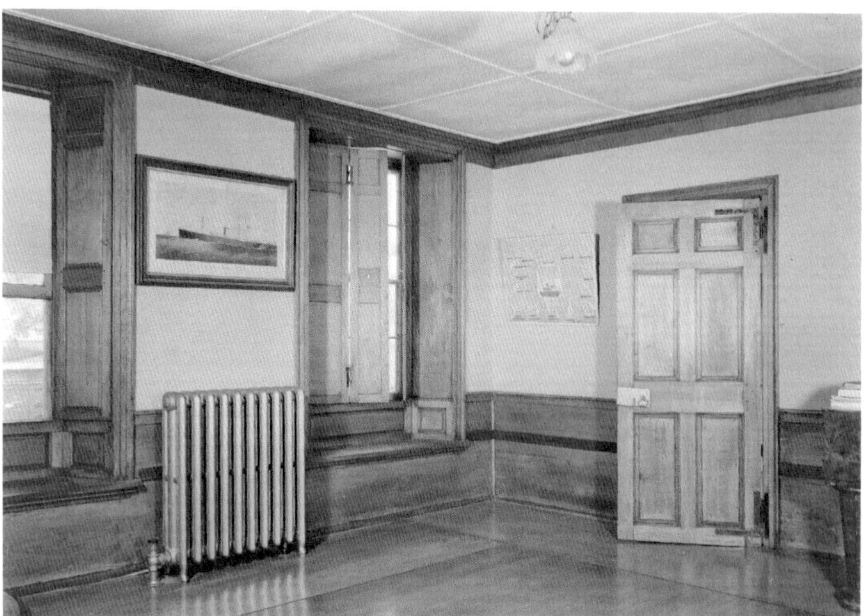

Northeast front room. Interior shutters are original. *Library of Congress, Historic American Buildings Survey. Ned Goode, photographer.*

Ship by ship, candle by candle, building lot by lot, the Rotch family grew very rich. In 1795, William's parents formally relocated to New Bedford and automatically became un-Quakerly royalty. In 1796, the Duc de la Rouchefoucald brought his carriage to William Rotch Sr.'s door.

By 1818, the family were considered noticeably grand. Young Anna Shoemaker visited the Hathaway family she would marry into and wrote home a letter that explained the growing view of the entire Rotch family: "We had a dinner not better, my dearest Richard, than many I've eat at thy hospitable board, not any better served or cooked and I began to think there is something in having a name as well as being wealthy; for every-one here looks up to them as if they were the princes of the land."

A precocious William Logan Fisher was sent from Philadelphia to apprentice with William Rotch Jr. He fell in love with and eventually married Mary Rodman. Years later, he described his courtship. His memoir was remarkably honest: "I was an extremely dull and stupid scholar, and the end of it all was that I learned little and that little was soon forgotten."

As a teenager, he was sent off to New Bedford. As an apprentice, he lived with the Rotch family as a quasi member of the family. He was expected to work. He also learned every corner of Bedford Village. Later, he remembered imported silver teapots and carpets being a wonder. He made friends, but there was always a line between them: "Such was the custom of the times, that I never knew what would now be called a tea party, nor was I ever invited to drink tea…even in a friendly way with these young people with whom almost as a matter of course I was expected to spend the evening."

Logan was invited to dinner with other members of the Rotch family but never received his own invitation. He sadly noted, "Yet I was on the most intimate footing with all the Rotch and Rodman families." Then Mary Rodman arrived, and Logan Fisher fell in love. It was 1796. The couple read improving books together. Under her influence, he read and read and made up for what he hadn't learned at school in Philadelphia. The young people were kept on short leashes, as he noted: "My master William Rotch wishes to have his house shut up at 10 o'clock, and I do not think that I was ever out a quarter of an hour after that time."

On November 25, 1802, Fisher and Mary Rodman married. He became a man of business: "I entered into commercial affairs, became part owner of several ships in the whale fishery, lived in a plain and unostentatious manner, kept my horse and chaise and had sufficient success in business to support my family."

New Bedford became a place that took gardens very seriously, and so did the young businessman. It was a way to forget ledgers and oil and candles. "I had one of the nicest gardens in that place, stocked with shrubbery, fruits and flowers."

Fisher suffered from mercury poisoning and an inability to use one arm. His health drove the family from New Bedford and back to Pennsylvania. There Mary Rodman Logan Fisher died in 1813, much too young, leaving a heartbroken husband and three children. Logan Fisher never forgot his years as a young Rotch apprentice.

Gaining any sense of how men and women actually lived in their time is often like trying to overhear whispered conversation in a locked room. Occasionally, a key turns up. In the case of New Bedford, there is Daniel Ricketson. He remembered and wrote and seems to have spent his life listening to other people's stories. In 1875, he looked back at 1825 New Bedford. Later, his children, Anna and Waldo, published his manuscript as *New Bedford of the Past*. It was a place a young boy could know as well as he knew his own face:

> *Every phase of human nature was to be seen; and New Bedford could then boast of its rare characters as well as now—men and women of those peculiarities which marked them from the rest. The shrewd man of business, the petty dealer, the miser and extortioner, as well as the philanthropic and open-handed; the pettifogger, the charlatan, as well as the grand jurist, counselor, and honorable and skillful physician, the calm dispenser of spiritual truths, and the ranter, the advocates of peace and those of war, the humorist, the practical joker (ever an abomination), as well as the dull and morose—these, and a great variety of other characters, were then seen, and stood out more prominently in a sparsely settled town than now.*

Unfortunately Ricketson does not name any names, yet he was extremely good at remembering and describing the rituals of 1825 New Bedford. Tea was the major daily social event, and Logan Fisher's exclusion really did place him in society as a family hanger-on. Ricketson spends a very long time describing the ritual. First he set the physical scene:

> *The domestic arrangements were far different from those of the present time. The usual fire was that of wood upon the open hearth, and only the houses of the wealthier had carpets; but curtains to the bed, now so generally discarded, were in general use, and truly ornamental, if not healthful were they, giving an air of comfort and coziness to the lodging-room.*

Ricketson sets the tea party in his parents' home. It most certainly was planned out in every detail:

> *The "east room" then was put in order, the bright Brussels carpets nicely swept, having first been sprinkled with wet tea leaves, the chairs, pier-tables, the great old-fashioned sofa, studded with brass-headed nails, the alabaster urns, and silver candlesticks, and snuffers with tray, dusted, an extra polish given to the high brass andirons, a great fire of oak and maple was kindled, blazing and crackling merrily, and the room nice and warm.*

Three o'clock was considered the proper time to arrive. Elderly members of the Society of Friends came first and were nested closest to the fire. By 4:00 p.m., everyone would have arrived:

> *In the meantime the tall spermaceti candles have been lighted, and with their soft light and that of the blazing wood fires, the rooms are brilliantly illuminated. On the tea table are candles duly arranged, the handsome urn of claret color and silver trimmings is in its place, and the fragrance of the tea and coffee pervades the room. The guests leave the parlor and cross the entry to the "keeping room," where they find my mother at her post. Nice short biscuit rolls, with quince marmalade and preserved plums, are succeeded by the usual variety of sponge and pound cake. The buzz of conversation is kept up with the clatter of cups and saucers. Questions are asked and answered, and the usual exclamations of surprise, and the hearty laugh, at times relieve the otherwise monotony of voices.*

Ricketson, who will turn up later as a major New Bedford historian and close friend of Henry David Thoreau, left a vivid description of Rotch:

> *"William Rotch, Jr.," as he always wrote his name, was a man of marked ability and dignity of manner. He always reminded me of the pictures of William Penn, to which his primitive dress in a good degree contributed. He was a large man, his height nearly six feet, and broad and stout in person. His countenance was less benign perhaps in expression than his father's, and his complexion florid. But he was a man of sterling integrity and worth, kind and hospitable, and though not perhaps generous from impulse was often so from principle.*

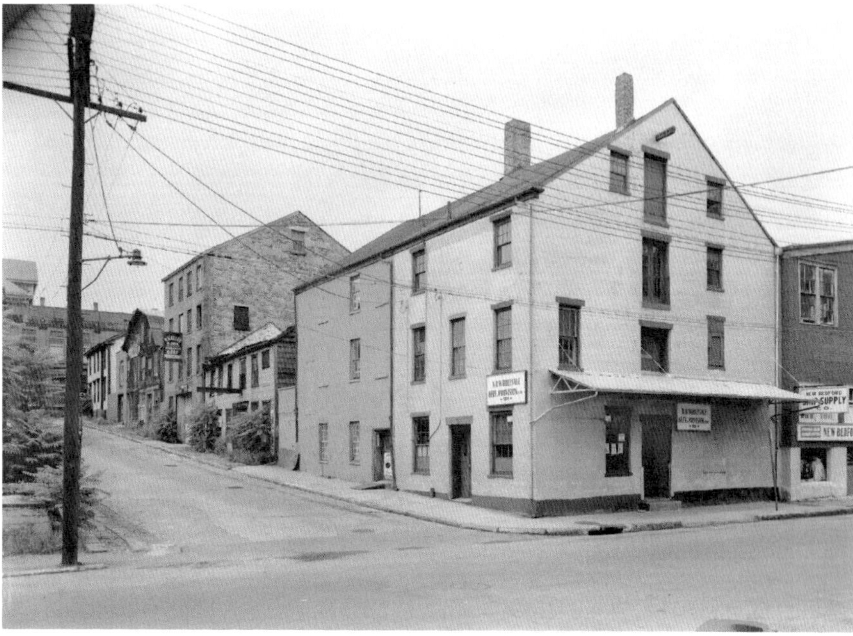

William Tallman Warehouse, 13 Centre Street, 1790. *Library of Congress, Historic American Buildings Survey. Ned Goode, photographer.*

Rotch's business grew. The house on the corner of North Water and William Street expanded with family members and then contracted as his daughter, Sarah, and sons married. Slowly the waterfront area became less and less a place to live. Candleworks were built and marine supply shops opened. There were ship smiths hammering out harpoons. Barrel makers were preparing casks to hold oil. It was a place for cold, hard business. It also smelled horribly. Gradually, Rotch's children moved up the hill to County Street to new homes. William Rotch Jr. stayed.

The year 1828 was not a joyous one for William Rotch Jr. On January 30, his wife, Elizabeth, died. On May 16, his father died at ninety-four, the most distinguished citizen in New Bedford. William Rotch Jr. had begun to be old at sixty-eight. He soon found himself a housekeeper for the house on Rotch's Hill. Lydia Scott was a childless widow who had been a family acquaintance for a number of years. Her father had been Job Scott, a great Quaker preacher. Within a year, the two were married, on April 25, 1829, in North Providence, Rhode Island, Lydia's former home. She was forty-six.

All of the family had known her for years, and yet the marriage seems not to have pleased the more conservative members of the family. Samuel

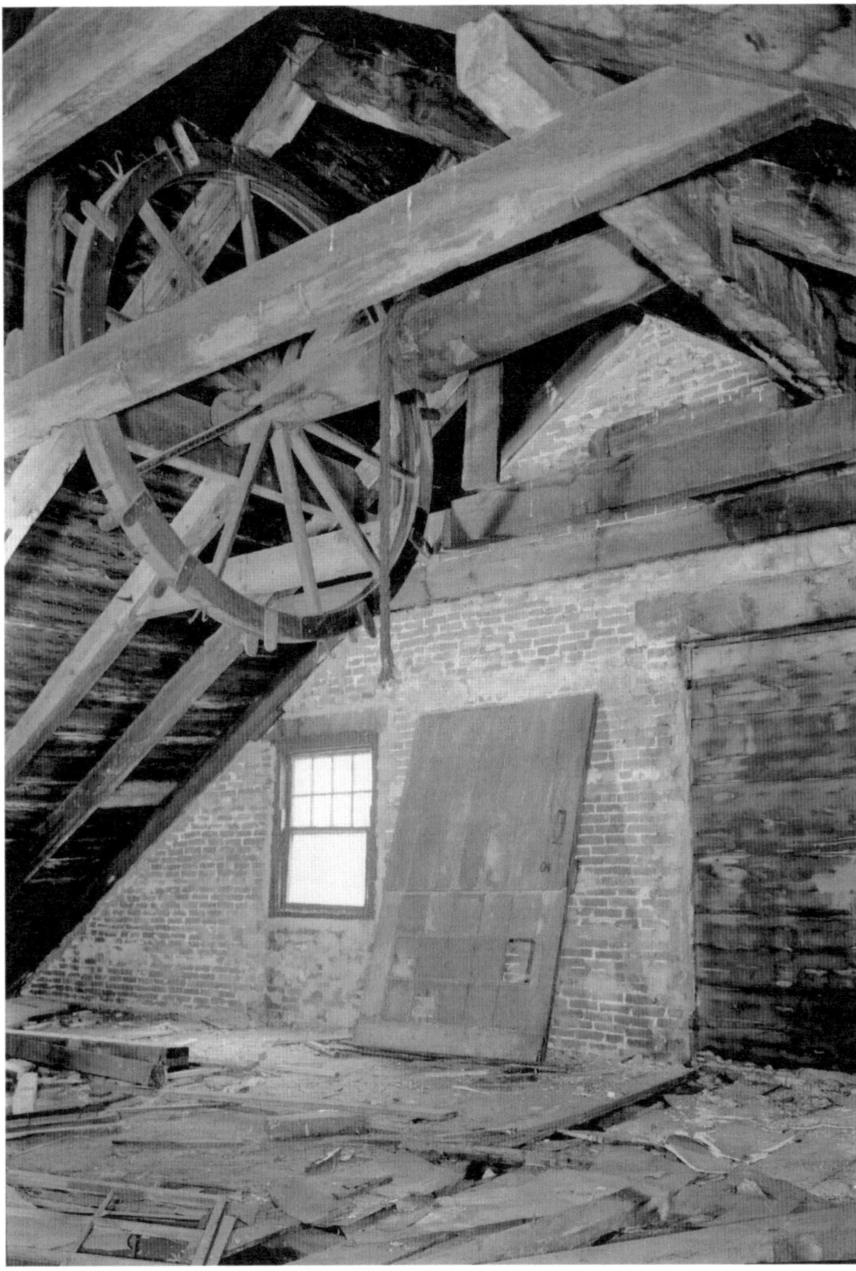

The hoisting wheel used to haul goods from the streets. *Library of Congress, Historic American Buildings Survey. Ned Goode, photographer.*

Rodman Jr., family critic and guardian of moral codes, made several entries in his diary on the subject of the marriage. The attitude seems to be that Rotch had married the kitchen under-maid: "April 5, 1829. The intentions of marriage of my uncle, William Rotch and Lydia Scott, was this day announced by Mr. Dewey to his congregation, to their great surprise."

The general New Bedford view was that Lydia wanted to get away from the smelly waterfront and up to County Street. Everyone else was building a mansion, she must have thought. Why not us? Rotch already owned the land for a proper home on County Street. It was a full city block. He inherited it as a part of his father's estate. It ran then (and still does in the twenty-first century) 204 feet, 6 inches on County Street; 226 feet on Madison Street; 203 feet, 6 inches on Seventh Street; and 207 feet on Cherry Street. By May 28, 1833, Rotch was paying builder Samuel Leonard "[t]wo hundred and Fifty dollars toward material for new house."

Samuel Leonard brought Rotch his architect. Richard Upjohn was a young Englishman who had apprenticed as a fine cabinetmaker. At twenty-seven, he came to America, first to Maine and then New Bedford. He began working for Leonard, a builder, lumber dealer and business associate of William Rotch Jr.

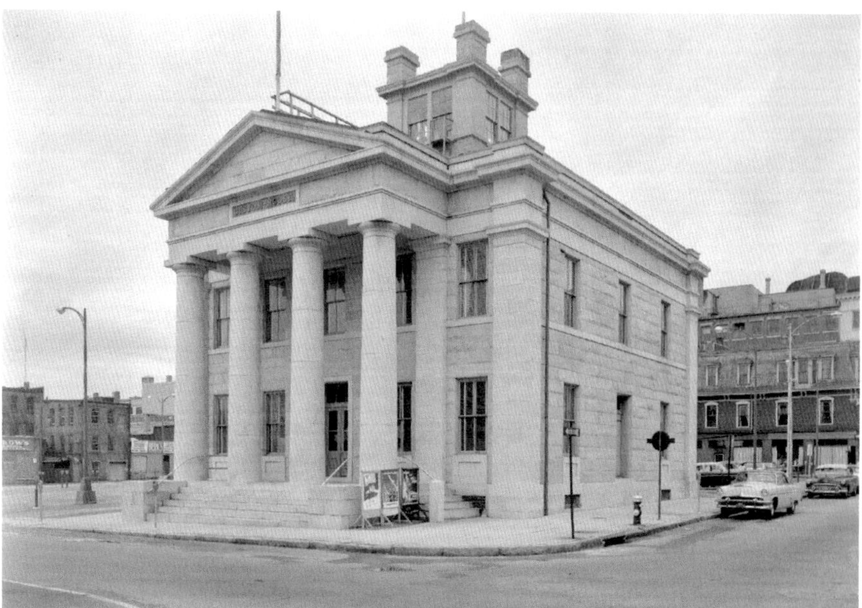

United States Custom House, Robert Mills, architect. *Library of Congress, Historic American Buildings Survey. Ned Goode, photographer.*

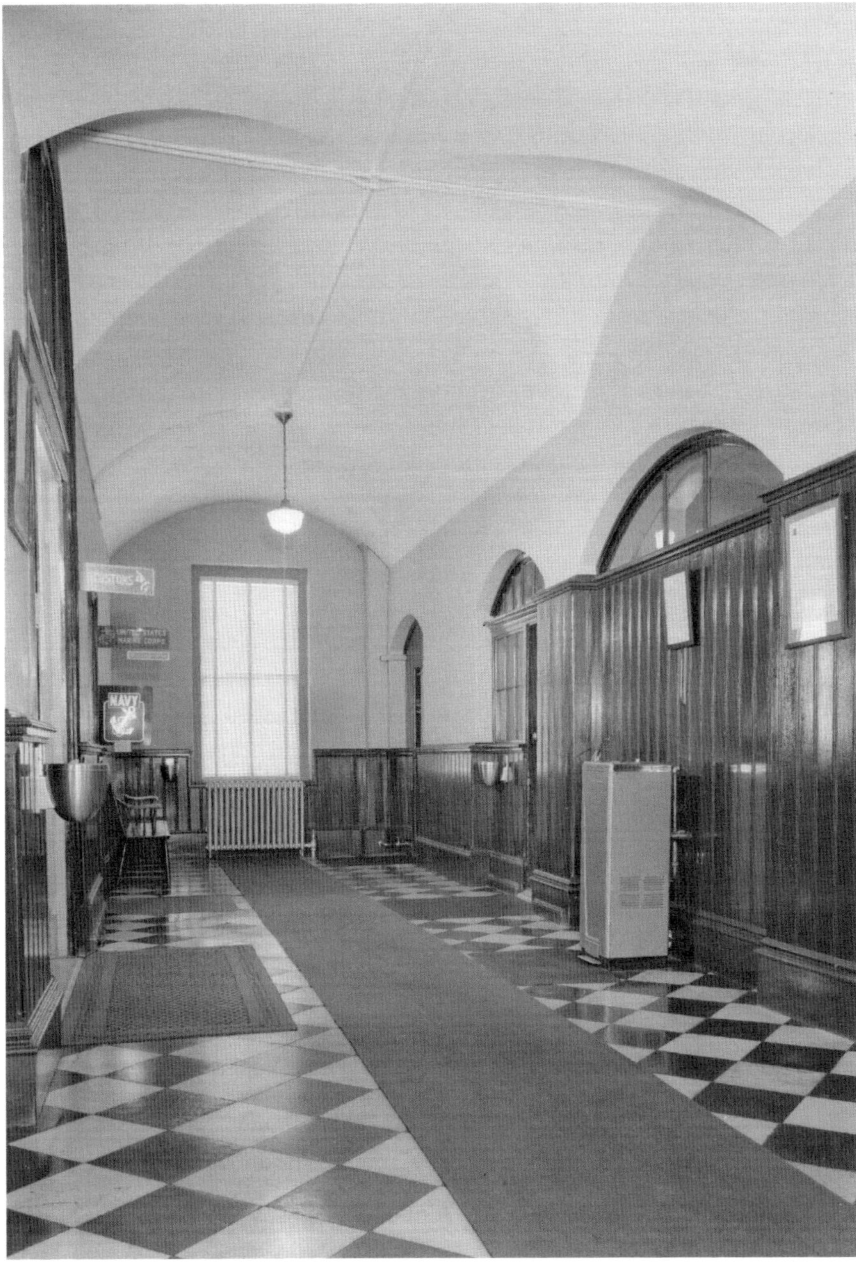

Custom House, center hall. *Library of Congress, Historic American Buildings Survey. Ned Goode, photographer.*

According to his grandson Everard Upjohn in his book, *Richard Upjohn, Architect and Churchman*: "One day a set of plans for a courthouse was brought into the office, in these the word architect was added to the name of the designer in the lower corner. On seeing this, Richard Upjohn exclaimed, 'If that's architecture then I am an architect, and after that I hung out my shingle.'" The *Mercury* printed an important advertisement on March 5, 1833: "Architectural Plans and Elevations Neatly Executed at Short Notice, by Richard Upjohn—Orders left at the Mechanics Hall, New Bedford."

Upjohn earned one dollar per day from Leonard and struggled to support his family. Designing a grand Greek Revival home for Rotch was his first commission. He designed an American masterpiece that is a National Historic Landmark. The house is notable for what it is not. Most Greek Revival mansions were built of granite. This house was clad in wood. It faces County Street with a single-story entrance porch with simple Doric columns.

We know it was completed by 1834 when Samuel Rodman Jr. made a family inspection:

> *September 30, 1834—Accompanied ma chere H.* [Hannah] *after dinner to see my Uncle William's new house which is very spacious and combines many conveniences and luxuries in its arrangement, but on a scale better adapted to the age of his wife than to his own age and for whose gratification mainly it may be presumed to have been built. The bedroom in the attic shows the turn of my uncle to investigate what is curious in nature.*

The Rotch house did not make Upjohn rich. He did become a founding member of the New Bedford Mechanics Association and, in 1833, designed its building. It is also believed that he designed a double town house on Prospect Hill (now Johnny Cake Hill) for Benjamin Mumford and William H. Taylor. Soon he moved to Boston, where one of his first projects was to design the gates for Boston Common. He quickly realized that he wanted to become a church architect. Surrounded by Gothic cathedrals in England, it is hardly surprising that he turned to working in the Gothic style.

In 1839, Upjohn was called to New York City and Trinity Church. Originally, he was merely to make few upgrades to the church. Eventually, the congregation decided that it wanted an entirely new church, and Upjohn received the commission that made his career. Trinity Church is still a New York landmark. Upjohn became a founder and first president of the American Institute of Architects. Along with Russell Warren, he became one of America's great architects.

Today, any listing of Upjohn's great buildings begins with the William Rotch Jr. house. Until 1982, the house lacked an architect, and Upjohn's role was unknown. A developer from New Jersey announced a plan to turn the Rotch house into a hotel/boardinghouse with a large bar and to asphalt large parts of the garden for parking.

My job, then, as a research historian for the City of New Bedford, was to support the struggle to save the house and to write its history. Assuming that it had to have been designed by a very great architect, I began searching. There were two possible men: Russell Warren and Richard Upjohn. Historic newspaper stories stated that it was an Upjohn. Finally, in Rotch's account books at the New Bedford Whaling Museum Library, I found two $40.00 payments to Richard Upjohn ($919.34 in 2013 dollars).

The developed plan was defeated. People came together in the neighborhood, the city and across the Northeast to save the house. In New Bedford, one magnificent woman made the difference: Sarah Delano, the president of Waterfront Historic Area League (WHALE). She was determined that the house be saved. One hot August night, hundreds jammed into city hall for what proved to be the end of the rooming house plan. Sarah Delano stood up before the crowd and said, "WHALE will buy the house." It did, and we now have the Rotch Jones Duff House and Garden Museum.

Every December, the Episcopal church liturgy delightfully celebrates and prays for two architects and one extraordinary designer, John Lafarge. It notes, in part, "Gracious God, we offer thanks for the vision of Ralph Adams Cram, John Lafarge and Richard Upjohn, whose harmonious revival of the Gothic enriched our churches with a sacramental understanding of reality in the face of secular materialism; and we pray that we may honor thy gifts of the beauty of holiness given through them." The service also includes a brief biography of each craftsman. Upjohn's notes:

> *Richard Upjohn was born in England in 1802 where he trained as a cabinetmaker. He immigrated to the United States in 1829 and eventually took up residence in Boston where he worked as a draftsman, art teacher, and eventually an architect. His first major commission was for a gothic-style building for St. John's Episcopal Church in Bangor, Maine, a building that was later destroyed by fire. He was commissioned in 1839 to design and supervise the construction of a new building for the Parish of Trinity Church, Wall Street, New York City. It was completed in 1846 and continues as Upjohn's most well known accomplishment.*

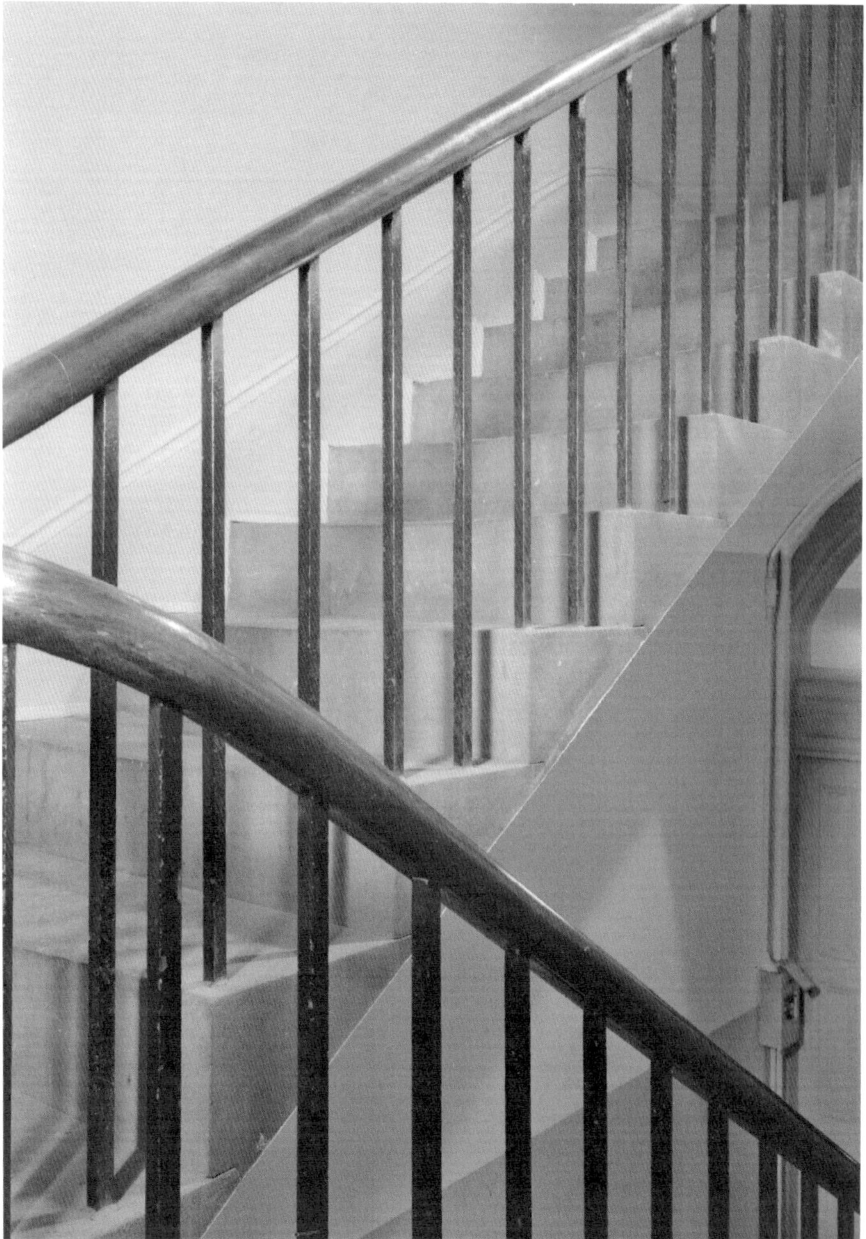

Custom House, stairway to second floor. *Library of Congress, Historic American Buildings Survey. Ned Goode, photographer.*

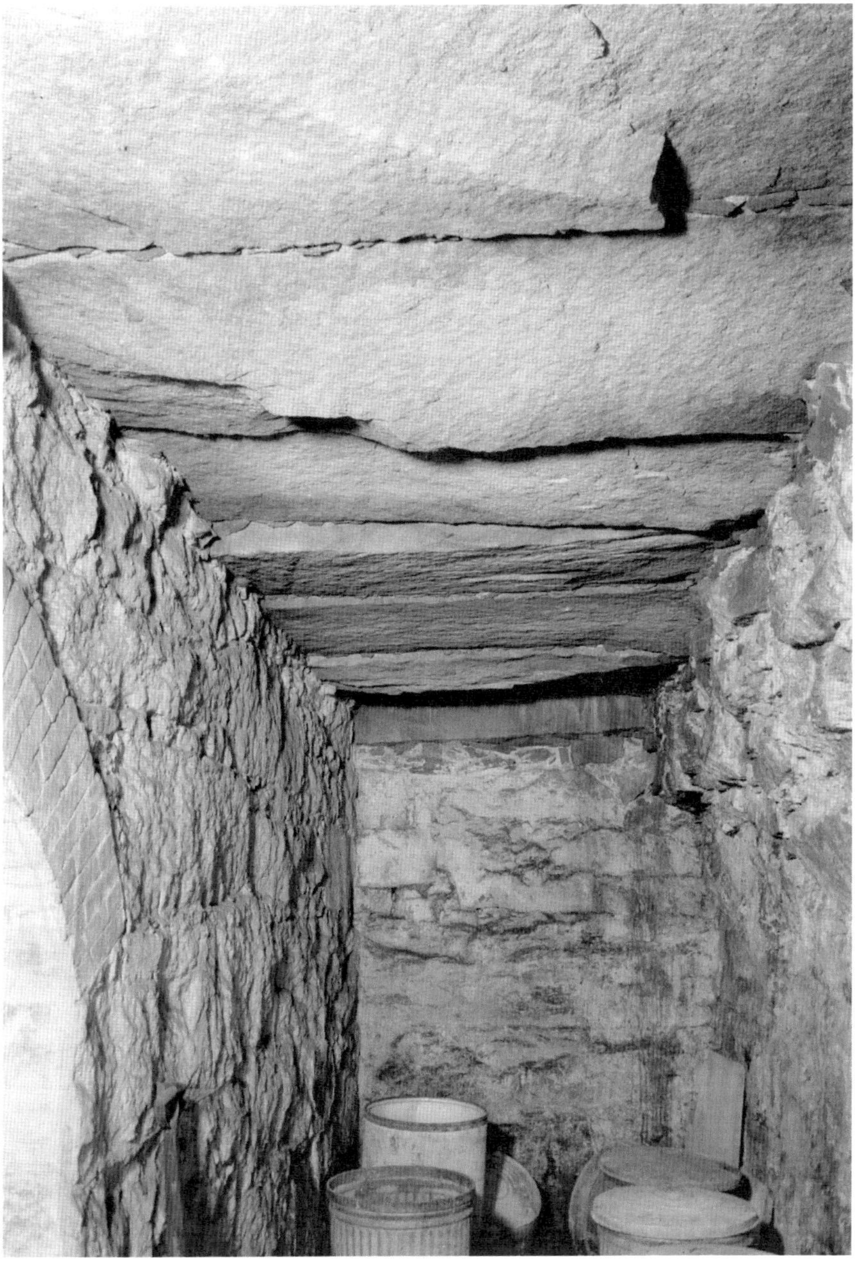

Custom House, granite blocks in basement under front portico. *Library of Congress, Historic American Buildings Survey. Ned Goode, photographer.*

There is one early glimpse of the house from William Wallace Crapo, later a congressman. According to his son, Henry Howland Crapo II, in *The Story of William Wallace Crapo*:

> *It was on a winter's day that William was sent by his father to deliver a document to the great man of the Town, William Rotch, Jr. The boy was timid about entering so grand a mansion. His timidity evaporated when he was shown into the back study and received with a cordiality which at once put him at his ease. Mr. Rotch, then about eighty years old, entered into conversation with him as if he were a grown up, and presented him with a jack knife. William troubled about the proper way of ending the interview, was immensely relieved by Mr. Rotch's suggestions, that, as he was about to go down town, William accompany him in his sleigh. The ride in the beautiful sleigh, behind a spirited horse and beside his distinguished host long remained in his memory as one of his most wonderful experiences.*

In 1850, William Rotch Jr. died at ninety. He and Lydia had been in the County Street house for sixteen years. Lydia disappeared from New Bedford afterward. As it turns out, she went to Boston, living on until the Civil War and dying on July 18, 1863, at eighty. Lydia had become a disciple of Swedenborg and left them a small fortune. It was administered by members of the Rotch family. She was blind at the end, and members of the Society of the New Jerusalem came to read to her daily.

Sarah Rotch Arnold gave her father's home to the New Bedford Port Society. It was moved by oxen to Johnny Cake Hill and became the Mariner's Home.

Chapter 2

The Houses of Rodman

Diaries, Weather and Loss

Samuel Rodman and Elizabeth Rotch Rodman had four sons. One, Thomas, died young of yellow fever in Cuba, but three survived. Each had a distinct and memorable personality. Each led a public life. Each built a house, and each of their houses remarkably survives.

William Rotch Rodman was the oldest, born in 1786. The mostly worldly of the brothers, he had paid a long visit as a child to English members of the Rotch family. One story has him set up on a table to show himself off. As an adult, he broke all of the Society of Friends rules—serving wine, dancing and building a truly glorious mansion on County Street. He held the very first ball in New Bedford history.

Samuel Jr. kept a diary from 1821 to 1859 that details his life and his city. He also left us a meticulous meteorological record of how New Bedford's weather was on any given day. It is now at the Blue Hills Observatory. The most devoted of the three, Samuel remained in the Society of Friends his entire life. Despite this, he was delightfully addicted to church hopping and went to services of every possible denomination—Baptist, Catholic, Unitarian and more. Because of his diary, it is easy to love Samuel Rodman Jr.

Benjamin was the youngest. He was a mystic, an abolitionist and a friend of Emerson and Hawthorne. He went to jail for his principles. His house was the first of the brothers' and was built on North Water Street. Going in reverse birth order, we start with Benjamin.

Benjamin's Federal home was built in 1820–21 (a New Bedford building year, as we'll see) and is the only original mansion remaining on its original foundation in the national park. With three stories of granite Quaker simplicity and a central entrance on North Second Street, it was topped with a Federal balustrade at the roof line and surrounded by gardens. It was a true town house for Benjamin, but his heart was in his farm, Woodlawn, set in the city's north end. There he raised short horn cattle and merino sheep and grew food for the poor. He was actually happiest there.

Benjamin married one of the Morgan girls, Susan Waln, a sister of Charles W. Morgan. He provided well for this wife, as expected from a good member of the Rotch Rodman clan. When things mattered, however, Benjamin could be very pragmatic. On December 29, 1819, he wrote to his uncle Thomas Rotch about his wedding plans: "Had you been nearer, you would have heard among the common reports & events of the day, of an engagement that exists between myself & Susan Morgan, of this City." His uncle lived on the Ohio frontier with his wife, Charity Rodman Rotch, and communication was slow:

> *It is nothing more than respectful on my part, to acquaint those who are as much interested in my general welfare, as I know you are, with a circumstance interesting to you because, important to me. In the conclusion, of which I now acquaint you I have not made haste—but with deliberation have examined it in all the points of view I am capable of, and have: one thus fear, not without the conviction of its propriety & suitableness—Susan is a sister of my brother's wife…so by a continuation of the same system, which the generation preceeding us, began, we may see three connections between the same two families.*

The prospective bridegroom seemed concerned about the multiple marriages:

> *The Morgans have not in their early youth, had their education directed in the same manner as ours, I can truly say there is scarcely a shade of variation in our (my own & my Susan's) sentiments in matters of principle & practice—for tho' young, she is far from being unacquainted with that restraining power of truth and the necessity of self-denial.*

He concluded the letter hopefully:

> *It was also her brother…that accompanied me to N Bedford, after my return from my western journey…. So that on many occasions, we have had to mingle our feelings, and after such an acquaintance it is, that I am willing to add a third link to the chain of connection between us.*

It was a happy marriage for Susan and Benjamin. The danger for the Rotch Rodman clan would come later and wreck friendships and family ties, creating a scandal that was unraveled only in the twenty-first century.

There is no doubt that the result of Benjamin's principles could be hard for his family. Henry David Thoreau spent one night in jail; Benjamin Rodman spent a hundred. He was desperately worried about young seamen thrown in jail for debt and clearly mad or alcoholic men and woman locked away as public nuisances without resources. Therefore, he refused to pay a small debt and moved into the Ash Street jail. There he stayed, making friends, offering aid and writing, writing, writing. He produced a small masterpiece, *A Voice from the Prison Being*:

> *It is my lot to be committed to Jail for debt. I am offered a release from this extremity by laying myself under obligations to my friends which I may not soon be able to repay though if I should appeal to their sympathies they would gladly advance me three fold the sum required.... I shall employ the leisure my position allows me in preparing a memorial which I hope will have some influence in expunging from the Statute Book the law which allows the incarceration of a man for no other crime than being poor.*

Imprisonment for debt was legal in Massachusetts, and Benjamin hoped by his example to end it:

> *First one word for myself. If any friend of mine has any as to the course I have taken let him come here and I will to satisfy him that I could not have taken any other than one I have chosen consistently with the honour and truth he has ever associated with my name. For those who are my friends I have no concern but to the world I will show my own case the most barbarous and oppressive acts of persecution that have ever marked the operation of this most abominable of imprisonment for debt.*

He remained in jail and eventually won. Imprisonment for debt was abolished:

> *Yet as regards improvement in the customs which govern the business of New Bedford this never can take place until some radical evils are removed There must lie a boarding house where the sailor may feel that he is a human being. This he cannot do where all feeling is drowned in Rum. He must have for friends and protectors the owners of the ships who will supply*

> *him with cheap and good clothing and these things will and must be the very hour that imprisonment for debt is abolished.*

Rodman's friends loved him well. In an 1894 issue of *The Century*, Sophia Hawthorne wrote to her mother:

> *September 7, 1851 Monday morning—My lamp grew so dim that I could not see to write any more last evening, dear mother. We have had several visits since I came home. One day I was most agreeably surprised by a call from Mr. and Mrs. Benjamin Rodman. Mr. Rodman was just as full of life and talk as ever. Last spring I had a very interesting letter from Mr. Rodman about "The House of Seven Gables" and "The Scarlet Letter."*

The youngest Rodman boy lived until September 1876. The New Bedford Free Public Library Report printed Reverend William James Potter's funeral sermon:

> *Not many knew how much he was doing to befriend the needy. Only by accident did his family discover many of his generosities. His extensive and pleasant grounds once quite out of town had become nearly surrounded by a factory village and the dwellings of the poorer class of people. Yet no gate barred free access to them. There worn women came to sit under the shade of his trees and enjoy his flowers and fruits and children played upon his lawns.*

Samuel Rodman Jr. was the brother who did not marry a Rotch or Morgan. Instead, he found Hannah Haydock Prior from Long Island and seems to have adored her all their lives. In his diary, he calls her "My chere" or "My chere H." Despite his Quaker principles, he spoiled his children outrageously and bought a favorite daughter a forbidden piano. He allowed them to attend very secular parties and even celebrated Christmas. Somehow the pleasures of the season made him smile reluctantly. Several of his January 1 entries mention calling on his cousin Sarah Arnold, helping his wife with holiday shopping and presenting small presents to his children.

On January 1, 1849, Mr. Rodman described a snowed-in and joyous New Bedford, although he did go into work at his counting house before visiting friends: "On my way I passed some of the streets thronged with coasters and spectators. The velocity of the sleds appeared to be equal to the railroad cars, though my old friend, James Scott…said that by his calculations and observation the speed was not more than six or seven miles an hour…Our three sons were till late at their coasting amusement."

Sometimes reading his diary, a reader wants to shake him. *You met John James Audubon? What was he like? Rembrandt Peale came from Boston to paint your parents. You knew William Lloyd Garrison and Margaret Fuller. Please tell us more.* He doesn't. He was only living his own life and writing about it as it happened. No one caught the small things about living better than he did.

Samuel Rodman Jr. told us about seeing Halley's Comet. He told us about his young son locking himself in his room and how a ladder had to be borrowed to get him out. It happened twice in one week. He also paid real attention to his children:

> *September 22 1837*
> *Our three youngest children were at Dr. Read's to tea. I called early to take them home. I believe it is about the first time that little Ellen has been out after dark. She was pleased with the brightness of the stars, which she called "lights up in the wall."*

In 1827, Rodman began building a new home for the family on the corner of County and Spring Street, up the hill from the waterfront. In 1935, the diary for that year was found in an attic and published. On March 28, 1827, he wrote from Boston, "Went to the State Prison and engaged my stones for my steps and front walls. Spent most of the afternoon with C. Coolidge looking at marble fireplaces, soap stones &C—prices for steps 58 cents, walls 52 cents, marbles 85 cents, full columns elegant, pilasters elegant 60 cents."

It seems that builders kept on hand architectural elements that could be ordered rather like from a Home Depot. Rodman had masons from Philadelphia come to New Bedford to construct his barn. Work went quickly, and by July 5, "The plasters began to cover the rooms and put the first coat on the North parlor and library,"

Always fascinated by new methods, Rodman decided to use a system that he had seen in Philadelphia for the exterior of the house. By July 21, "The masons completed the west and east side with the finish in imitation of granite. The imitation is very good and if the coating should withstand the frosts of our climate and retain its fine appearance the mode will probably be considerably practiced." (It wasn't practiced, and today the Rodman house is painted Quaker brown.) By December 12, it was nearly finished. "Took mother to see the former, the carpenters having left it about complete in their work."

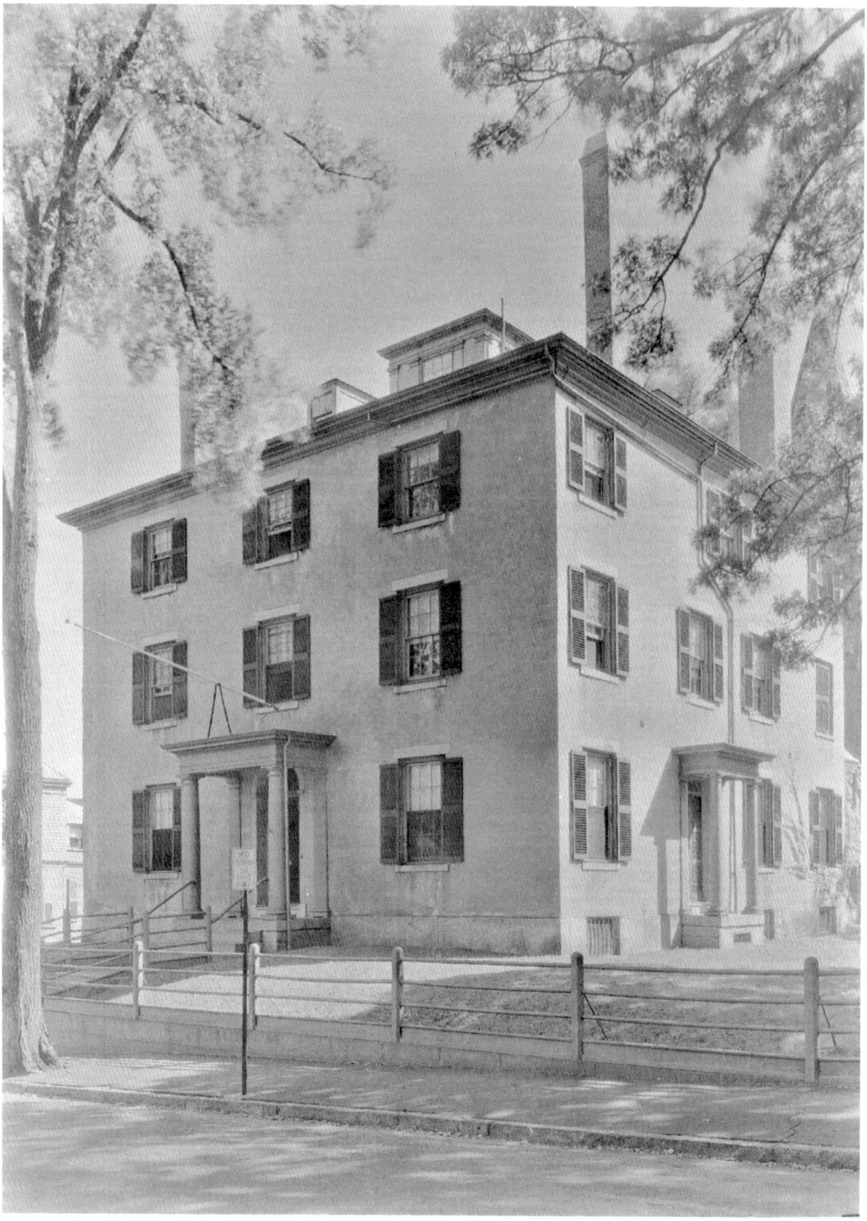

Samuel Rodman Jr. House, Spring and County Streets. *Library of Congress, Historic American Buildings Survey.*

The entire family moved in in January 1838. On the eleventh, the front door was hung, and by the fourteenth, he had recorded, "Devoted most of the day to the business at my new house, preparing to removing there this week." Furniture was moved up the hill by wagon, and the children were sent to their grandmother Rodman to keep them out of the way. On the seventeenth, he said goodbye to his first home: "We expect to leave this dwelling tomorrow. My notes hereafter will be made at another place."

Samuel Rodman Jr.'s pride was the cupola atop the house. This was his meteorological observation point and his place to view the stars and planets:

> *February 22, 1828*
> *Spent most of the day at the counting house, though not too much purpose as I had two of my little prattlers through the afternoon. Evening at home. Observed the planet Saturn with his splined ring from my observatory, as did Sister Eliza and most of the family.*

In 1927, the largest part of Rodman's diary was published, edited by Zephaniah W. Pease. In his introduction, Pease described the cupola, which still existed: "In the ceiling of this four square observatory was the compass, still there, which indicated the direction of the wind and a fine telescope. There were seats around the cupola and on the north side was a built in desk. A pipe leading from below stairs furnished heat in winter. The room perched on the roof was a family resort and the owner's children and grandchildren were often there with him." It was without doubt the most elaborate and most used cupola in all New Bedford. Rodman ended his diary in 1859. He continued his daily meteorological observations until his death in 1876. In 1929, when the diary was published, members of the family still lived in the house.

Samuel Rodman Jr. loved his family passionately. Although he remained in the Society of Friends, every member of the family left to join Grace Episcopal Church. He was present, as even Hannah was accepted into the congregation. Grace Episcopal Church on County Street was built on the site of his garden with money left in his will.

William Rotch Rodman was the most flamboyant and worldly of the Rodman brothers. He believed in living well and built New Bedford's grandest and most important remaining mansion. Designed by Russell Warren, who was possibly America's major Greek Revival architect, the Rodman commission truly made New Bedford a city of palaces.

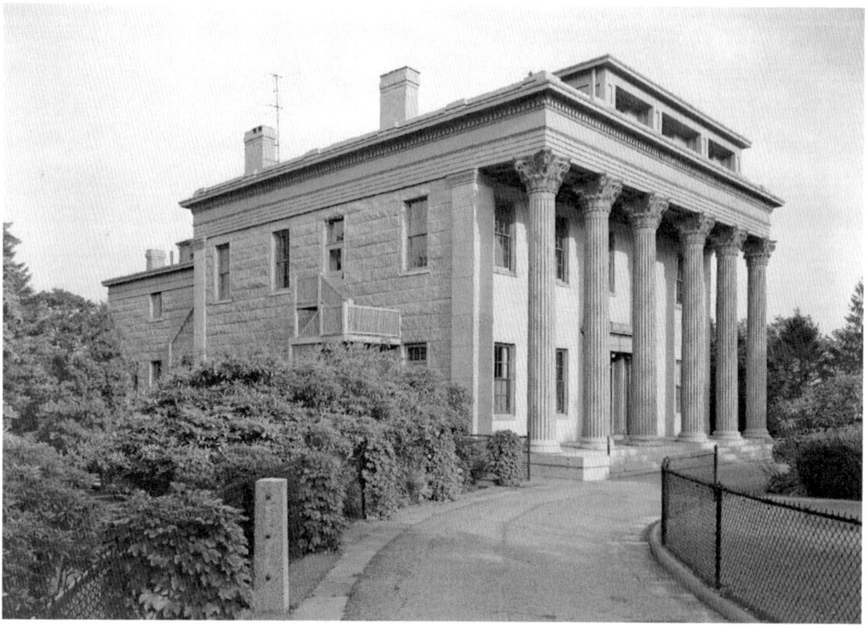

William R. Rodman's mansion, 388 County Street, New Bedford. *Library of Congress, Historic American Buildings Survey. Ned Goode, photographer.*

Public comments on William R. Rodman were mixed. A somewhat sarcastic book published in 1852, *Names and Sketches of the Richest Men of Massachusetts,* described him as worth $500,000:

> *A son of old Samuel, and a go-ahead, gain-or-lose sort of man. He owns in everything, from a sheep-farm in Australia to a part of the St. Charles Hotel in New Orleans; has whalers out of Havre, and business everywhere in the world. Many think he will "make a spoon," and many that he will "spoil a horn"; these things lie in the womb of time. Meanwhile he is affable when he pleases, pays his bills when he pleases, and does as he pleases generally.*

In 1917, Henry H. Crapo delivered a paper at the Old Dartmouth Historical Society on city banks. He made sure to mention William R. Rodman: "Mr. Rodman was essentially an aristocrat. He had a somewhat haughty manner, and consequently was not generally popular."

Rodman was a bank president and had lured Russell Warren to New Bedford. Here he built the glorious Double Bank building at the foot of

North Water Street: "One day Mr. Rodman was superintending the lifting of a heavy safe into the second story of this building…one Philip Groves, a blacksmith and an exhorting Methodist, who said to Mr. Rodman; 'Lay up for yourself treasures in heaven; where your Treasure is. There will your heart be also.'"

The Methodist picked the wrong man to preach at: "Mr. Rodman turned to Mr. Gibbs and said; 'Who is this offensive fellow?' Mr. Rodman's manner was largely only manner and not indicative of his character, which was kindly and generous. He was a man of rather more scholarly attainments than many of his business contemporaries."

Crapo, one of New Bedford's many amateur historians, closed by noting that Rodman took great pride in racing his horse and carriage between the city and his Fall River cotton mill: "He used to make fabulous time on these journeys and prides himself on the speed of his horses."

Backtracking, at sixteen William was sent to England to receive a proper Quaker education. He was looked after by members of the English Rotch family. There he met his cousin Francis Rotch, who would later cause heartbreaking problems to the New Bedford families.

On January 2, 1800, Eliza Rotch wrote back to New Bedford:

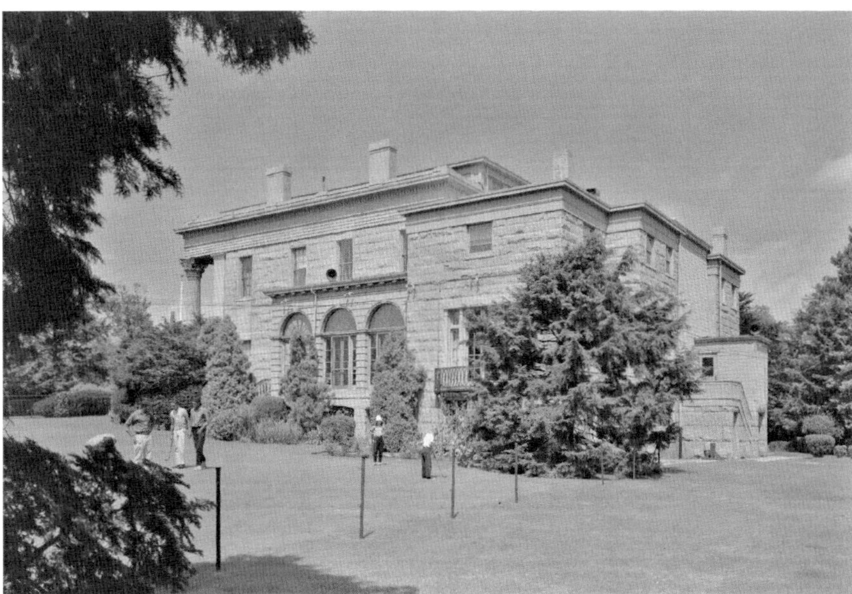

William R. Rodman's mansion, east elevation. *Library of Congress, Historic American Buildings Survey. Ned Goode, photographer.*

> *I have now taken up the pen while William, Frank, Eliza and Ben having just finished a romp at blind man's buff, are quietly set down to play a game at grammatical forfeits, they are now all talking to-gether & Joanna the loudest to silence them, so if I make some mistakes I trust thou wilt forgive it. William & Francis have been home a week yesterday...I have just had a kiss on my cheek as I sit writing which I suppose is the redeeming of a forfeit.*

At first William's American clothes were considered so unusual that people turned to stare at him in the London Streets. His aunt soon rectified the situation:

> *My mother readily sympathized with the feeling of embarrassment this must occasion to a shy youth of sixteen, and she persuaded my father to order a suit of dark clothes for his nephew. When attired in these, he looked so handsome, that he still attracted much attention, but of this he was not aware.*

After whirlwind sightseeing in London, the boys were sent off to a proper school in Reading. The pleasures of the city made more of an impression on both boys than the somber Quaker rule did. By at least 1814, William Rodman had returned to America and soon had gotten into major financial difficulties. Initially, he moved to Pennsylvania and spent far too much time with Francis Rotch.

William, Benjamin and Francis Rotch each married one of Charles W. Morgan's sisters. The Morgan girls had been orphaned early, and all their lives they protected one another and adored their brother, Charles. William had married Rebecca in Philadelphia. It wasn't until 1829 that he settled in New Bedford. Samuel wrote on September 27, "William and his family arrived from Northampton at father's. They will probably make this their place of residence." It seems that Samuel and Benjamin did not really know their brother well. For each single note in Samuel's diary about brother William, there are scores about his closest friends, his brother Benjamin, Charles W. Morgan and Andrew Robeson.

It did not surprise anyone when William decided to build a grand mansion and hired Russell Warren to design it. The land at the foot of Hawthorne Street on County had come from their mother. Warren had already begun to reshape New Bedford when he began work for William. His twin granite mansions for Joseph Grinnell and Joseph Anthony were completed, as was the John Avery Parker Mansion.

Rodman wanted something special, and he got it. It was nearly unheard of to find a building contract officially registered, but William Rodman

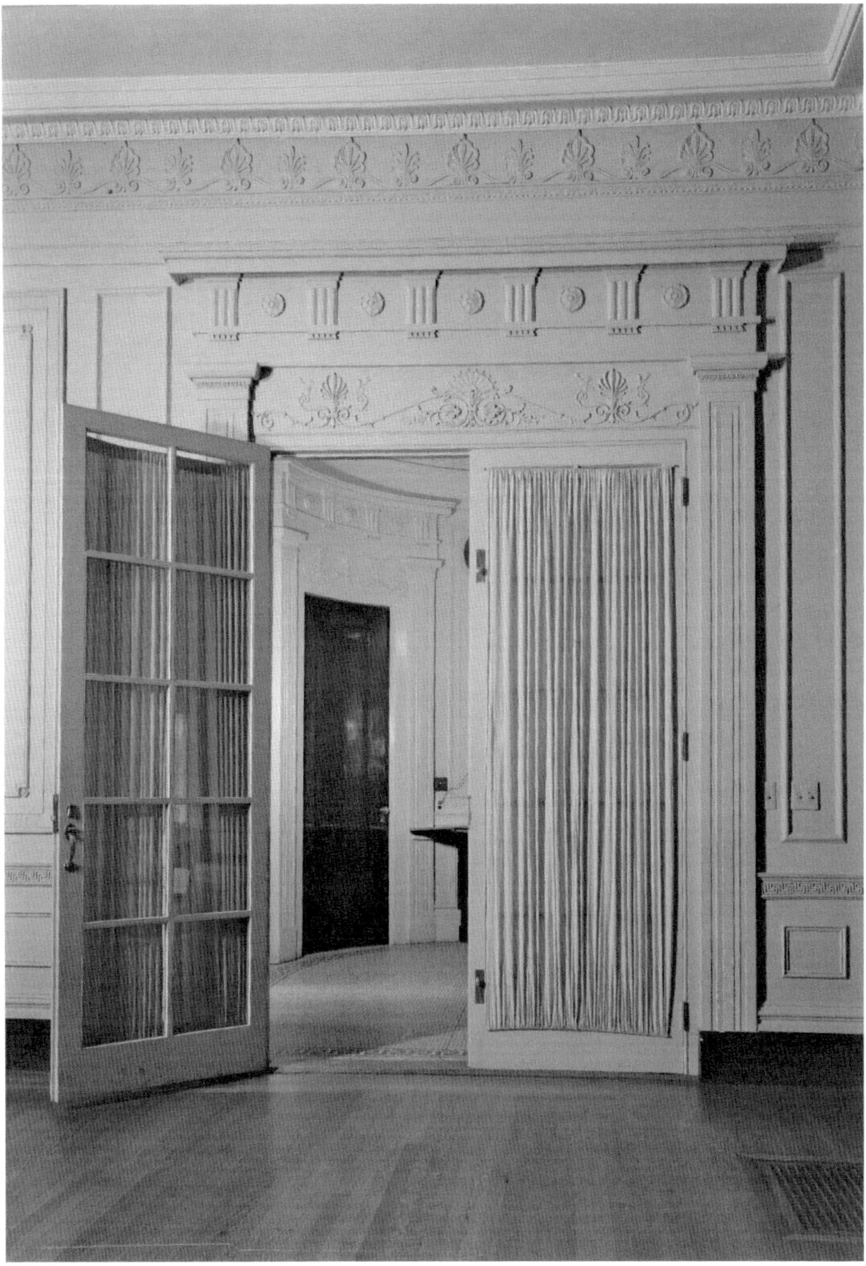

William R. Rodman's south drawing room. *Library of Congress, Historic American Buildings Survey. Ned Goode, photographer.*

did exactly that—he wanted no doubts about the duties of his builder. On February 3, 1834, he recorded his contract with Nathaniel Potter of Rhode Island. The date of recording seems to have been after the work was completed, since the date usually assigned to the Rodman Mansion is 1833. Potter's duty was to "do the Mason work and find the materials for a dwelling house comfortable to specifications to which are affixed the signatures of the parties and further that said house shall be completed and finished as fast as the carpenters work will allow." He was to receive a total $8,500 in stages:

- *$500 when the walls and chimnies are completed to the first floor*
- *$2,000 when walls and chimnies are comfortable to the second floor*
- *$2,000 when the walls and chimnies are comfortable to the third floor*
- *$1,000 when the steps are complete*
- *$1,000 when all the brown mortar was put on and the balance $2,000 when the house was comfortably finished*

> *All the materials to be furnished by the said party of the second part shall be considered as the property of the first part when delivered upon the lot where said house is to be erected.*

Adjusting for inflation, the construction cost $195,366.09 in 2013 dollars. This amount does not take into account Warren's fee, landscaping what became elaborate gardens and furnishing the house.

Even today, standing on County Street and staring up at the elegant two-story portico, with its six fluted Corinthian columns, there is no doubt that Warren designed a palace. It would be at home in London. In 1909, the *Morning Mercury* remembered, "The wooden columns in front of the house were then regarded as something very ornate as indeed they were. They were built in Providence and were shipped to the city in a sloop. They were unloaded at one of the wharves and carried to the house where they were placed in position."

The front façade is smooth, light-gray granite, and the sides are rough-hewn granite that catches light and shadow. The house has five bays, with six-over-six windows that reach nearly floor to ceiling. Originally it was built in a "U" shape, with rear projecting wings. Inside, it was a house made for entertaining. Stepping through the front door, your eye is pulled toward the double staircase built against the rear wall. It is one of very few in New Bedford. Public rooms were on the first floor, with spacious bedrooms on the second floor.

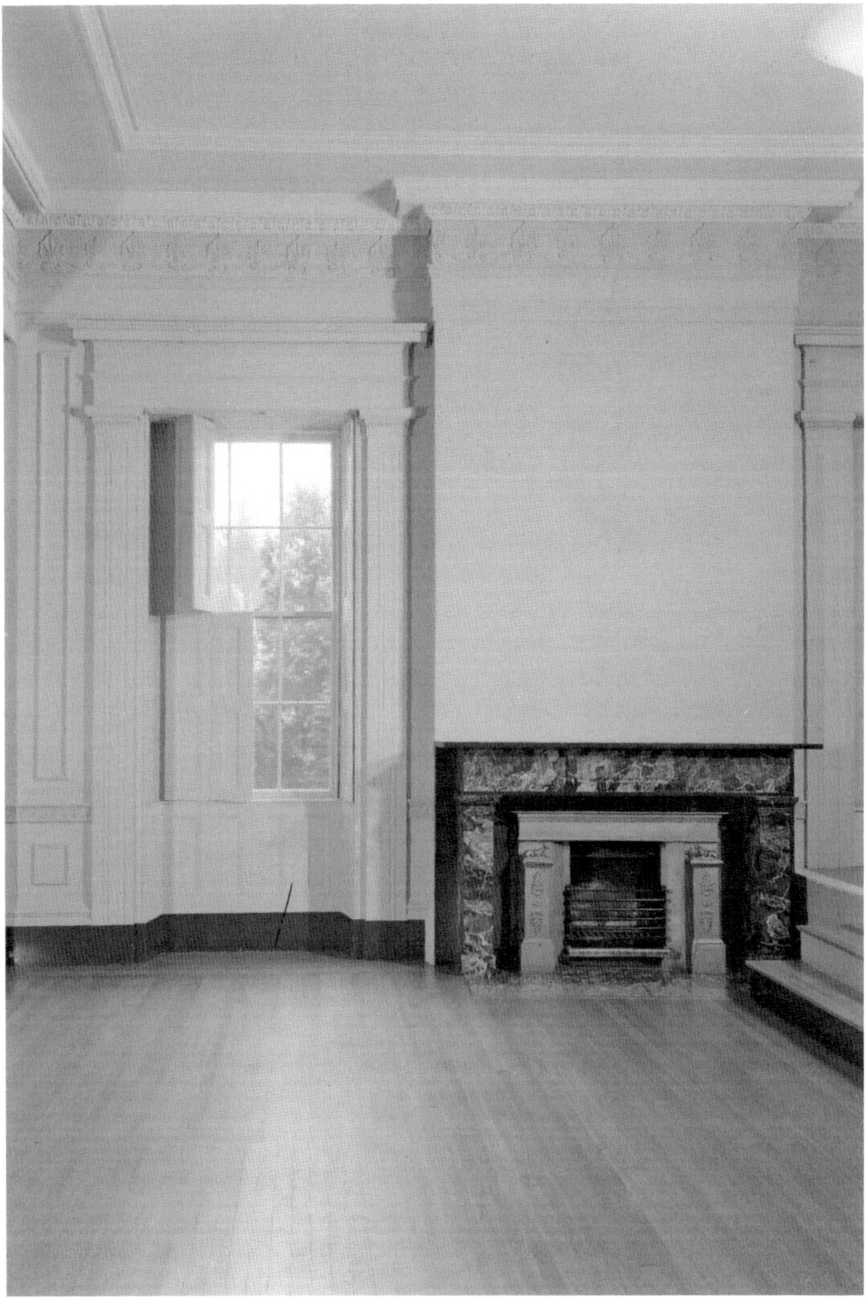

William R. Rodman's mansion detail of fireplace, window and shutter in drawing room. *Library of Congress, Historic American Buildings Survey. Ned Goode, photographer.*

Among the guests hosted by William and Rebecca Rodman was Washington Irving, then at the height of his fame. On July 4, 1836, Samuel Rodman noted, "At brother William's to meet others of the family assembled there to see and be introduced to Washington Irving of New York whose literary works have been so generally admired…His appearance is that of an amiable and polished gentleman of fine physiognomy and person."

Rebecca Rodman died in 1848, leaving William alone in the echoing mansion. Without warning, William R. Rodman died in 1855. Samuel wrote between March 26 and April 1, "This has been a week of sadness and sorrow. The sudden death of the brother William has spread a pall of gloom over our family circle and has extended its melancholy influence through the place and to the extent of his widely extended mercantile reputation and business relations that the tiding have yet reached."

That morning, William had visited their mother and had tea with his children. After dinner, he had visited a friend on nearby Seventh Street and simply dropped dead there. It seems to have been a massive heart attack.

Rodman's grown children wanted to immediately sell what they seemed to view as their father's folly. There was also a persistent rumor that William had died in the arms of a mistress in a house on Seventh Street. They also moved out of New Bedford to live permanently in Boston. Samuel wrote, "My brother William's children are desirous to sell with out delay his splendid mansion as it is on a scale of magnificence which neither of them wish to posses."

The mansion was sold to Abraham H. Howland, New Bedford's first mayor. It was an incongruous sale since Howland made great claims about being a man of the people; moving into the grand mansion didn't quite fit the image. Howland sputtered that he was offered such a great deal he couldn't refuse.

William's death was a sad ending for the worldliest of the Rodman brothers, but then he certainly seemed to have enjoyed his life.

Chapter 3

The House of Arnold

A Gentleman Out of Providence

James and Sarah Arnold were the absolute best of the second generation of their families—and perhaps the saddest. Their 1821 Federal home was the center of New Bedford's social and public life. Their extraordinary gardens were described in every major horticultural magazine in the country. At his death, James Arnold endowed the Arnold Arboretum. A passionate book collector, Arnold purchased no. 74 of Audubon's "Double Elephant Folio," *Birds of America.* Most of all, they were bred-in-the-bone abolitionists. James and Sarah Rotch Arnold's opposition to slavery can be traced to their upbringing and the knowledge that James's mother, Mary Brown Arnold, had been a slaveholder.

James Arnold was born on September 9, 1781, and raised in Providence, Rhode Island. His mother, Mary Brown Arnold, was the first cousin and sister-in-law of Moses and John Brown. The Brown brothers were Providence's wealthiest and most controversial family. Their fortune was based on every possible eighteenth-century business, including the whaling industry. This brought them into contact with the Rotch family.

The Browns were also outright, unapologetic slave traders. Rhode Island's wealth was built on the trade, especially in Bristol, Newport and Providence. John Brown stubbornly refused to apologize for his actions and successfully defended them in court. Moses Brown became a member of the Society of Friends, freed his slaves and twice sued John for running with the trade. His friend Thomas Arnold assisted in the suits. They lost both times in Newport Courts, delighting John Brown inordinately.

Thomas Arnold, James's father, was the first of his family to attend any college. He became a lawyer, to the delight of his family. He then infuriated them at the time of his marriage to Mary Brown when he joined the Society of Friends and gave up the practice of the law.

Sarah Rotch was the first child of William Rotch Jr. and Elizabeth Rodman Rotch. She was born on Nantucket on June 3, 1786. Shortly afterward, the family relocated to New Bedford.

In 1800, Sarah's uncle Thomas Rotch and his wife, Charity Rodman Rotch, left New Bedford and eventually settled in Kendal, Ohio. Their move to what was then the western frontier led to an extraordinary collection of letters to Charity Rotch from her New Bedford Rotch Rodman family. The women formed a circle of loving friends to write weekly to Charity. The chain of letters began in 1800 and ended only with her death in 1824. These lifelines thrown out into the wilderness are everything a lonely woman wanted—gossip, news and affection. The letters also document the life of Sarah Arnold from the age of eighteen in 1804 through the building of the Arnold Mansion.

The collection is owned by the Massillon Ohio Free Public Library as the Rotch-Wales Collection. Each letter has been scanned and is available at Massillon Memory. In her first letter, in 1805, Sarah wrote:

> *Dear Aunt Charity*
>
> *Having made thy proposition to some of the younger branches of our families to give thee weekly information of the transactions in our Village, we have concluded to make out a list, & each write in our turn.*
>
> *I believe the intention is to supply the place of the "Courier," but my communications will bear a stronger resemblance to the "Medley"—however I have thy assurance that any thing will be interesting.*

Sarah later described a visit to a dying woman that marked her forever. Hearing that the woman needed help, Sarah went to find her. What she saw in the shack shocked her:

> *As I gave her my hand she burst into tears & was as much agitated as I ever saw a person...the gratitude she felt for our visit quite overpowered the little remaining strength & a long time elapsed ere she was able to speak. Her bed was a miserable thing...three or four little children were crawling about their mother who was by no means in a situation to bear their noise. She*

has 7 or 8 children, one only that can earn anything for their subsistence... she concluded with saying if I would take her little Betsy about 5 years of age that she could die in peace—my heart felt so much for the poor creature that I had at most fixed to take her without recollecting I had Parents to consult in a step so important—however I relieved her by assuring her I would attend to the disposal of her favorite.

This may have been the first time in her life that Sarah came face to face with real poverty and death. She wanted to have her father do something for the poor immediately:

New Bedford May 7, 1805

[B]*ut when after my excursion I mentioned a wish that a suitable building might be directly erected & proper care taken of those miserable little creatures, my Father answered 10,000 dollars must first be collected, which he deemed impracticable in our little Village, that there seems but a gloomy prospect of their being very soon placed in a more eligible situation...I hope at some future period the minds of a larger part of the community may be turned towards them tho' at present it seems to occupy but a small part of their attention.*

Sarah Arnold never forgot that Dartmouth family. As an adult, when she was able to give, she gave time and money. On October 29, 1807, in New

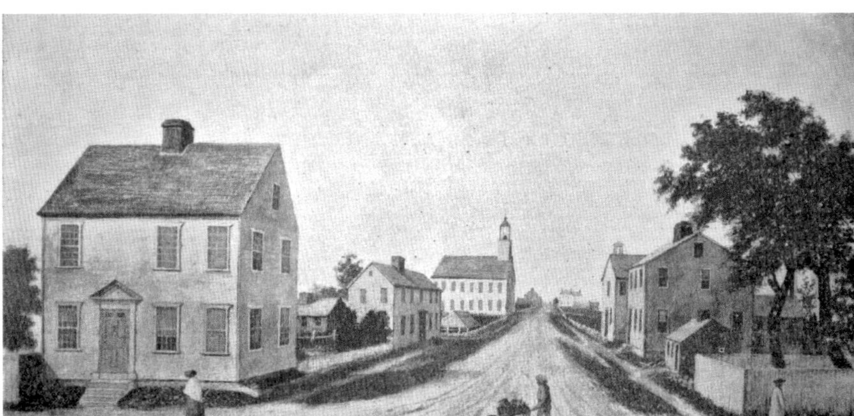

Purchase Street, 1820. Every New Bedford family walked this growing street every day. *Collection of author. Courtesy of Arthur P. Motta.*

Bedford, she married James Arnold, and on January 17, 1809, her only child, Elizabeth, was born. By 1821, the Arnold family was ready to move away from their home near the counting house.

Although James Arnold did not hire an architect for his home, he knew what he wanted having grown up in Providence. He wanted a Federal mansion and got a nearly perfect one. We know the contractor and masonry subcontractor because they bragged about the job. Charles M. Pierce received the masonry contract from Dudley Davenport for the Arnold Mansion. Since the house was constructed of brick, he was responsible for the majority of the contract. Davenport later worked with Russell Warren on the Double Bank Building for the Merchants Bank. He also was the contractor for most of New Bedford's other large 1830s projects.

The completion of the Arnold Mansion can be dated to exactly May 20, 1821. As Zephaniah W. Pease explained in *The Arnold Mansion & Its Traditions*, an Old Dartmouth Historical Society sketch, it's a great example of how history is passed on:

> *Dudley Davenport, a housewright, was the contractor and he sub-contracted with Charles M. Pierce for the mason work, James Wheaton, a journeyman mason, told Mr. Denham's father that while he was at work on the house, one afternoon, toward night, he "turned the arch" over the front entrance of the house. Immediately after the day's work he drove over to Rehoboth and married Lydia Pearce, coming back to New Bedford that night. In order to get the date Mr. Denham wrote to the town clerk of Rehoboth for the date of the marriage and found it to be May 20, 1821.*

Pease also interviewed a family member, who described the completed house:

> *The original mansion was of brick two stories high. Mrs. Francis M. Stone, a daughter of the late William J. Rotch furnishes a few details from recollections of childhood visits. In the south room wing was a room called "the cabinet," surrounded with mahogany cases filled with shells, "a rather dark and awesome room," as Mrs. Stone remembers. In a room on the north side was an office and large store closets. On a long table at the center of the room were heaped grapes from the hot houses, ready to be sent to friends or invalids who would appreciate them especially, and Mrs. Stone recalls the delicious scent of the fruit which always filled the room.*

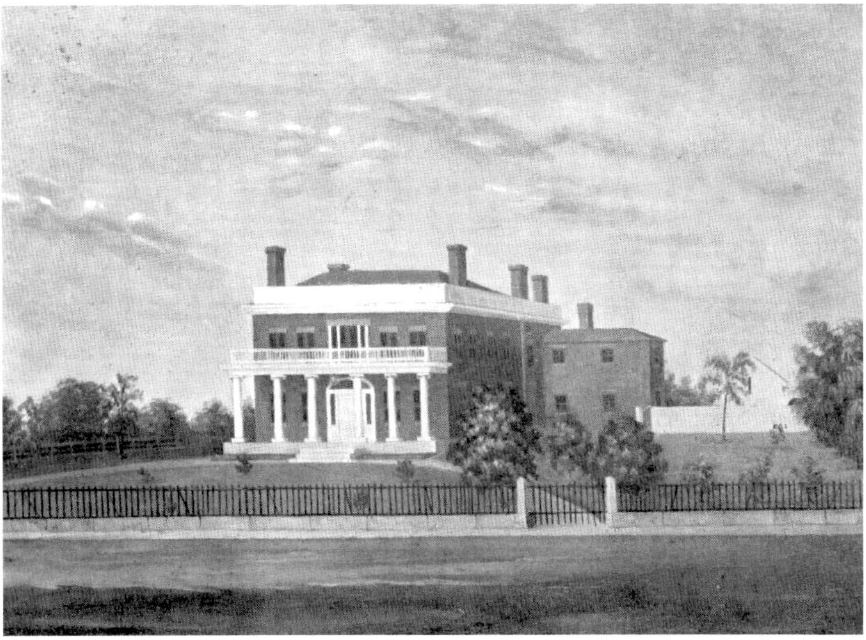

The only known image of the James Arnold Mansion as it looked in 1821. *Courtesy of the Library Trustees, New Bedford Free Public Library.*

Meanwhile, on November 11, 1821, Sarah wrote to Charity, "Our house is nearly finished, but we do not think of removing until some time in the spring—Andrew Robeson is nearly as forward & cousin Benjamin's finished, they commenced housekeeping yesterday. Houses are still very scarce here."

Between Sarah's frail health, stays in Boston and finishing the interior of the house, moving in took a while. It wasn't until January 16, 1823, that she wrote:

> *I have been out more & have had most of my acquaintances to dine or take tea with me—I make one more party of elderly people, our neighbors Russells &c. &c.—and then my "house warming" will be over, & since I am upon the subject of warmth, I recollect Father desired me to inform Uncle Thomas how our entry stove proved & I gladly testify to its being the greatest comfort to our house it warms it throughout.*
>
> *My parents dined with us last 5th day, thermometer at 6 degrees & wind high...When the parlor doors were open, the heat from the entry was felt very sensibly—I am thus minute because I was desired to be. We sleep in a*

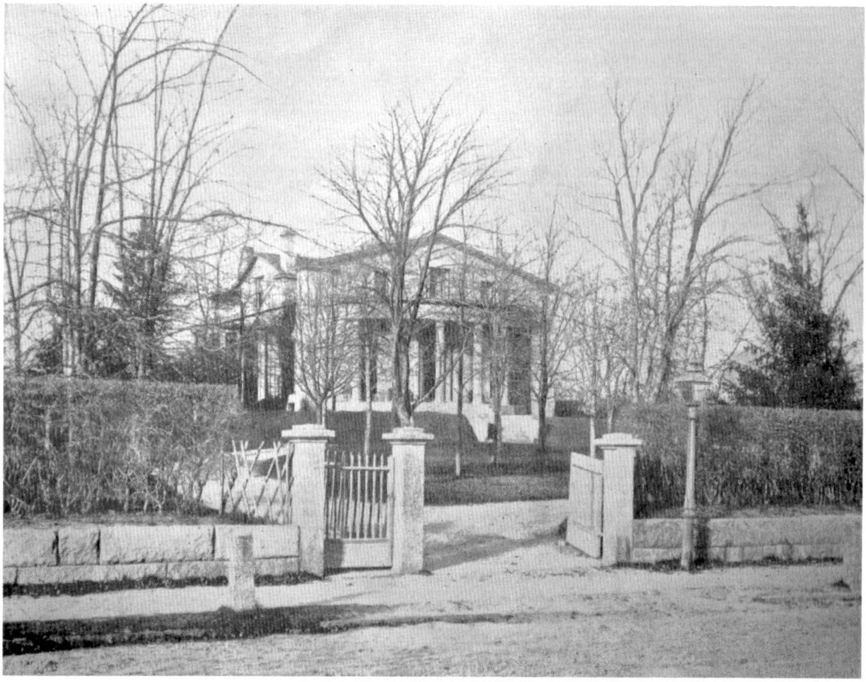

Thomas R. Robeson Mansion, built by Andrew Robeson's son. The family eventually moved business to Fall River. *Collection of author. Courtesy of Arthur P. Motta.*

> *very large chamber over our back parlor which we cannot warm these short mornings from the fire place, but by opening our door into the entry we feel a warm current from the stove below.*

Sarah seemed fondest of her bath just off her bedroom—a real luxury in 1821:

> [T]*he most complete little bathing room thou canst conceive of. Here we have a little stove that heats the air to 60 degrees in 15 minutes & there I dress and undress, wash &c. The boiler lined with tin holds water enough for 3 baths & heats in 20 minutes. A pump leads up into it from a cistern in the cellar supplied by pipes either from our rain or well water pumps. The latter is both soft to wash with & good to drink—a large stone sink is inserted in the floor at one end of which is our shower bath—This is the greatest luxury of our establishment & has been just what was necessary for my comfort, bathing having been very salutary & recommended by all our physicians.*

The original 1821 core of the mansion still remains on County Street, with additions made when it become the Wamsutta Club.

The Arnold family's new home was a perfect five-bay, brick Federal mansion on a granite foundation, with a fully excavated basement. Six slim Ionic columns ran across the front façade, supporting a deck with delicate Chippendale balustrade with alternating panels and balusters. An entrance from the second-floor center window gave access to the deck. A full balustrade extended around the house. There were four end chimneys.

The house had a center entrance with an elliptical fanlight with three-over-four sidelights. Windows were six-over-six with granite lintels and sills. The house would have had exterior shutters with two paneled louvers. The second-floor center window had full-length sidelights.

The interior layout of the Arnold Mansion was a basic four-room-per-floor plan, with public rooms leading off a central hallway. The staircase was set at the rear of the hall. Leading from the left side of the hall were two identical double parlors eighteen feet, three inches wide by twenty-two feet. Sliding pocket doors with an opened measurement of nine feet, four inches allowed the rooms to be opened as one space for social gatherings or closed to conserve heat and create intimacy. The two white Italian marble mantels imported by James Arnold around 1850 were and still are sited on the south wall. Each measures six feet, four inches in width.

To the right of the hall were two slightly smaller rooms, one behind the other. The room to the immediate right of the hall remains largely original and measured sixteen feet, three inches wide and sixteen feet long. Five-foot, six-inch black Federal mantels remain on the north wall, as do the original interior shutters. Using historic descriptions of the house as reference points, this room was Mr. Arnold's office. The second room measured sixteen feet, three inches and would have had similar six-over-six windows with interior shutters. From her description, Sarah Arnold's bedroom was directly over the southwest parlor. The second floor of the mansion's original core still retains the basic layout and a number of original features, including fireplace mantels and interior shutters.

It is highly probable that the third floor was part of the original Arnold Mansion. The mansion had a hipped roof with projecting dormers largely hidden by balustrades. There are indications that there were additional rooms in this area. The second- to third-floor staircase and elliptical plasterwork remaining in the mansion have Federal detail. Third-floor bedrooms in the Arnold core have Federal fireplaces and paneled interior shutters. The cellar core of the Arnold Mansion contains portions of the beautifully cut and laid stone flagging.

During the 1830s, the lives of all three Arnolds were ruined by what came to be called the Great Rotch Scandal. It involved the long betrayal of family trust and ties. Elizabeth Arnold was seduced by her much older cousin, Francis Rotch. It started when she was a child and ended in a scandal that rocked New Bedford, Boston and country houses in England. Charles Francis Adams, President John Quincy Adams's son, wrote about it in his diaries. Elizabeth Palmer Peabody, the great Transcendentalist teacher, was driven out of Boston for a time because of her involvement. Samuel Rodman described it in his diary, although the entries were kept out of the published edition. John Morgan Bullard included it as a chapter in *The Rotches* using false names.

In 2005, Megan Marshall in her book *The Peabody Sisters: Three Women Who Ignited American Romanticism* put all the letters, diaries and hints together. She wrote, "By winter, scandal had broken out. All of New Bedford—and soon after, all of Boston—knew about 'The Great Rotch Scandal,' which painted little Frank's father, Francis Rotch, as a sexual predator."

Ms. Marshall goes on:

> *There was no disputing the facts of the case. The senior Francis Rotch had secretly made a mistress of his cousin Elizabeth Rotch Arnold, a girl twenty one years younger than he. On the eve of her wedding to another man, the tearful Elizabeth Arnold confessed the two-year affair to her father, Rotch's mentor in business, knowing full well that the news would prevent her marrying. The enraged Arnold made the story public and ran Francis Rotch out of town leaving young Frank's mother a temporary widow and nearly hysterical with grief and shame. Of course Elizabeth Peabody tried to help her.*

Ms. Marshall unveils the hints that Mr. Bullard gave. In a clearly sexist twist, years of New Bedford histories had made it clear that it was an Arnold family tragedy yet shielded Francis Rotch. Mr. Bullard wrote in *The Rotches*, "The scandal and the events leading up to it occurred in New Bedford in the first third of the nineteenth century, more than a hundred years ago.... One of the participants in this particular scandal bore the name of Rotch. The other had a Rotch mother, but bore another name."

Deepening the family tragedy, Francis Rotch's wife was Ann Waln Morgan. Her brother, Charles W. Morgan, was the Arnolds' neighbor on County Street. Her sister, Susan, was married to Benjamin Rodman. William Rodman's wife was another of the Morgan sisters. One far too cynical and charming young man raised in England, although born on Nantucket, devastated his family.

John M. Bullard reprinted a letter from "someone not in the family to someone in St. Michael's Azores, dated at Fairhaven describing the methods used by Rotch":

> *He has been giving her improper books to tread to poison her mind so as to be able to accomplish his diabolical purposes and it seems she has been his mistress for upwards of two years without her friends mistrusting either of them and when she has expostulated with him he has even threatened her life. She was engaged to Mr. T a fine young man from Boston and a member of one of the oldest and most respected families in the city—she was to have been married this winter but of course now it will never take place.*
>
> *...I wonder they did not try to conceal the matter but Casanova* [Francis] *thought and said to someone who spoke to him on the subject that Mr. Arnold would not dare expose him.*

The letter, most likely sent to one of the Dabney family, who had close ties to New Bedford, continued: "I never liked the man as he always had a sarcastic smile on his features." At the height of the scandal, Charles Francis Adams wrote a cryptic diary note that is fully explained in the diary footnote:

> *Sunday 28th November 1830*
>
> *I attended Divine Service all day and heard Mr. Stetson preach a very able and useful Sermon upon the practice of Slander and Gossip which is so prevalent among us. I like that kind of address for it is probable that not a single person sat in that Meeting house to whom his words did not in some degree apply.*

A footnote continues:

> *Both the sermon on slander and gossip and CFA's strongly approving reaction to the choice of subject may have had a topical significance beyond the general suitability of the lesson: "Boston has been in a state of consternation owing to a little scandalous peccadillo which has occurred and crushed all the interest of the European News and almost of internal politics. It is as high in its grade as the Knap murder and conducted with*

all the deliberation, which rendered that incident so awful. The Lovelace [Rotch, Francis] *began with bad books at the age of twelve and completed the Seduction at fourteen and it has come out on the eve of the marriage of the lassy aged twenty-two because she would not agree to infringe the rights of matrimony. It is a New Bedford affair. The Mother gone distracted." Louisa Catherine Johnson Adams, wife of John Quincy Adams, Charles's mother writing to Mary Catherine Helen Adams.*

Francis Rotch was always a bit too charming for his own good—or for anyone whose path he managed to cross. While technically an American, he was raised and spoiled as a gentleman in England. After his father lost most of his money, Francis, then in his late twenties, was sent to America. He planned originally to settle and farm in Illinois. Somehow he was introduced to the Morgan family and fell in love with Anne Morgan.

As early as 1818, Charles W. Morgan was expressing his quiet doubts about his future brother-in-law, Francis, in his diary:

Philadelphia December 1818
We have received long letters from Francis Rotch which has dispelled the many fears we had begun to entertain on several accounts—His letter is written to Sister with all that elegance and refinement of style that marks every sentence he utters—and breathes a sincere and ardent attachment for my sister to whom I believe he is altogether devoted…It wants something however and what is this something—it has elegance of composition, warmth of feeling—beauty of description—and elevated morality to recommend it but he seems anything but a Quaker and seems ready to become even less than he is.

By 1820, the "sort of Quaker" had married Anne and brought her to New Bedford, as both the Rotch and Rodman families demanded. Even while writing to Charity, a firmly convinced Quaker, his view of Arnold as a bit of a fool shines clearly: "Warren Gifford and James Arnold are on a religious visit to Philadelphia…James has felt it is his duty to make many communications to his friends in their several meetings and has appeared more than once in prayer. He is careless of dress and sits in the gallery with a high crowned hat on his head—an offence beyond doubt to the outward formalist—but James takes little heed as to what he puts on."

Francis, of course, escaped tarring and instead moved his family to New York. His daughter, Anna, was later a belle in Cambridge and friend of

Margaret Fuller. Margaret even visited the estate in New York and seemed charmed by Francis. Charles W. Morgan and William Rotch Rodman were furious that Anne was taken away to New York and never forgave James Arnold. The Arnolds were left to somehow remake their lives.

Elizabeth Arnold survived her molestation by Francis Rotch. Her life after the winter of 1830–31 was, however, not the one she or her parents expected for her. After Rotch's actions had been made public, it would have made sense if the family had left immediately for Europe. Instead, James Arnold was determined to face down the world and New Bedford society.

In the *Diary of Charles Francis Adams*, he described a September 1835 visit to New Bedford with his father, former president John Quincy Adams:

> *We went on to Mr. Arnold's where we stopped. He took us over his garden, which has been laid out with great taste. The presence of a female with taste is perceptible in it. Having gone through it we were ushered into the house and found Mrs. Arnold, her daughter, and his sister to whom we were introduced. The melancholy story which has saddened this family for life made me feel surprised to see Miss Arnold. But I conversed with her for some time and found her a woman whose mind will always prevent her from being despicable in any body's eyes. Mrs. Arnold too is a lady as there are not many.*

Finally, in 1837, Arnold allowed the family to escape. They sailed for Europe, touring from Scotland to Rome until 1839. While in Rome, Robert Scott Lauder painted the entire Arnold family, and James Arnold sat for the bust that is now in the New Bedford Free Public Library Art Room. In Paris, Narcisse Othon did sketches of each member of the family that are owned by Harvard. James Arnold looks exactly like a gentleman out of something by Anthony Trollope.

In London, Elizabeth may have fallen in love. We do know that Pliny Earle, a pioneer of humane treatment for the mentally ill, fell in love with her. Earle noted in his diary:

> *May 31.—At a meeting appointed by Sarah Grubb I met James, Sally and Elizabeth Arnold (of New Bedford, in New England). They had left Paris a few days earlier than I…In the evening I called upon the Arnolds. James's daughter Elizabeth is without exception the most highly educated young lady I have met on this side of the Atlantic. She is not handsome; but one is charmed by the fluency and polish of her conversation, in which*

> *she draws from the resources of a mind largely stored with literary and scientific knowledge.... She speaks French well.*

Franklin B. Sanborn, in his book *Memoirs of Pliny Earle, M.D.*, wrote, "In Paris Dr. Earle met a lady from New Bedford, with whom he soon became intimate. Why they never married is not known; the acquaintance continued for many years; and the recollection of Elizabeth Arnold may have prevented any subsequent engagement." Elizabeth and Earle wrote each other to the end of Elizabeth's life.

On St. Patrick's Day 1859, Elizabeth did marry. She was fifty, and it would have been impossible for her to bear children. She married Dr. Charles Martin Tuttle from Littleton, New Hampshire. He had been married, divorced and had custody of his two daughters, Alice and Mary Belle. Standard family history says that the Arnolds did not approve. Elizabeth married him despite their feelings. She proudly used her married name, Elizabeth Arnold Tuttle, in making donations to the New Bedford Free Public Library. Elizabeth had very little time left. She died on October 26, 1860. Tuttle married a third time and named his daughter Elizabeth Arnold Tuttle in her memory.

In 1843, President Adams and Charles Francis Adams returned to New Bedford: "And our third visit was to Mr. and Mrs. Arnold, in the same house where we met an evening party in September 1835. The year after which they went to Europe, and traveled there three years. Their house was then graceful and comfortable, and furnished with elegance and at great cost. It is now embellished with many articles of exquisite luxury from Italy, so that it is like a second princely palace."

In 1857, the Arnolds joined the always impossible effort to help Bronson Alcott and his at times literally starving family. The charming educator, philosopher and professional genius refused to work at any job after he was forced to give up the Temple School in Boston. He did agree, however, that he *would* accept money for conversations and eventually toured the country giving them. A close friend of New Bedford historian Daniel Ricketson, in April 1857 Alcott came to New Bedford and gave three conversations in the Arnold double parlors.

On April 7, Alcott wrote to his long-suffering wife, "I dined on Saturday with the Arnolds...They offer their spacious drawing rooms for the Conversations, and their invitations are sent out for our first gathering on Thursday evening coming—some sixty or more—the best families—the Rotch's, Morgans, Rodmans, etc. are to comprise our Company." Historian Sally Sapienza quoted the letter in her typescript lecture on Mr. Arnold.

Richard Henry Dana Sr. once had a reputation far greater than his son, who became famous for his autobiographical book, *Two Years Before the Mast.* Dana Sr. was the son of the chief justice of the Massachusetts Supreme Court. He had been tossed out of Harvard after a small riot and was later allowed back in. He became a non-practicing lawyer and a writer, poet and critic. He often lectured in New Bedford and stayed with the Arnolds. His letters to Sarah Arnold are informal and delightful. One is even quoted in *The Letters of Charles Dickens*. To Mrs. Sarah Arnold, he wrote on February 14:

> *No sooner was it known that the steamer with Dickens on board, was in sight, than the Town was pouring itself out on the wharf; and when this remarkable man reached the Boston side, the "hacknies" were all calling out, each anxious to have the honor of carrying "Boz." And for days the streets were a flutter with ribbons and feathers.... When my eyes first fell upon him I was disappointed. But the instant his face was turned toward me, there was a change. He has the finest of eyes; and his whole countenance speaks life and action—the face seems to flicker with the heart's and mind's activity. You cannot tell how dead the faces near him seemed.*

Later, he shared with her his real sadness when, following the wrong family tradition, Richard Jr. was also ordered to take leave from Harvard. Writing in the *New England Quarterly*, "The Education of Richard Henry Dana, Jr.," James David Hart noted, "Although the elder Dana had been rusticated for a similar offense twenty-four years previous to this, the punishment of his son, and his own melancholy temper made him extremely despondent. In letters to the family friend, Mrs. Sarah Arnold he wrote of 'my banished boy' and 'Richard's exile.'" The Arnolds and the Danas spent a great deal of time together both in New Bedford and Boston. Richard Henry Dana Jr. in his journals seems to have been a bit infatuated with Sarah.

On June 30, 1842, at the age of twenty-six and already famous because of *Two Years Before the Mast*, Dana wrote, "Dined at Mrs. Arnold's. Mrs. Arnold is the most charming & dignified of women. There is something about her which interest your feelings, makes you love to be near her, & at the same time commands your highest respect & insures without enforcing it the most deferential address & manner in all who approach her." Only a pair of cherished copper beeches remain of the Arnold gardens.

They had made horticultural history, however. The following description was published in *Magazine Horticulture* in October 1840:

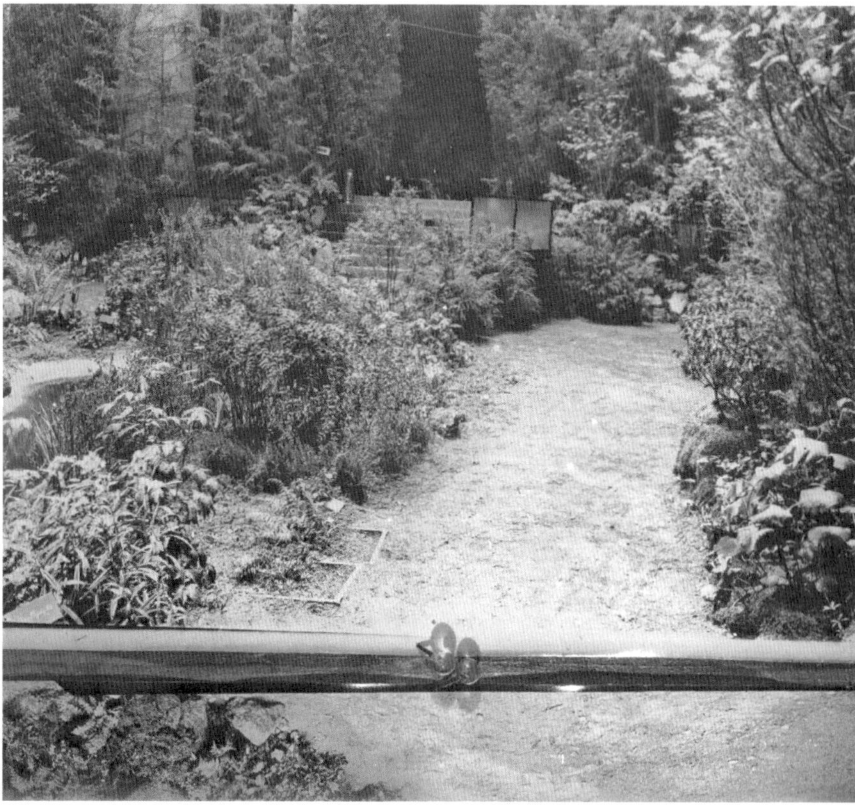

Wildflower exhibition garden at Horticultural Hall Boston, similar to James Arnold's informal cutting garden. *Library of Congress. Frances Benjamin Johnston, photographer.*

ART. 1. Notes on Gardens and Gardening, in New Bedford, Mass. By the Editor

August 24th.—The delightful grounds of Mr. Arnold are situated on the west side of County street, nearly opposite the head of Union street. The site is one of the most elevated in the street, and commands a view of the harbor, and beyond, on the opposite side of the river, the neat and flourishing village of Fairhaven; to the west stretches out a vast extent of country, well wooded, and in some directions presenting varied and interesting views… which are laid out in a pleasure ground, a flower garden, vegetable garden, orchard, &c.

The house stands about one hundred and fifty feet from the street; a broad carriage-way enters on one side, and, sweeping by the entrance to

> *the house, in a semicircular form, opens to the street on the opposite side. Between this carriage-way and street there is a fine lawn; this is varied by two or three elegant groups of trees, which break the view of the house from the street.... From the approach, on the south side of the house, about two thirds of the distance from the entrance, a walk leads up to the conservatory, the back of which stands up against a wall running west from the rear of the house. In front of the conservatory is a fine flower garden, laid out with dug beds on turf. This garden is bounded by a wall on the west, and by the back of the grapery on the south; and, to screen the latter building from the eye, a vigorous and luxuriant growth of the woodbine has covered it so completely, as to scarcely leave an open space. A rock-work, in a small way, hut erected mostly with rare specimens of quartz, &c., and covered with verbenas and petunias, is an interesting feature of this garden. The work was executed by Mr. Jones, formerly gardener to Mr. Arnold.*
>
> *Continuing through the winding walks, shady bowers, and umbrageous retreats, through which rustic seats were placed, we arrived at the shell grotto. This is an ingenious piece of work, finely executed under the direction of Mr. Arnold. The roof is supported by columns of rough trunks of trees, the outer part of the roof thatched, and the ceiling elegantly inlaid with shells, quartz, &c. A rustic sofa and table are the only articles in the interior. So secluded is this grotto, that the robin has built its nest and reared its young in some of the niches left for that purpose.*

Andrew Jackson Downing, perhaps the single greatest influence on gardens and appropriate houses in the nineteenth century, included the Arnold gardens in *A Treatise on the Theory and Practice of Landscape Gardening*.

In 1890, Arnold was still remembered and still made good copy in *The New England Magazine: An Illustrated Monthly*:

> *"Tarry at Home Travel" III—Edward E. Hale, D.D.*
>
> *Dear Mr. Arnold! I remember him so well! He was always so good to me, as he was to everybody. The true princes are always good to everybody, and he was one of the true princes, one of that New Bedford dynasty. It exists to this hour. The house was a palace with the comforts of a log cabin and that is more than you can say of all palaces, and he and all his were so cordial to everyone who came in.*
>
> *Please let me tell the story of his dog and then I will tell you about the Arboretum. The dog was a magnificent fellow, Newfoundland I think.*

But he grew very old. He seemed to enjoy nothing, and had as many sores and ailments as poor Lazarus himself; and so Mr. Arnold said to his right hand man one day: "It will be a mercy to kill him. Life is a burden to him. Shoot him some day when you can be sure of your mark, and we will put him out of him misery." Upon which the dog rose from that place between the door where he used to lie, and left the house and grounds, and was seen no more of men for weeks on weeks...after many weeks the poor creature returned, nearly starved this time, and with that imploring eye which said, better than words, "I know you'll not shoot me now." And they did not shoot him. He lived till he died, and if you go to New Bedford, you may see his memorial stone.

Now as I say, Mr. Arnold has this beautiful place, which you may call an arboretum of his own. That was where I first saw a Spanish chestnut growing—and why other men in Southern New England do not have Spanish chestnuts I do not know. It seems to me that he told me that the nut it came from grew in Mt. Vernon, and that some general of the Revolution planted it, perhaps General Cobb, possibly Lafayette.

James Arnold's wife, Sarah, died on May 9, 1860. His daughter, Elizabeth, died the following October on the twenty-sixth. Arnold died on December 3, 1868. With both his wife and daughter dead before him, in the chilling words of the Chad Brown Memorial, "The line is extinct."

Chapter 4

The House of Russell

Winning and Losing Great Fortune

Benjamin Russell lost everything. He was a spoiled, blithe young man who drew pointed cartoons of his elderly bank bosses, but that came to an end. On August 14, 1835, the *New Bedford Mercury* ran this notice:

> *Dwelling House and Lot on Tuesday, August 18th, at 10 o'clock, on the premises unless previously disposed of at private sale.*
>
> *That commodious House and Lot situated on County Street, recently occupied by Benjamin Russell. The house is built of first rate materials and is thoroughly furnished from the cellar to garret.*
>
> *The Lot contains 382 rods of land and is in a high state of cultivation. The entire premises will be sold together with a large and convenient stable nearly new.*
>
> *The above offers a rare chance, for a person wishing to purchase a healthy situation within 10 minutes walk from the business parts of the town.*
>
> *An indisputable title will be given.*
>
> *Terms 6 and 9 months approved endorsed paper payable at Bank with interest.*
>
> *The premises can be examined at any time by calling for the key at G.R. Thornton's counting room Parker's Buildings.*

The House of Russell was bankrupt. Samuel Rodman Jr. reported on that crash: "December 30, 1835—Engaged at the Bank & counting house. The difficulties incident on the failures of Charles Russell & George Tyson,

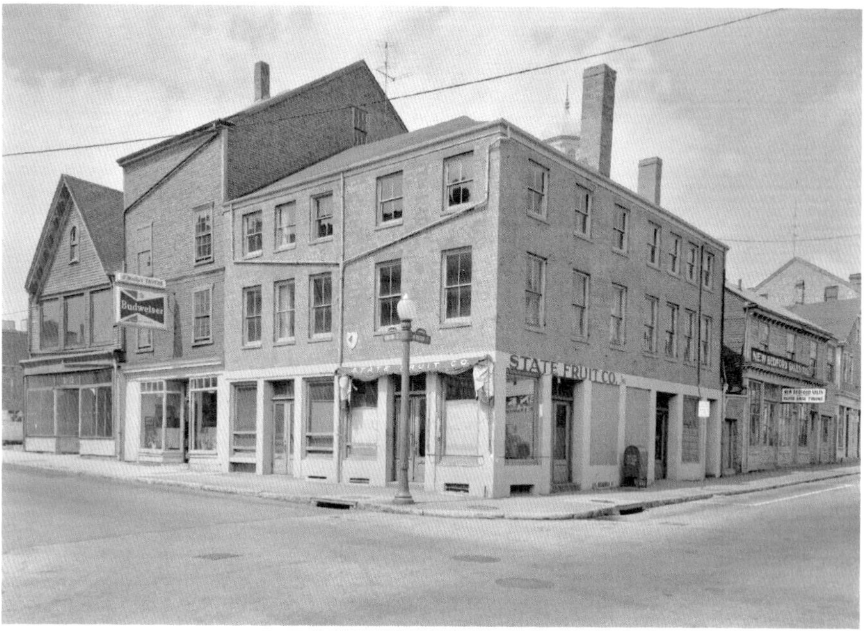

Charles and Seth Russell's Sundial Building, Union and Water Streets, 1820. Lost when the family failed. *Library of Congress, Historic American Buildings Survey.*

and the assignment of Seth Russell making the principal business, a special meeting of the Directors being also held in the afternoon."

America has always been prone to financial panics, and in 1833, a really nasty one hit. New Bedford banks called in all their mortgages. The Rodman family was barely able to find enough cash to save both Samuel and his brother, Benjamin.

The Russell family wasn't that lucky, as historian Edmund Wood explained in a 1911 whaling museum paper discussing Benjamin and his family. There were clearly the lucky Rotches, and then there were the Russells. Seth Russell was Benjamin's father and Charles his uncle: "On the other hand were Seth and Charles Russell, who had recently increased the prestige of that family and were rich and powerful. Some of their foreign ventures in commerce were brilliant, they carried a large bank balance in London, they owned many merchant ships and whaleships, and they had also acquired a large amount of real estate within the town."

Wood also hinted at something else: "There was some rivalry between some of the older merchants and these two brothers, Seth and Charles Russell. The latter were called progressive, they took long chances and with

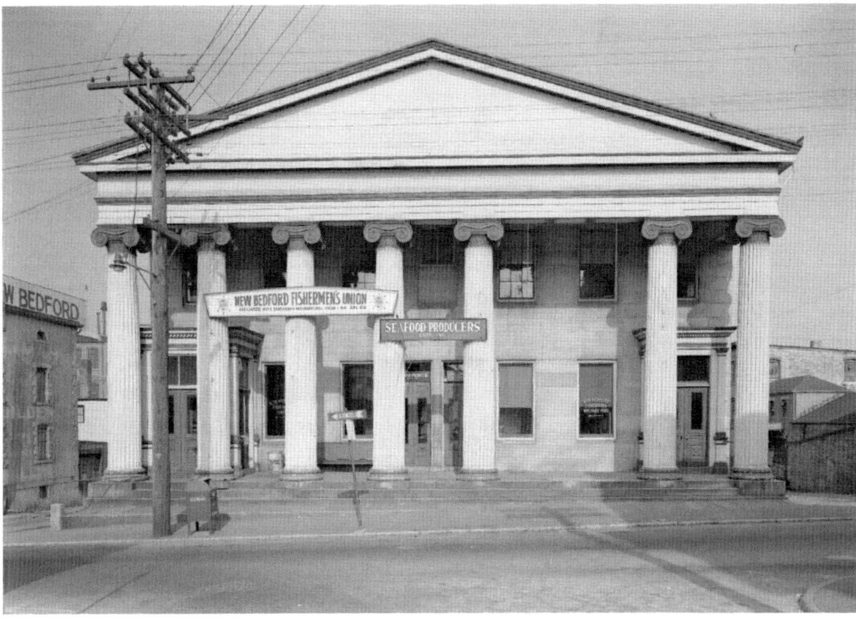

Russell Warren's Double Bank, built jointly by Merchants and Mechanics Banks. *Library of Congress, Historic American Buildings Survey. Ned Goode, photographer.*

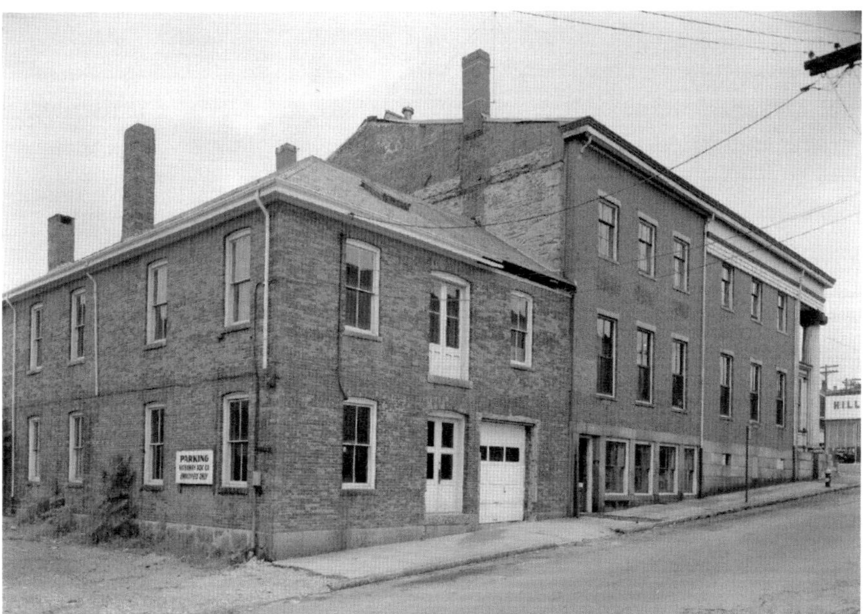

The Double Bank, North and East Elevations. *Library of Congress, Historic American Buildings Survey. Ned Goode, photographer.*

uniform success. But soon there came reverses, then the tide seemed to turn against them and finally came the crash when the brothers failed, and much property and real estate in the city changed hands."

Benjamin was a watercolorist and sketcher even as a very young man. He had a whimsical side, as illustrated by the charming "Sarah" cartoons owned by the New Bedford Whaling Museum. Identifying Sarah is difficult, however. She was not Russell's mother, sister or daughter. There is one possibility: Sarah Swain Hathaway Forbes. She was a niece of William W. Swain, and Russell was one of his nephews. They would have grown up together in New Bedford and remained in contact after her marriage to the enormously wealthy John Murray Forbes of Milton and Naushon Island.

Russell's penchant for quick sketching is noted in an early Old Dartmouth Historical Society paper by Edmund Wood. He noted, "There is a story that he drew an interesting caricature of one of the directors' meetings, which was remarkably true to the life. In it the almost life-long president of that institution was represented as seated at the head of the table on a cake of ice. This picture was said to be exceedingly popular with certain disappointed applicants for discount, who had been chilled by the presidential atmosphere." The bank president, Joseph Grinnell, was not someone to make an enemy.

The Whaling Museum owns a letter from George Howland sent in 1839 dunning Benjamin: "This oil was sold thee after thy failure, with a full expectation it would have been attended to agreeable to contract and I believe it is over two years since thee has said a word on the subject voluntarily…I very much dislike to have unsettled matters hanging along so."

With wife Hannah Howland Russell, two daughters and a son to support, Benjamin Russell signed on as cooper on the *Kutusoff* and went whaling from 1841 to 1845. Even before he left the harbor, every cent he might earn was pledged to pay debts. He was thirty-seven. That voyage was his making as an artist. He returned knowing a whale ship inch by inch. He came home understanding the vastly complicated system of setting sails. He learned how whales were caught and rendered. Art saved him.

Russell began by painting portraits of ships and selling them to ship owners and whaling masters. He issued a series of prints that seems to have been moderately successful; today they are priceless. Then he hit on an idea that might remake his fortunes. It had to be something large. Something that people would want to see and, even better, pay to see. Something that no one had ever done better. He knew whaling, and he'd been out there. Why not something that would use what he knew? He decided on what came to be known as the *Grand Panorama of a Whaling Voyage Round the World*.

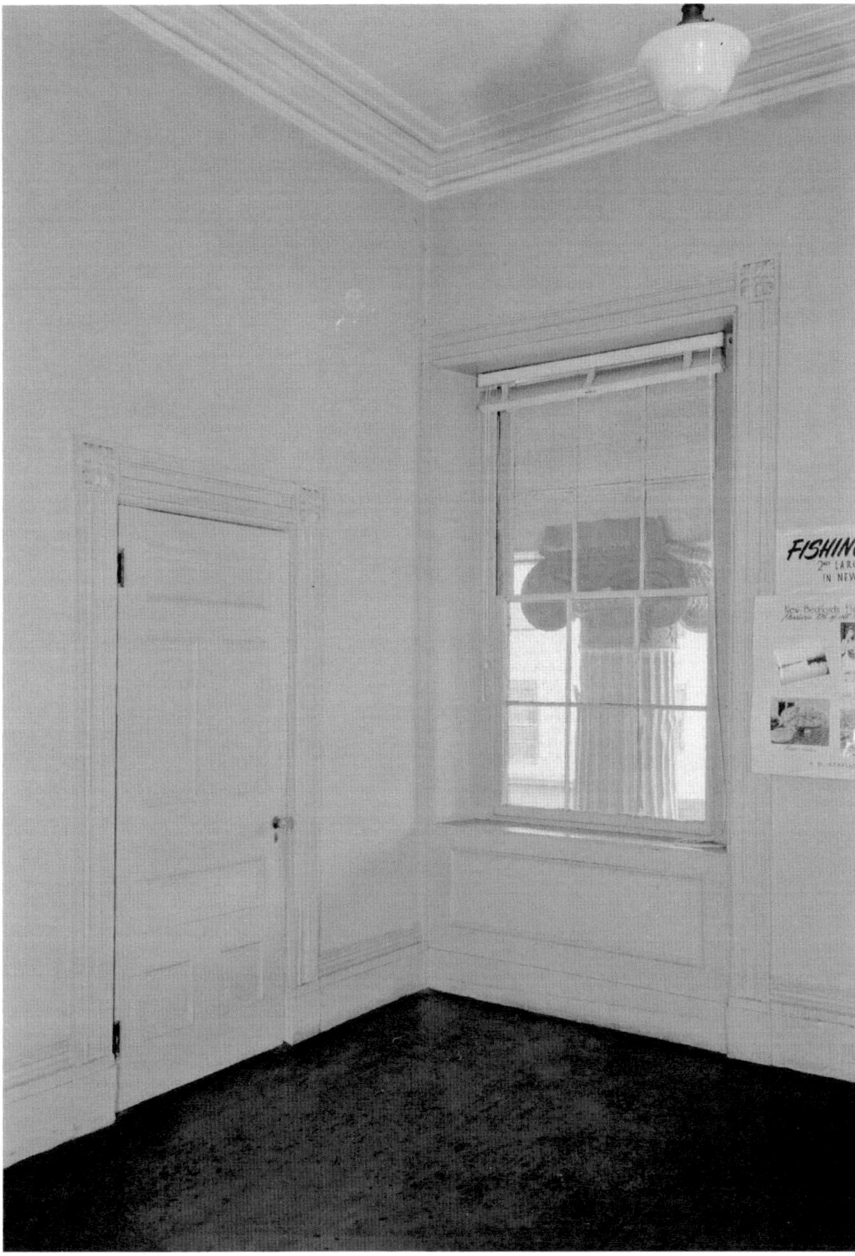

Double Bank, northeast front room, second floor. Note the capitol through the window. *Library of Congress, Historic American Buildings Survey. Ned Goode, photographer.*

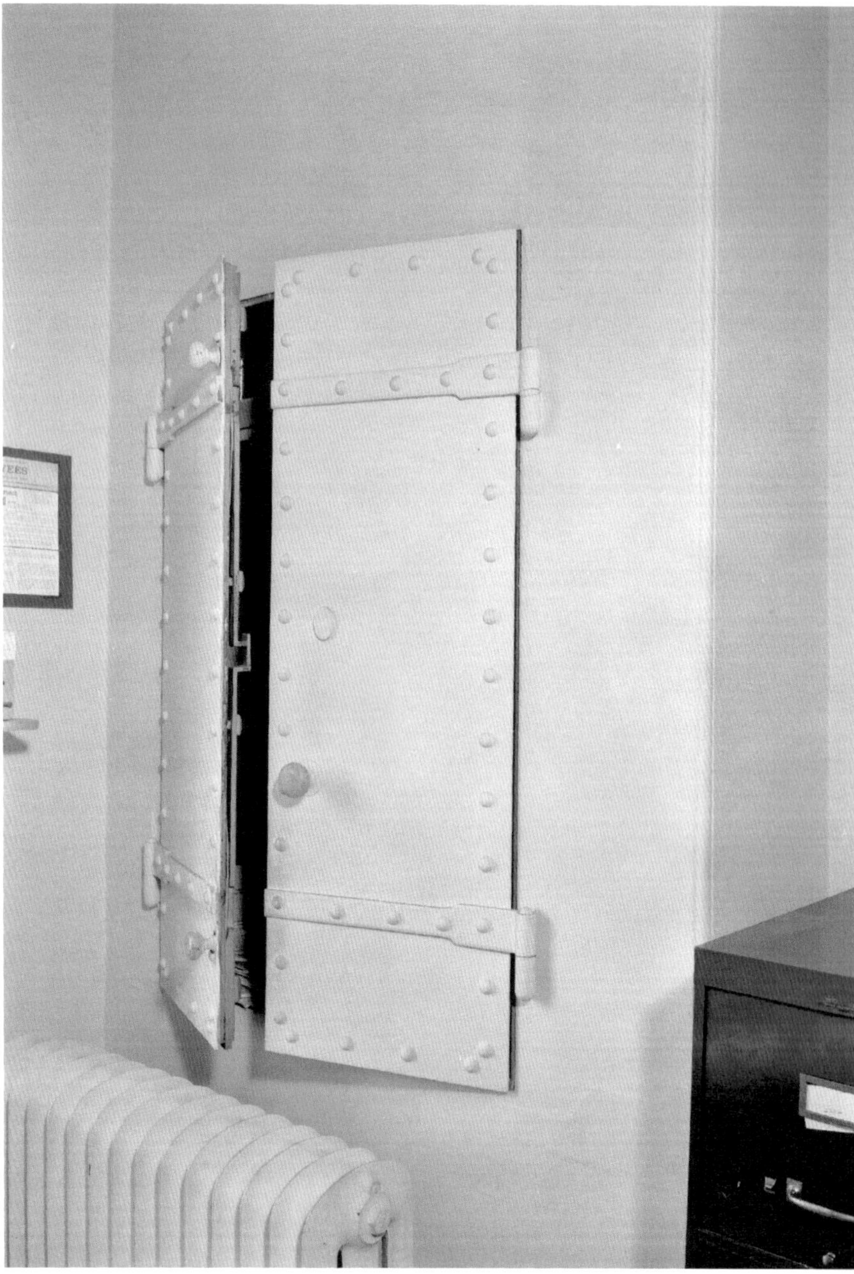

Double Bank, metal safe on second floor. *Library of Congress, Historic American Buildings Survey. Ned Goode, photographer.*

To produce such an enormous piece, Russell had Caleb Purrington partner with him. The general assumption is that Russell sketched out the entire panorama, and Purrington did most of the painting on sheeting cut to the proper length—1,275 feet long and 8½ feet tall.

The *New Bedford Mercury* announced on November 17, 1848:

> *We understand that the extensive Panorama of a "Voyage Round the World"...is now nearly completed and will shortly be exhibited in the principal cities of the Union. Some idea of the extent and variety of scenery presented in this immense painting may be formed from the fact that it opens with a graphic view of the departure of whaleships from the port of New Bedford, following their course through the stormy gulf to the Cape Verde Islands, thence round Cape Horn to the various Island of the Pacific resorted to by our Whaleman, and the return home view St. Helena.*

What this description can't capture is how very beautiful the panorama actually is. Writing in 1980, marine historian Samuel Eliot Morison called it "the masterpiece of the panoramic art." In a time without radio, television, electric light or, of course, computers, an evening at the panorama was the equivalent of a really grand 3D movie. You could see the "Burning of Moscow," the "Battle of Gettysburg" or a "Journey Down the Mississippi." Best of all, a panorama was educational, and even the most staid churchgoers could see it.

A narrator as flamboyant as P.T. Barnum explained the show. Writing in 1918 in the *Boston Daily Globe*, reporter Zephaniah W. Pease described the spiel of Stephen W. Booth, who worked for Russell on the show. Booth would say, "Here we see the good ship Niger of New Bedford anchored in the harbor of Fayal. At her masthead floats the American flag. All Nations respect it. When they don't we make 'em."

For your twenty-five-cent admission, you also got sound effects. "A storm at sea was one of the thrillers. The lights were turned down, the sheet iron devices rolled out thunder and the flashes of lightning furnished a thrill to the unsophisticated audience of that day." It was a grand event that played well on the East Coast, and Russell even took it as far west as Ohio. Showings for schoolchildren were arranged.

In 1897, John Munroe described viewing "A Trip to Venice": "So now where everything was seen or unseen, was new and strange, and the imagination was quite free to rove, the charm was more intense. We stood and gazed upon the moving panorama like persons in a trance." Most amazing of all, according to writer Mary Jean Blasdale in her exhaustive *Artists of New Bedford*, the panorama was Russell's first and earliest known work.

The *Voyage Round the World* didn't make Russell a fortune, but it allowed him to survive and become a truly important marine artist. Today, a Benjamin Russell is worth a small fortune and is best seen in museums. In 2014, the New Bedford Whaling Museum began an extensive restoration of the panorama, and visitors can watch the work being done.

Benjamin Russell, the man who lost everything and found himself as an artist, died on March 3, 1885, at the home of his daughter in Warren, Rhode Island.

Chapter 5

The House of Morgan

Owning the Last Whaling Ship in the World

Charles W. Morgan came to New Bedford for love. He stayed to build a family, a home and, incidentally, a whaling business. Most everyone has seen the elderly man in the daguerreotype and knows of his most famous ship, the *Charles W. Morgan.* The eager young man from a good Pennsylvania family desperate to marry his Sally has been largely forgotten.

Happily, Charles W. Morgan kept a diary. Through it we can discover the beginnings of the man—young, impetuous, a shrewd judge of character and bad with money. He was Welsh tempered and wanted only to get to his Sarah ("Sally") Rodman in New Bedford. He loved the story that he was related to Henry Morgan, the buccaneer.

His parents were Thomas and Anne Waln Morgan. Both died young, leaving Charles the head of the family well before he was twenty-two. Although the family always kept ties to Pennsylvania, their lives would be spent in New Bedford because of a remarkable series of marriages. Anne Morgan married Francis Rotch. Susan married Benjamin Rodman. William R. Rodman married Rebecca. Eventually, Charles was to marry Sarah Rodman. All his life, Charles passionately looked after his sisters.

By the time his diary begins in 1818, Rebecca had already married William R. Rodman, brother of Samuel Rodman Jr. and Benjamin Rodman. Young Anne was being courted by Francis Rotch. Charles was caught in Philadelphia. His uncle, also named Charles Waln Morgan, was procrastinating endlessly about settling Charles's inheritance. Without the

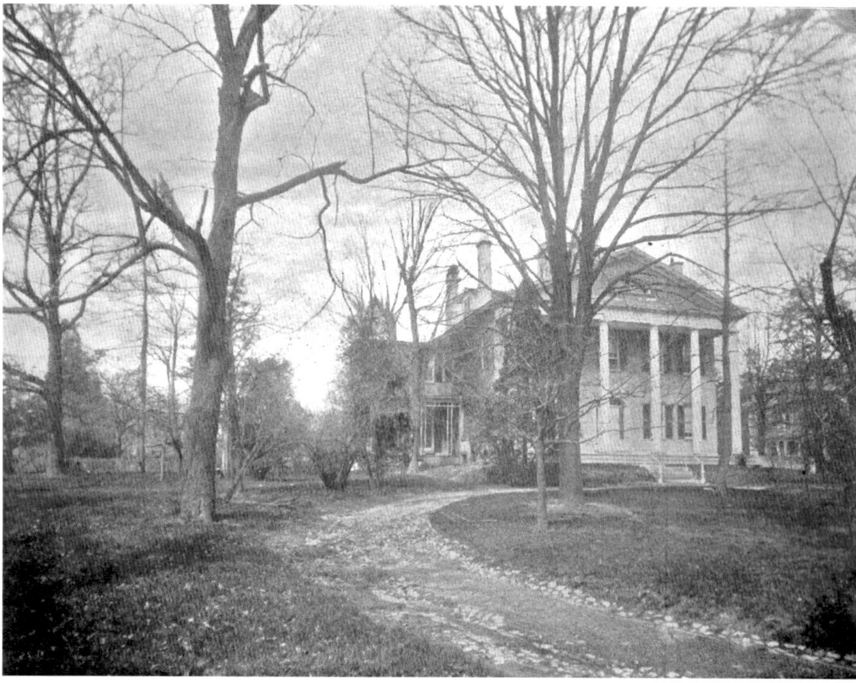

Morgan Mansion. From the steps, it was possible to look directly down William Street to the Double Bank. *Collection of author. Courtesy of Arthur P. Motta.*

money, he couldn't marry Sarah. He was not a happy young man. The Morgan diary is at Mystic Seaport and available online.

> *NOVEMBER 1, 1818*
> *On the 1st of the eleventh month I sit down to commence a Journal, which it is my intention to keep (should my life and health be spared), for many years to come. I am twenty two years of age I was born on the 14th day of the 9th month 1796 at ½ past two in the morning—It is my intention to note all events here that are at all of an interesting nature so that it may serve as a reference at some future day.*

> *NOVEMBER 2, 1818*
> *I left meeting before its adjournment to see if there was not a letter from my Sarah—and one was handed to my anxious inquiry—of that sweetly soothing nature which my excited feelings so much needed—This first epistle from my darling girl was full of all that tenderness,*

that fond affection which my heart was aching to know and feel and I have been calmed by the perusal and the depression of my spirits has been lightened.

NOVEMBER 4, 1818
I have been this morning paying some visits to a few of my old acquaintances, they received me coolly because I had not been before…the tie is now broken…I am an exile from my sisters—and my friendships my intimacies are declining…The pang of parting here will not be bitter, the bitterness will have been experienced long before it arrives—the thread is even now snapped I have made a violent exertion to do it and I do not wish to rejoin it…No I am desolate I am dissatisfied—I am afraid too I am at a stand in the road to reformation of heart—my temper feels irritable—I have no conversation and few good ideas—I never remember such a state of mind as I now experience.

Charles was forgetting that at the time his sister Sarah and her husband, William Rodman, were living in the same city. At his age, unhappiness lasts forever.

NOVEMBER 13, 1818
This has been a day of no pleasing sensations to me I have done nothing in every sense of the word…I went today to a dinner party at Thos. Rotch and a miserable time I have had.

Francis Rotch, who weaves through this book like a weak thread, caused Charles additional worries. He had become fascinated by an odd con man named Morris Birkbeck and wanted to move west with Ann Morgan. Charles had his doubts.

NOVEMBER 20, 1818
I have looked at the subject with some anxiety and interest but these are not satisfied…I cannot think his an honest heart—and I fear the influence of his cold mind on the untutored one of our Francis.

Eventually, Francis gave up the plan. At the same time, Charles was having difficulties with his brother-in-law William R. Rodman. Later in New Bedford, they would become close friends, but not in 1818.

NOVEMBER 21, 1818
Rodman's enmity towards me seems to continue unabated towards me—I called there as is my custom this morning and found him at home most unexpectedly—he took no kind of notice of me—and I felt disagreeable enough in being thus unavoidably with him in his own house—his conduct towards me seems unaccountable to us all.

The cause of the coldness has been lost to history. Whatever it was rankled Charles during his last months in Philadelphia.

NOVEMBER 26, 1818
I was invited by Sister R to dine with her but the idea of dining with William and in his own house was so unpleasant to me in his present state of feelings towards me that I passed on home.

On the Anne and Francis front, things seemed better.

DECEMBER 5, 1818
We have received long letters from Francis Rotch which has dispelled the many fears we had begun to entertain on several accounts—His letter is written to Sister with all that elegance and refinement of style that marks every sentence he utters...It wants something however and what is this something—it has elegance of composition, warmth of feeling—beauty of description—and elevated morality to recommend it but he seems anything but a quaker and seems ready to become even less than he is.

Charles was a better judge of character than he realized. The marriage of Francis and Anne would be a disaster. Francis would eventually cause the Great Rotch Scandal. His seduction of a child rocked New Bedford, split the entire interconnected Rotch Rodman and Morgan families and drove Francis from New Bedford. The bitterness that Morgan felt at having his sister taken away would blight him emotionally and financially.

DECEMBER 9, 1812
Oh how freely can I now fly to my darling Sarah—and the repose of Bedford—nothing detains me here but the interested plots of William Rodman—which it has hitherto baffled me to fathom, his coldness towards me still continues—but how do I pity him he is so perplexed

> *with business of my spirits has been lightened—Oh may I continue to more and more deserve this jewel, this treasure—and then I shall the more enjoy it.*

Charles would always have problems with money. In 1848, he was forced to sell the *Charles W. Morgan*, and he was in debt when he died. His uncle was finally ready to settle with Charles, and the result was not what he had assumed.

> *JANUARY 6, 1819*
> *I have observed with sorrow that I never was worth as much as I had an idea of—and have been spending as if my income was $1000 when in fact it is not near that sum—so that I have been encroaching on the principal and this has proceeded from the unjustifiable detention of these accounts—and deluding me with the idea that my situation was really better than it is.*

The Rotch and Rodman families were extremely tight with their money and would expect the same of Charles. He would be expected to explain in New Bedford what had become of the Morgan fortune. Was he worthy to marry Sarah?

> *JANUARY 15, 1819*
> *Now I am free and I only want to get to New Bedford and make final interesting arrangements.*

> *JANUARY 23, 1819*
> *Two more days and…I will be on my way to my dear home—the weather continues dark, damp and cloudy rendering the roads as bad as possible—I did not feel well today and took some medicine which is operating and I feel relieved from a nausea and sickness that oppressed me—I intend to change my habits.*

Finally, Charles W. Morgan did get to New Bedford and married Sarah Rodman in Quaker Meeting on June 3, 1819. According to his descendant, Reverend Alfred Hussey, in his *Life of Charles W. Morgan*, the result of the wrangling with his uncle had given Morgan about $14,000, some stocks and $4,000 invested in the ship *Enterprise*.

He entered the whaling industry first with the family Rotch Rodman firm and then on his own. He stopped keeping his diary for a number of years but

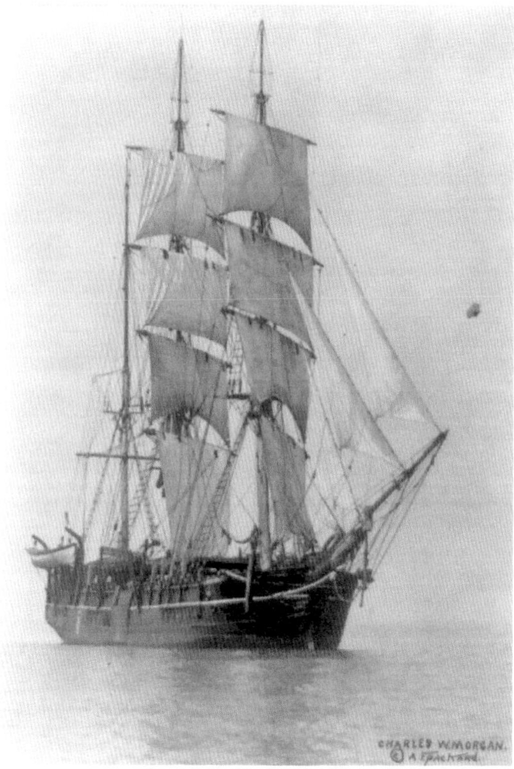

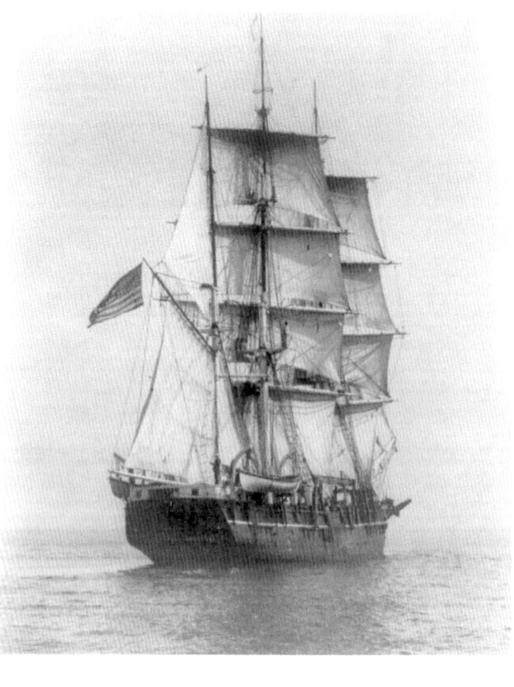

took it up again in 1848. Morgan and his family would eventually leave the Society of Friends. In 1821, close to his then friend James Arnold on County Street, Morgan built his own home facing down William Street toward the harbor. It was one end of a perfect axis, with the Double Bank at the other. That same view can be found today from the highest step of the New Bedford School Department building, constructed later as New Bedford High School.

In that house, his growing family celebrated Christmas with a tree and gifts. They experimented with table tapping. Morgan bought two John James Audubon paintings and read Thackeray, Defoe and the Bronte sisters. He followed the infamous Parkman-Webster murder at Harvard and actually went to Boston to sit in on the trial. Morgan

Above: Drying sails: the *Charles W. Morgan* in dock, December 12, 1927. *Library of Congress Prints & Photographs Division.*

Left: The *Charles W. Morgan*, circa 1924. *Library of Congress Prints & Photographs Division. A.E. Packard, photographer.*

was as shocked as everyone else was when Webster confessed just before his hanging. He helped establish the New Bedford Lyceum and gave two important natural history lectures on a subject he knew well: the whale.

Young Mr. Morgan became the older public figure Charles W. Morgan. This Mr. Morgan built and launched a certain ship in 1841, the *Charles W. Morgan*. Revisiting a young, eager Charles Morgan gives us a sense of the man he would become.

Charles W. Morgan felt abused by James Arnold, County Street neighbor and former friend, calling him "a man totally devoid of sensibility and true kindness of feeling." Morgan often had financial problems in his own right and was forced to sell his glorious and profitable ship, the *Charles W. Morgan*, to the Howland family. It is today a National Historic Landmark and the last existing whaling ship.

> *TUESDAY. APRIL 2 1850*
> *Busy all this day making financial arrangements, in which I shall succeed notwithstanding a cold & cruel attempt to crush & dishonour me…I may forgive it & its authors—but I will never forget and they shall know my mind, when I am properly prepared.*

His anger grew and exploded the next day.

> *APRIL 3, 1850*
> *Had the pleasure of paying off a very heavy note to the Bedford Commercial Bank this day—which or any part of which they utterly refused to renew—although they told me there was money enough…this from an institution where I had kept my principal account for 30 years—Sat as director 20 years—have had transactions to the amount of over 6 millions of dollars—Kept a good & active account—while at the other banks what I asked was granted kindly, promptly and cheerfully where I had no claim—but that of responsibility common citizenship & a common humanity—I therefore brand this proceeding here as one of the most cold blooded & cruel attempts to crush a man without rhyme or reason as affected the bank—not so individuals—one man sat at that board—a professing Christian a plain coated elder—who had in years gone by sworn, as much as a Quaker could swear revenge—and who has since had an opportunity of venting it on several of our family…I brand George Howland President & James Arnold as director with an attempt to destroy me & injure W.R Rodman my endorser—without*

> *cause except on the one part the gratification of revenge & the other of the most cold hearted selfishness—which would not lift a finger to save me from destruction—henceforth I have no sympathies or fellowship with these men—I shall not act against them but I shall avoid & shun them—I have no common feeling with them—I hope to forgive them—I cannot forget.*

Adding to Morgan's fury was the fact that he blamed James Arnold for driving his beloved sister Anne from New Bedford. It seems not to have occurred to him that Francis Rotch had ruined Elizabeth Arnold's life. James Arnold and Charles W. Morgan were never close again.

Chapter 6

The House of Grinnell

The Congressman and the Tastemaker

Russell Warren built any number of masterpieces in New Bedford. His most austere was the Greek Revival expression of pure power in the house he gave Joseph Grinnell. If anyone in New Bedford was famous outside the city, it was Joseph Grinnell—founder of one of New York's greatest shipping firms, Grinnell and Minturn; congressman who brought Abraham Lincoln to New Bedford; father-in-law of a great nineteenth-century tastemaker and writer, Nathaniel Parker Willis; and founder and owner of the Wamsutta Mill, the most famous and long lasting of New Bedford's textile mills. Some people dared to call him "Uncle Joe" but in reality he was always "Congressman," the Honorable Joseph Grinnell. Born in 1788, Grinnell outlived the War of 1812 and the Civil War. He died at ninety-three in 1885, having lived well in two centuries.

Grinnell would probably have considered raising his brother Cornelius's daughter to be his greatest, most loving accomplishment. Cornelius hung himself in December 1830. Cornelia was five. Joseph and his wife, Sarah Russell Grinnell, immediately adopted her. She was their only child. She grew up to be an extraordinary woman.

By 1830, Joseph Grinnell had already had a massively profitable career in New York City. During the War of 1812, he owned merchant ships with an uncle. They lost most of their ships to the British navy. By 1815, he was back in business with his cousin, the delightfully named Preserved Fish. Preserved was named for his father—it is not known if he had a sense of humor about the name. Fish and Grinnell did very well. Fish retired early. Joseph invited

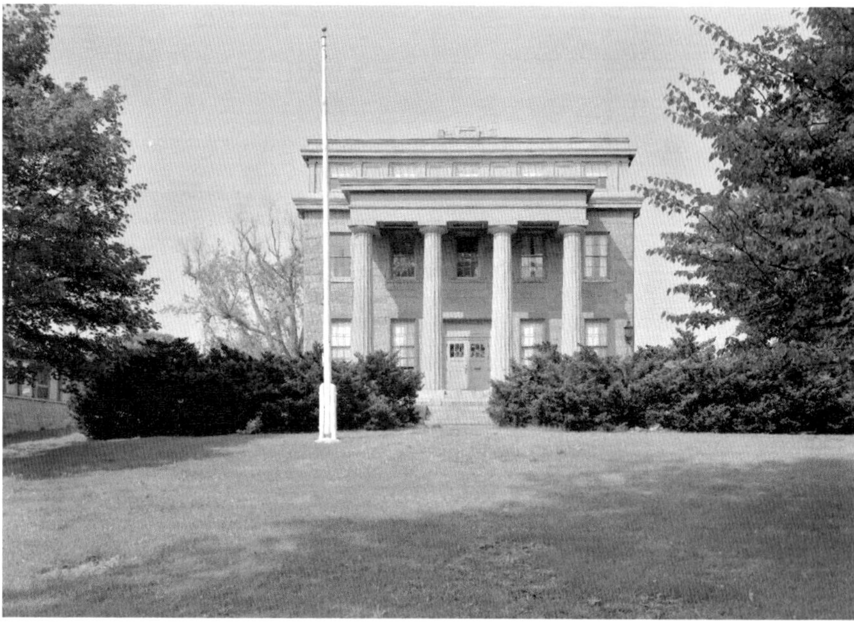

Joseph Grinnell Mansion, 379 County Street. Warren's most subdued design. Russell Warren, architect. *Library of Congress, Historic American Buildings Survey. Ned Goode, photographer.*

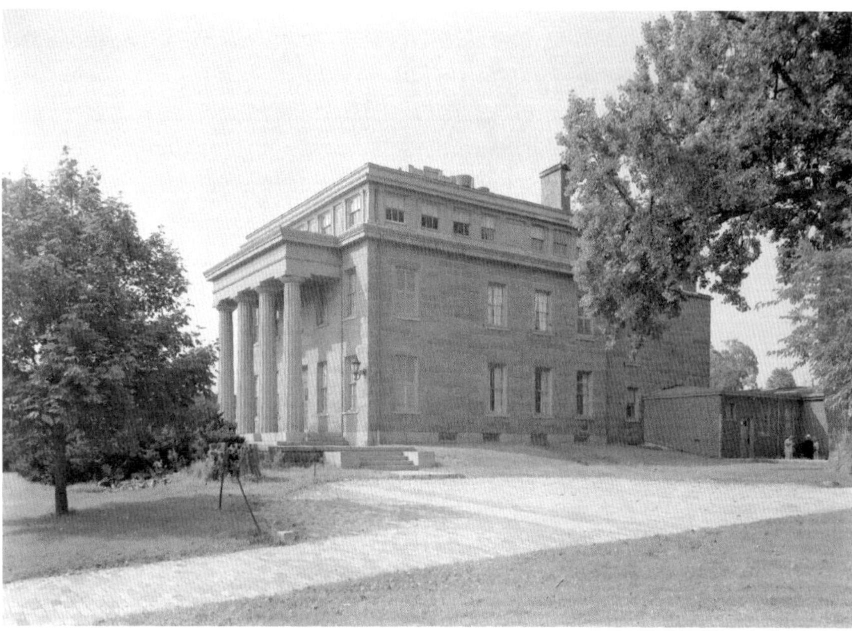

Grinnell Mansion, front and side elevations. *Library of Congress, Historic American Buildings Survey. Ned Goode, photographer.*

his two brothers, Moses and Henry, in as partners. By 1828, Joseph was able to retire back to New Bedford. Henry Grinnell invited his brother-in-law, Robert Minturn, to join the firm. It became internationally known, respected and feared as Grinnell, Minturn & Company.

Joseph, Rebecca and little Cornelia sailed for a European grand tour. In Florence, Cornelia was introduced to the American wonder Nathaniel Parker Willis; both were sculpted by Horatio Greenough. According to Zephaniah W. Pease both pieces were carved from the same block of fine marble. The two would come together years later.

After the tour, Grinnell returned to business, this time at home in New Bedford. He had his entire hand in banking, railroads, ship building and, of course, the textile industry. He served in Congress from 1843 to 1851.

In 1848, deciding that he needed some election support, he invited a young fellow congressman to campaign in New Bedford for him. Since a Massachusetts tour on behalf of presidential candidate General Zachary Taylor was already planned, he agreed to a New Bedford stop. On September 14, 1848, Abraham Lincoln spoke at Liberty Hall and spent the night at the Grinnell Mansion. Samuel Rodman Jr. wasn't terribly impressed: "In the

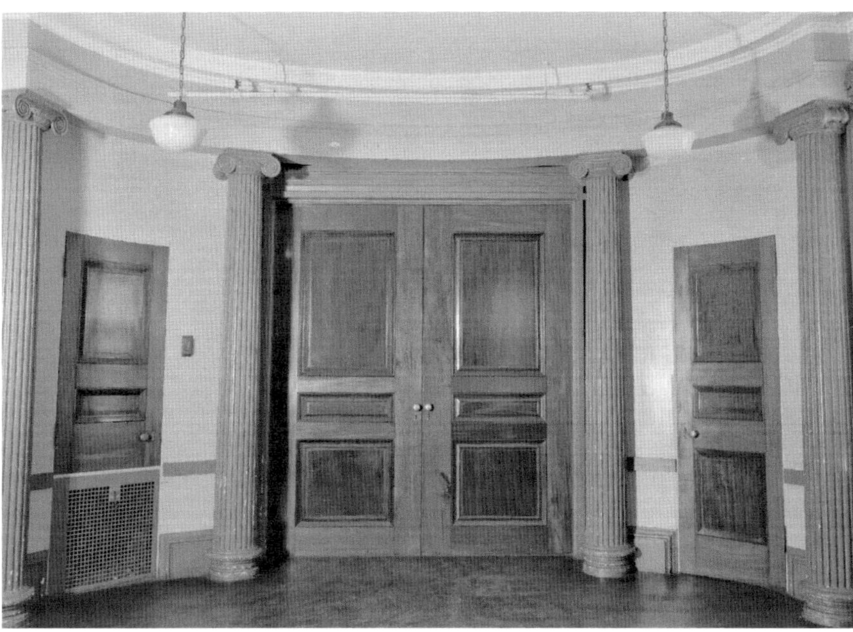

Joseph Grinnell Mansion, first-floor entrance hall. *Library of Congress, Historic American Buildings Survey. Ned Goode, photographer.*

evening went to the Whip meeting which was addressed by Mr. Lincoln of Illinois. It was a pretty sound, but not a tasteful speech." In contrast, the *Daily Mercury* called it "marked by great originality, clear, conclusive, convincing, reasoning and enlivened by frequent flashed of genuine, racy, western wit." Lincoln was introduced by John H.W. Page, a politics-adoring attorney. Page turns up later as a friend of John James Audubon.

By the time Cornelia Grinnell and Nathaniel Parker Willis saw each other again in Washington, he had become a literary star. Willis was as famous and famously read as his friends Charles Dickens and Edgar Allan Poe.

Born in 1806, Willis was the son of a newspaper owner and a Yale graduate. In 1835, he married Mary Stace, the daughter of a British general, and moved temporarily to England. He became known by a serious of sparkling, name-dropping letters from all over Europe. Charles Dickens took him up, and he knew Ada Byron, Lord Bryon's daughter and a founder of computer science, well enough to introduce her to Henry Wadsworth Longfellow.

Back in New York, Willis became a close friend of Edgar Allan Poe. Poe actually wrote a favorable piece about Willis in his American writers series. Poe could be a killing critic but was fond of Willis. He caught Willis perfectly: "It has been the fate of this gentleman to be alternately condemned *ad infinitum*, and lauded *ad nauseam*—a fact which speaks much in his praise. We know of no American writer who has evinced greater versatility of talent; that is to say, of high talent, often amounting to genius; and we know of none who has more narrowly missed placing himself at the head of our letters."

Poe, who knew a lot about literary strategy, noted that his friend

> *pushed himself, went much into the world, made friends with the gentler sex, "delivered" poetical addresses, wrote "scriptural" poems, traveled, sought the intimacy of noted women, and got into quarrels with notorious men. All these things served his purpose—if, indeed, I am right in supposing that he had any purpose at all…As a writer of "sketches," properly so called, Mr. Willis is unequaled. Sketches—especially of society—are his forte, and they are so for no other reason than that they afford him the best opportunity of introducing the personal Willis.*

Best of all, Poe caught the essence of Willis's "Hurrygraphs":

> *His style proper may be called extravagant, bizarre, pointed, epigrammatic without being antithetical (this is very rarely the case), but, through all its whimsicalities, graceful, classic and accurate. He is very seldom to*

> *be caught tripping in the minor morals. His English is correct; his most outrageous imagery is, at all events, unmixed.*

When Poe died horribly in Baltimore on October 7, 1849, a series of sharks circled to defame him. Willis defended his friend in the *Home Journal* on October 20, 1849. Willis did not pretend that his friend had no faults:

> *Residing as he did in the country, we never met Mr. Poe in hours of leisure; but he frequently called on us afterwards at our place of business, and we met him often in the street—invariably the same sad-mannered, winning and refined gentleman, such as we had always known him. It was by rumor only, up to the day of his death, that we knew of any other development of manner or character. We heard, from one who knew him well (what should be stated in all mention of his lamentable irregularities), that, with a single glass of wine, his whole nature was reversed, the demon became uppermost, and, though none of the usual signs of intoxication were visible, his will was palpably insane. Possessing his reasoning faculties in excited activity, at such times, and seeking his acquaintances with his wonted look and memory, he easily seemed personating only another phase of his natural character, and was accused, accordingly, of insulting arrogance and bad-heartedness. In this reversed character, we repeat, it was never our chance to see him.*

Nathaniel Parker Willis knew that he was not a genius. He did know how to recognize one and had no doubts about Poe. In the meantime, Willis's first wife had died, and he found a most extraordinary nanny for his children, Harriet Jacobs, an escaped slave who had spent years hiding in an attic in fear of being sent back south. Jacobs would later write *Incidents in the Life of a Slave Girl.* Although Jacobs did not like Willis and thought him sneering, she did love Cornelia and her children. They would be tied to one another for their entire lives.

On October 1, 1846, Cornelia Grinnell married Nathaniel Park Willis in New Bedford at the Unitarian Church. He was forty years older than his bride, yet it was a happy marriage. Willis found a kind of second father in Joseph Grinnell. The former congressman and his writer son-in-law often traveled together for pleasure. His *Sketches of Scenery, Celebrities and Society, Taken from Life* is, in fact, the same subject of this book. Willis wrote about New Bedford in the early 1850s as well as anyone ever did:

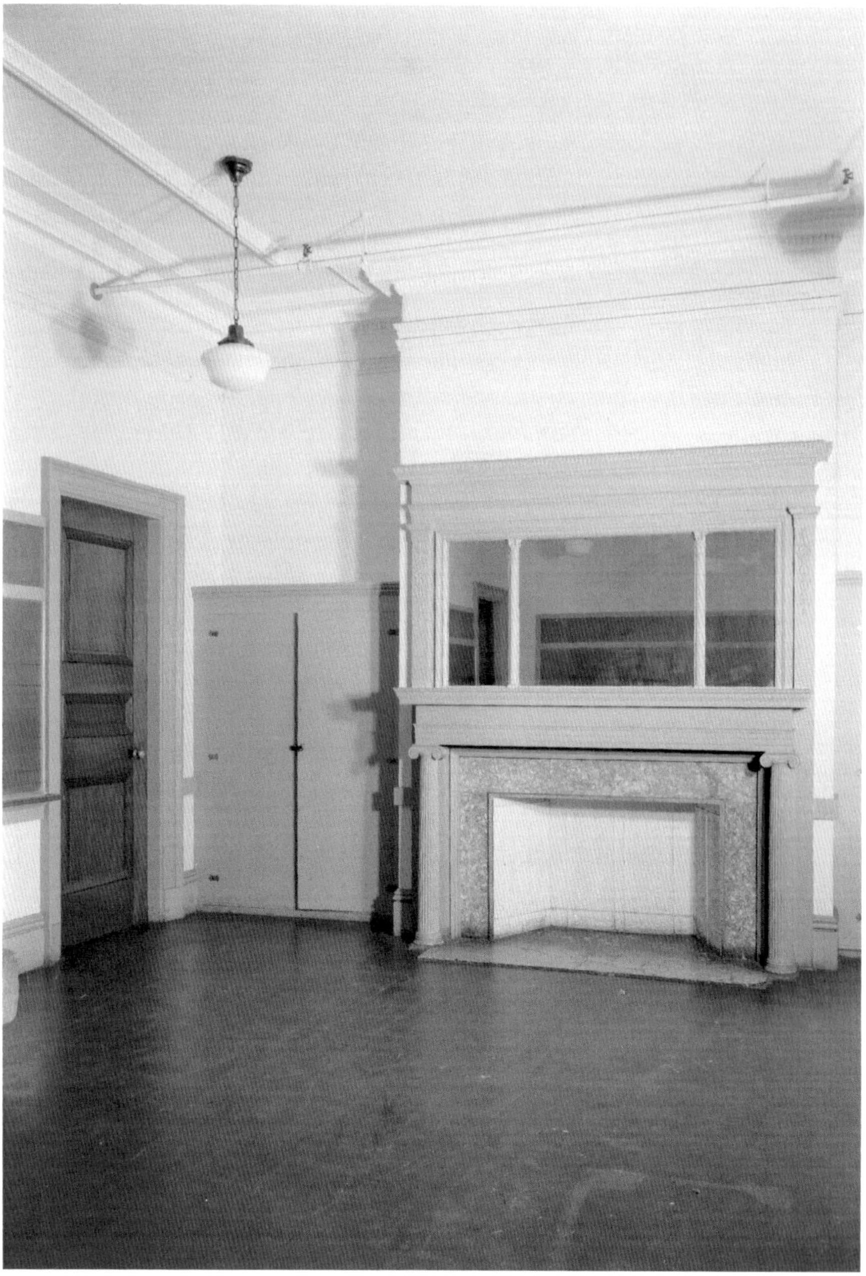

Joseph Grinnell Mansion, first-floor interior. This was probably the kitchen. *Library of Congress, Historic American Buildings Survey. Ned Goode, photographer.*

Luxurious as the town is now however and few and far between as are the lead colored bonnets and drab cut away coats there is a strong tincture of Quaker precision and simplicity in the manners of the wealthier class in New Bedford and among the nautical class it mixes up very curiously with the tarpaulin carelessness and ease. The railroad which has brought Boston within two hours distance is fast cosmopolizing away the local peculiarities.

Describing County Street, Willis pointed out:

On the table summit of the precipitous hill which rises immediately behind the town stands one of the finest arrays of dwelling houses in this country an extensive neighborhood of costly villas with each its ample surrounding of grounds and garden and this part of New Bedford reminds one of the Isle of Wight or English Clifton.

He noticed what everyone knew but only the wisest thought much about:

In the beautiful houses where many of these easily suited persons are now growing old is to be found luxury in its most refined shapes and costliest superfluities so readily in this mobile country of ours do classes and customs undergo changes the most improbable. Whaling as every one knows has been the principal commerce and industry of the town since its first settlement. The large fortunes possessed here have been mostly made in this trade and the majority of the inhabitants even now are mostly dependent on it in one shape or another.

He closed by throwing a bouquet to his father-in-law and his granite mill:

The establishment of the Wamsutta Steam Cotton Factory which has lately been put into operation at New Bedford with a capital of three hundred thousand dollars and in which a sailor's daughter for example who else might be painfully dependent or compelled to leave home and go out to service may earn four dollars a week by independent and undergrading labor. This is the average of the present earnings of two hundred operatives in this new factory and as the investment is already proved to be a good one other factories will doubtless be built and the industry of New Bedford turned remedy to provide new conduits against their natural or accidental depletion. New Bedford is indebted for this to its able Representative in Congress Hon Joseph Grinnell.

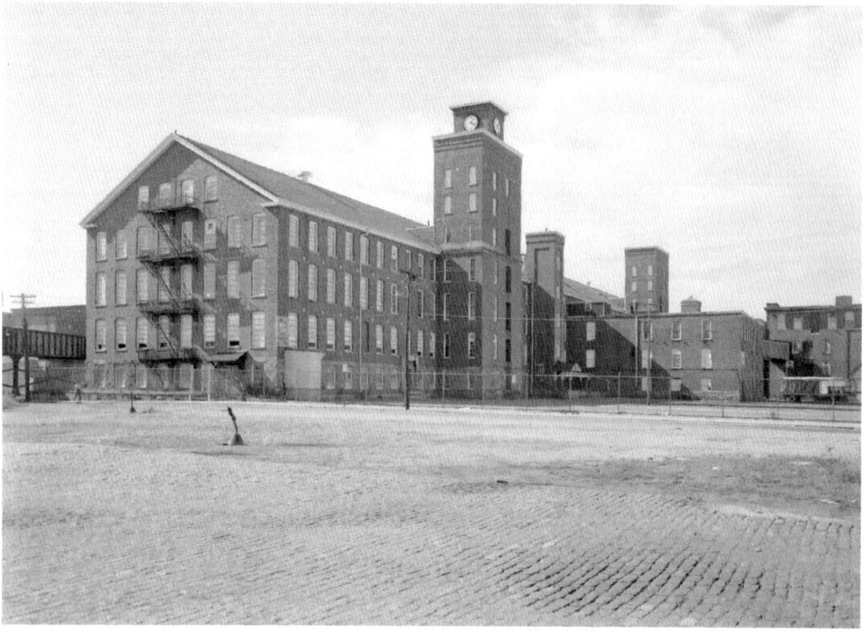

Grinnell's Wamsutta Mill. *Library of Congress, Historic American Buildings Survey. Jack E. Boucher, photographer.*

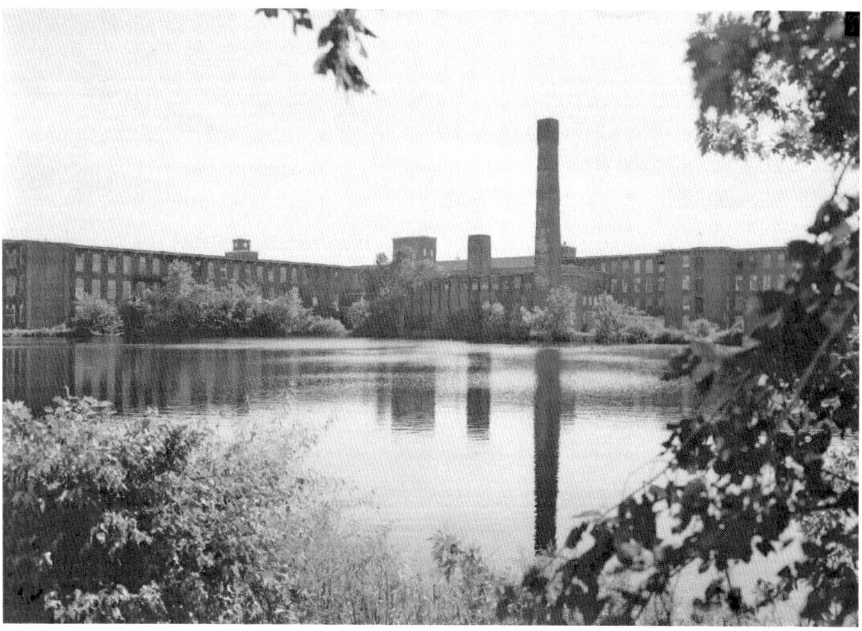

Wamsutta Mills holding pond. *Library of Congress, Historic American Buildings Survey. Jack E. Boucher, photographer.*

Both Willis and Joseph Grinnell were correct. New Bedford's later wealth lay in the textile mills.

One of the bravest things Joseph Grinnell ever did was to shelter Harriet Jacobs when she was being hunted by her former owner. As an escaped slave, she would be sent back south if caught. He had Cornelia send Harriet and the Willis children to New Bedford, where they would not be found. The County Street mansion kept them safe. In the meantime, Cornelia personally paid Harriet's owner $300 for her freedom.

Willis eventually developed severe epilepsy. Joseph Grinnell took him south, trying to improve his health. Nothing helped, and on his sixty-first birthday, January 20, 1867, Willis died. Cornelia and her children returned often to New Bedford. When anyone in the family was ill, Harriet Jacobs came to nurse them. Every one of the children remained close to Jacobs as adults.

The Russell Warren Mansion remained in the Grinnell family until the mid-twentieth century. It became a Catholic school and then was deserted by the church. The portico and columns burned. Preservationist Peter Grinnell, one of the last children to grow up in the mansion, was heartbroken. Shortly before his death, a film was made that showed him walking down the steps of the mansion. He said, "I still remember the sound of the massive doors closing in this house." Although he never knew it, the Grinnell Mansion was saved and restored. It is today congregate housing for the elderly.

Chapter 7

The Outsider

John Avery Parker Tops Them All

No one could have invented John Avery Parker. His entire life reads like something from Charles Dickens. His astonishing financial career did not begin well, however, as the *Cleveland Plain Dealer* pointed out in 1858: "The late John Avery Parker, a successful merchant of New Bedford, was at one time 'warned' to leave Westport, Massachusetts, under the old law or custom of warning strangers who were likely to become a public charge. He died worth $1,300,000 [about $34,495,000 in 2013 dollars]." The moral? Don't ever insult someone temporarily out of cash, as you'll be sure to regret it later.

If anyone in New Bedford could ever be said to mint money, it was John Avery Parker. He understood how to make money, make it work for him and then make more. He made sure to live well and seems to have vastly enjoyed his life and being fawned over. Even well after his death, the *History of Bristol County* was doling out rave reviews:

> *As a shrewd and energetic business man, Mr. Parker had few equals and was among the first merchants in New Bedford to set the wise example of engaging in other enterprises than the principal one of this city at that time. The large operations in which he engaged required excellent judgment and foresight and that he possessed those qualities in no slight degree is proved by the almost uniform success which attended his transactions. At the time of his death he was president of the Merchants Bank in this city having served gratuitously from the commencement of the corporation a period of twenty*

> *eight years. Possessed of such ample means it was in the power of Mr. Parker very often to assist those who were just starting in business or who had met with disappointment in their affairs. We believe it is within the personal knowledge of many that this assistance was often and cheerfully rendered and that too sometimes when the relief thus extended was not perhaps strictly within the limits of an over cautious prudence Mr. Parker was one of the earliest supporters of common schools and though under the district system he was heavily taxed for their support he always met the obligation thus imposed upon him with cheerfulness.*

Parker built and owned a series of ships—first for the merchant trade carrying goods from port to port and then, inevitably, for whaling. Among them were the *Alexander Barclay* (ship), the *Averick* (ship), the *Dragon* (bark) and the *Franklin* (brig). He owned the Lionet Iron Mill in Wareham and the Merchant Bank for all practical purposes.

He married well in 1788 to Averick Standish, a direct descendant of Miles Standish of Longfellow courtship fame. The couple had two sons: Avery Parker, who was lost at sea, and Frederick Parker, who became his father's business partner. There were seven daughters who lived to grow up and marry into New Bedford society. The family needed a large home, and here he had perfect taste. John Avery Parker found Russell Warren.

Warren had already designed for Parker the Merchants Bank, the Double Bank building. The Merchants and Mechanics Bank shared what is perhaps New Bedford's finest surviving commercial building. The Greek Revival temple owns its site at the foot of William Street. It is safe to assume that if it had been demolished, as one New Bedford mayor wanted, there would be no New Bedford Whaling National Historical Park. The value of the park would never have existed.

The Parker Mansion was generally considered one of the most beautiful homes built in America. Critic Joy Wheeler Dow wrote in 1904:

> *I suppose the finest specimen of Transitional domestic architecture extant in the United States is the Parker (Bennett) house on County Street in New Bedford, erected about 1840….*
>
> *There is nothing disappointing about this Transitional exemplar; it was one of those grateful notes of hope at a season of national melancholia. Wonderfully imposing from its great size, it will grieve the reader to learn that the magnificent pile is already crumbling from lack of appreciation, and it will not be long before the dealer in second hand building materials*

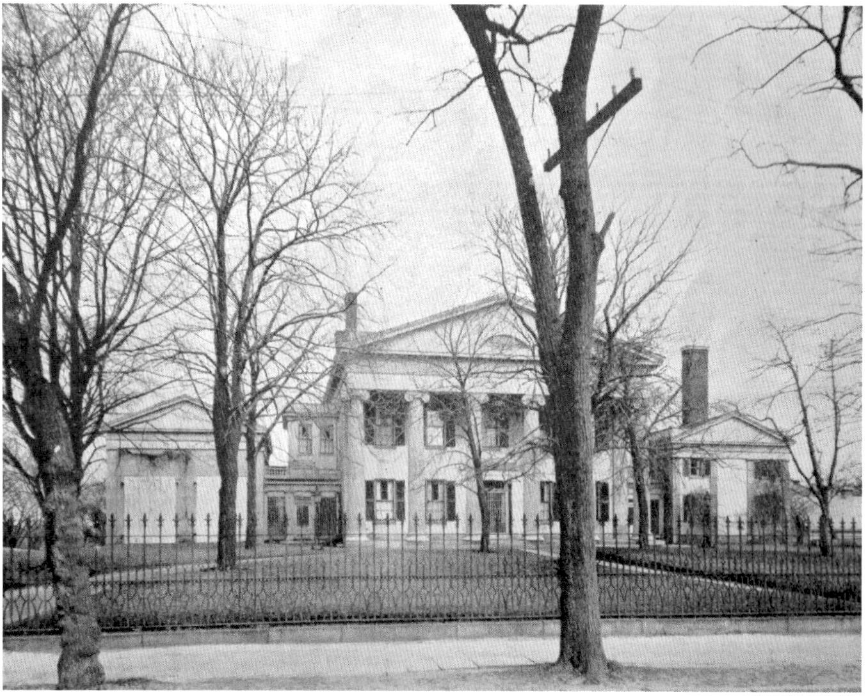

The John Avery Parker Mansion. Russell Warren, architect. One of America's most lavish private homes. *Collection of author. Courtesy of Arthur P. Motta.*

> *carries it away, piece by piece, to his yard, so little do the people of New Bedford care for the most interesting building by far that their city posses today.... The Parker (Bennett House) is the only successful adaption of the Greek temple motive, pure and simple, to domestic purposes that has come to my knowledge.*

The History of Bristol County described it this way:

> *The most imposing house ever constructed in New Bedford and one of the masterpieces of Russell Warren, was built by John Avery Parker, on the corner of County and Pearl streets.... The west façade somewhat resembled that of the W.R. Rodman house* [no surprise since Warren designed the Rodman Mansion], *but the east side was the most elaborate. There was ample space to the east, and as the house was painted white that was no suggestion of heaviness in its appearance.*

The view from below was particularly satisfying. It would be easy for one who had seen this house to understand how it and the famous Colt house of Bristol were designed by the same architect.... This structure is reported to have cost Mr. Parker $100,000.

Zephaniah W. Pease, who had seen the house, wrote about it in his *History of New Bedford*: "In 1834 Mr. Parker built the splendid mansion of granite on Willis and County Streets...Not only did the mansion have granite exterior walls, but it had as its interior finish solid mahogany paneling. From 1834... it was the showplace in New Bedford." Even the workers who built it knew how important the mansion was. When it was demolished, a board behind a mantel noted, "Whoever tears this down recollect that it was in the best style when it was built." We have photographs of the Parker Mansion and descriptions. One wing, built for servants, was moved to Willis Street. All else is gone.

Parker was not finished with Warren. No one can ever say that New Bedford didn't know how to open a hotel. In the nineteenth century, New Bedford threw parties for a new one, and everyone had a grand slightly drunken time.

Warren had made New Bedford a "City of Palaces." When Warren built Parker his grand mansion, there was a question of what to do with his

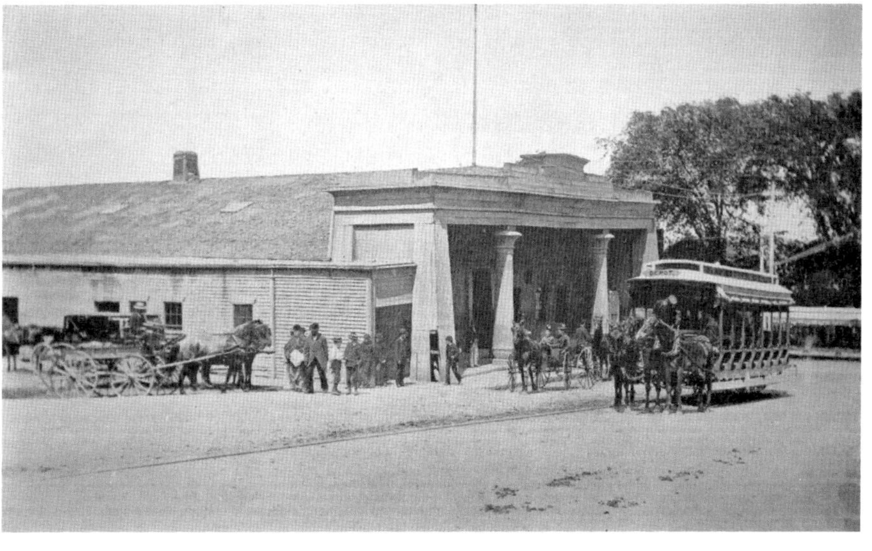

New Bedford Railroad Terminal, "The Tombs." Russell Warren, architect. A rare example of Egyptian Revival architecture. *Collection of author. Courtesy of Arthur P. Motta.*

downtown place, and wonderfully enough, it included Russell Warren. The *New Bedford Mercury* reported a scoop on Friday, April 23, 1841:

> *New Public House—We learn that the Hon. John A, Parker has made arrangement for the erection of a new and commodious public house in this town upon the site of the old mansion house formerly occupied by himself at the corner of Purchase and Middle streets. The building, as we understand, will be three stories high and will extend on Purchase street the whole distance from Middle to Elm street; affording a spacious dining hall, with private parlors and lodging rooms for the ample accommodation of more than one hundred boarders. The contracts for the work have already been made and is believed that it will be completed during the ensuing season.*

Part of the *Mercury* story came from Rhode Island. The *Providence Journal* wrote:

> *We have had the pleasure of seeing the plan of the proposed establishment, drawn by our townsman, Major Russell Warren, and have no hesitation in saying, that, if the building correspond with the drawings, it will be one of the most commodious and beautiful edifices of the kind in any part of the country. We congratulate the citizens of New Bedford and travelling public, upon the prospect of a speedy completion of this splined edifice.*

By Friday, November 12, 1841, the *Mercury* had revealed more information about the soon-to-open hotel:

> *This new and splendid Hotel was commenced in May last, by the Hon. John A. Parker, whose name it bears, and the work is now so far advanced, that it will probably be opened in the Fall for the reception of company. When completed according to the plan, which was drawn by Major Russell Warren of Providence, it will be one of the most spacious and commodious public houses in the country. It is four stories high including the basement, containing a dining hall, twenty-four feet wide and, seventy-two feet long, one hundred and ten rooms beside and a large bathing establishment. The front portico is thirty feet long, projects seven feet, and is supported by four columns with ornamental caps. There is also a private entrance on the north. An observatory on the top of the North wing commands a fine prospect of the town, harbor and bay.*

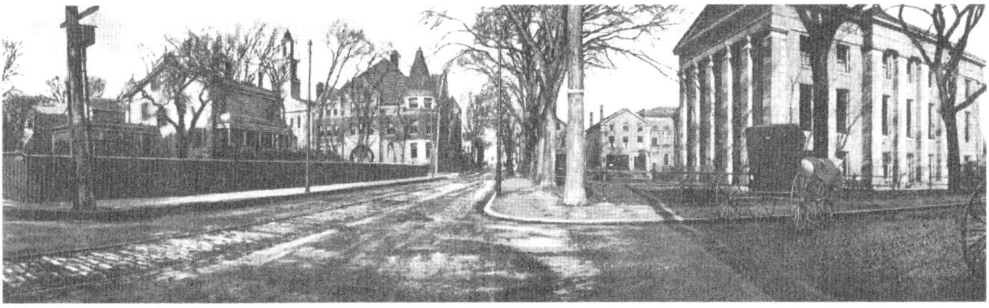

Rear view of Warren City Hall behind horse-drawn carriage, circa 1906. Blanchard and Young panorama. *Library of Congress.*

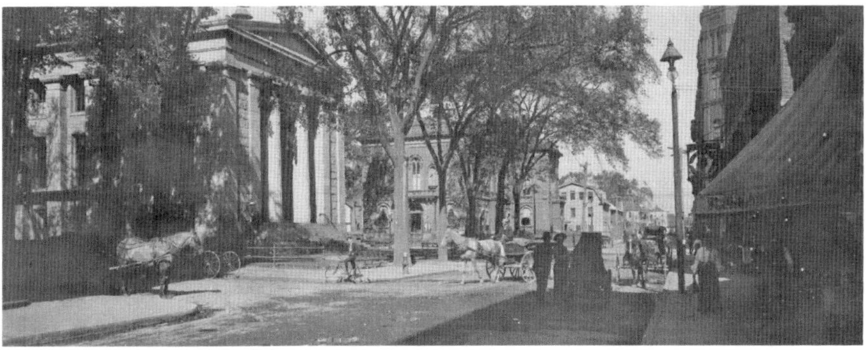

Pleasant Street scene in New Bedford, Massachusetts, circa 1900. City hall and library. *Library of Congress.*

The paper was slightly off on its estimate. The Parker House officially opened on Thursday, February 10, 1842. An unknown lucky member of the *Mercury* staff got to attend. From his report, it seems that he also got to enjoy the dinner and lavish drinking. There were two hundred guests, with a number coming from Taunton, Boston and Worcester. If you were male and well known, you got to make a toast to John Avery Parker and the Parker House. Future Massachusetts governor John Henry Clifford was the toastmaster or "President" of the evening:

> *We regret that we cannot give a full report of the many excellent remarks and brilliant repartees. We submit some of the toasts given on the occasion.*
>
> *By the President—*
>
> *The Parker House—We can wish for it no better success than that its merits shall equal the enterprise of its founders.*

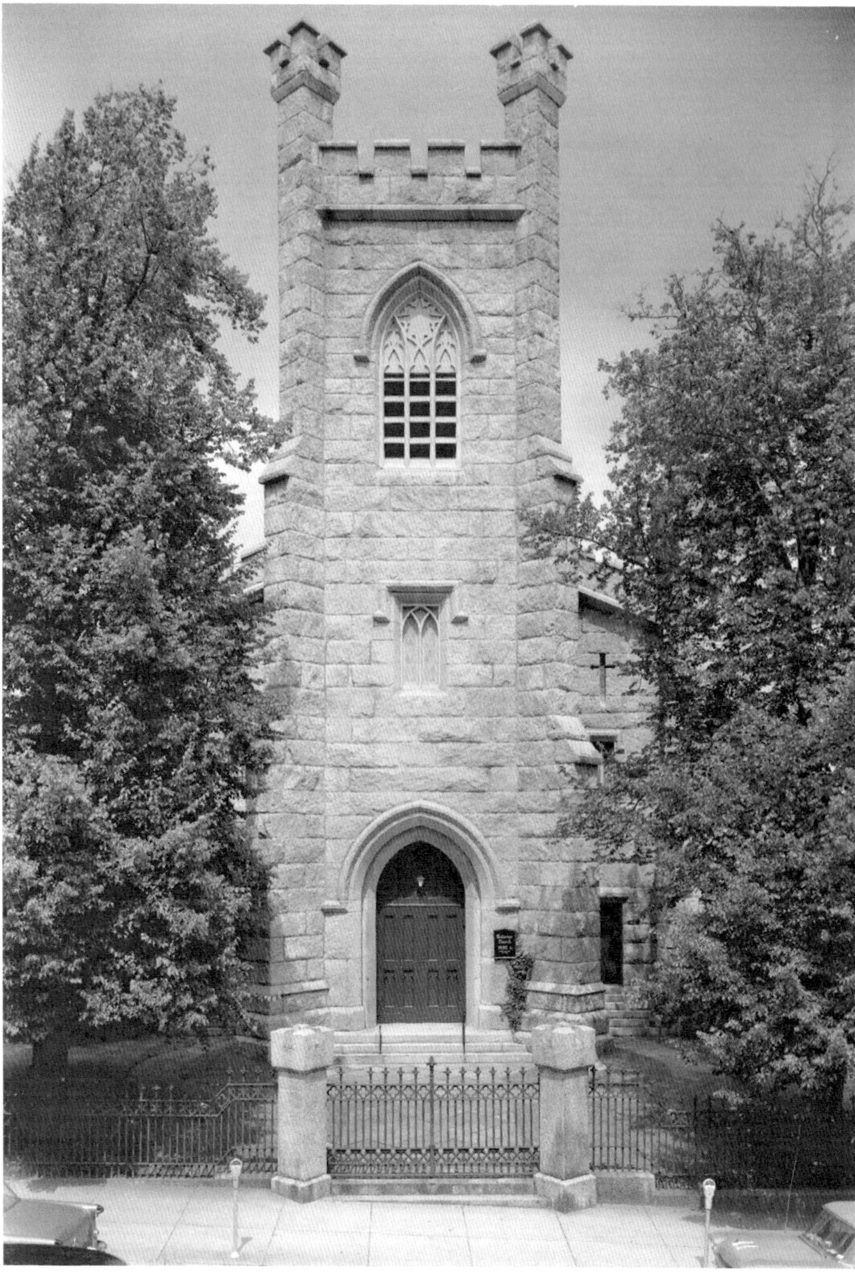

The Unitarian Church, Union and Eighth Streets, A.J. Davis and Russell Warren, architects. *Library of Congress, Historic American Buildings Survey. Ned Goode, photographer.*

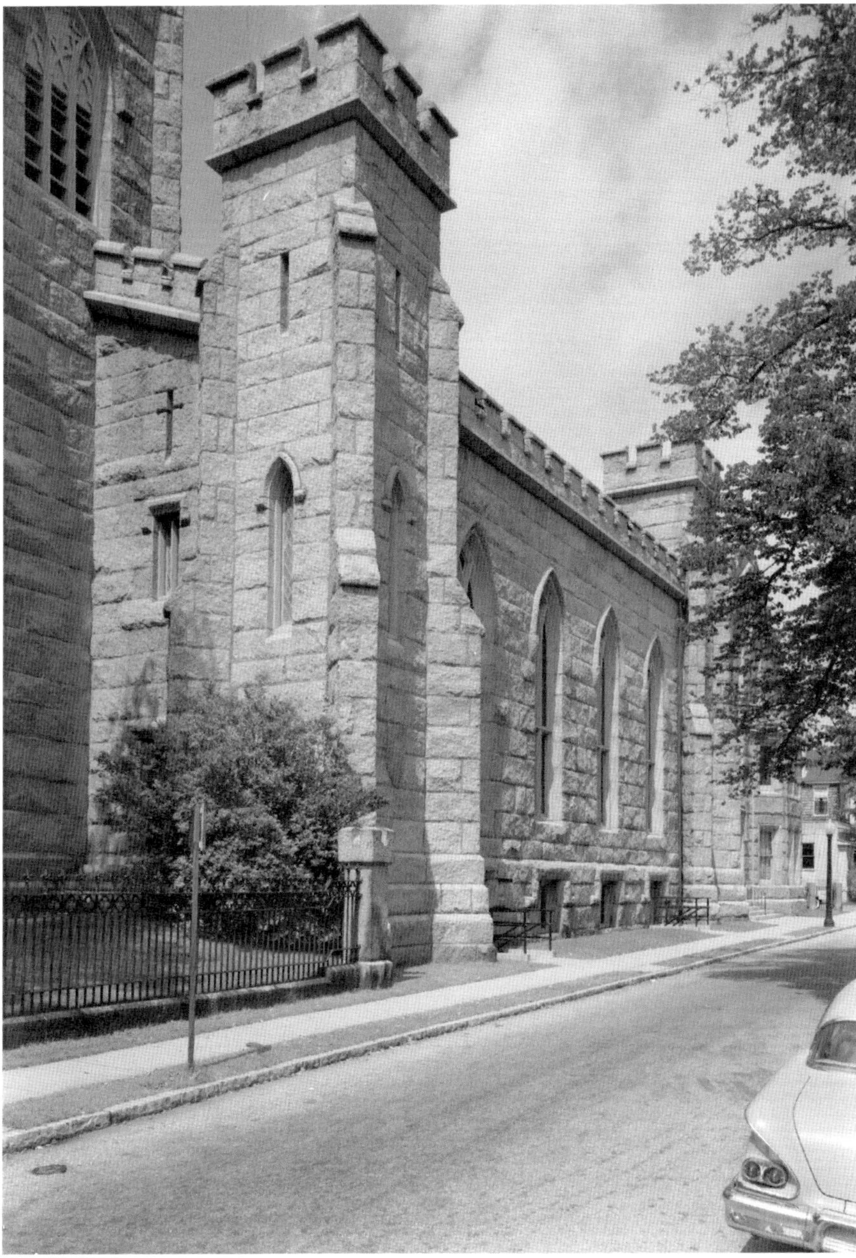

Families who left Quaker Meeting owned pews in the Unitarian Church. *Library of Congress, Historic American Buildings Survey. Ned Goode, photographer.*

J.A. Parker, Esq. responded to this toast by tendering to the guests a cordial welcome.

The Honorable Joseph Grinnell, of course, had his own Warren building drank to:

Yankee Enterprise—Ever conducing to the public welfare—and looking at the profits of the pocket.

My favorite toast had obviously been worked out well in advance by William Eddy and probably even presented to the unknown reporter to make sure it made the paper:

Our Host—A great anomaly. Though inclined to peace, an instigator of **fowl** *murders, and a promoter of* **broils**, *though no gambler yet greatly given to appropriate* **steaks**, *though never on change, yet nobody watches closer the state of the market, though his dinners have disqualified him from* **running**, *the dinners themselves are peculiarly* **racy**, *though a member of the bar, he is an honest man. May his shadow never be less, and while he keeps the Parker House may the Parker House, as in duty bound keep him.*

I think you had to be there to really get it. According to Leonard Bolles Ellis, in his *History of New Bedford*, Eddy was the editor of not one but two newspapers, the *Daily Evening Bulletin* and the *Semi Weekly*. Finally, the reporter missed the most important person there. His speech came a bit late in the toasting order:

By the President—
The City of Providence—Her architects have made is a "City of Palaces"...Maj. Warren of Providence responded to this toast in some remarks that did not reach our ear.

The *one* person I really wanted to hear from, as a historian, was Russell Warren, and the reporter blew it. There is a New Bedford game of finding Russell Warren buildings. As far as I know, the Parker House was the one building in New Bedford *not* attributed to Russell Warren. When John Avery Parker died on December 30, 1853, the city lost a man who was already a legend. No one could ever top Parker.

Chapter 8

Young Mr. Rotch Shocks the Neighborhood

William James Rotch was perhaps the last of the lucky Rotches, and he lived accordingly. He didn't realize he was commissioning a masterpiece when he first wrote to Alexander Jackson Davis of New York City in April 1845. Rotch needed a house, and his brother-in-law, Joseph Angier, had suggested Davis.

Rotch was twenty-six in 1845, and his wife, Emily, was twenty-four. They had one child, William, who had been born in 1844. A second son, Charles Waln Morgan Rotch, named for his grandfather, Charles W. Morgan, had died that January. Emily Rotch very probably wanted to leave the house they were then living in at 109 Elm Street. It had not been built for the Rotches and cannot have held pleasant memories.

William James Rotch's father, Joseph, a son of William Rotch Jr., did not usually please the more conservative members of the family. John M. Bullard, writing in the twentieth century, had a difficult time describing Joseph: "Joseph Rotch, the beautiful, one of the handsomest men ever born, Joseph Rotch, the bad or at least weak, if you can judge by the comments of the worthy members of the Rodman family and their descendants, Joseph Rotch the very loving and human husband and father, if you can judge from his own letters; it is hard to write of Joseph Rotch."

Joseph was later famous in New Bedford for his very fast sleigh, his attempt a running a silk factory and his most charming wife. He married Anne Smith, a totally convinced member of the Society of Friends. That

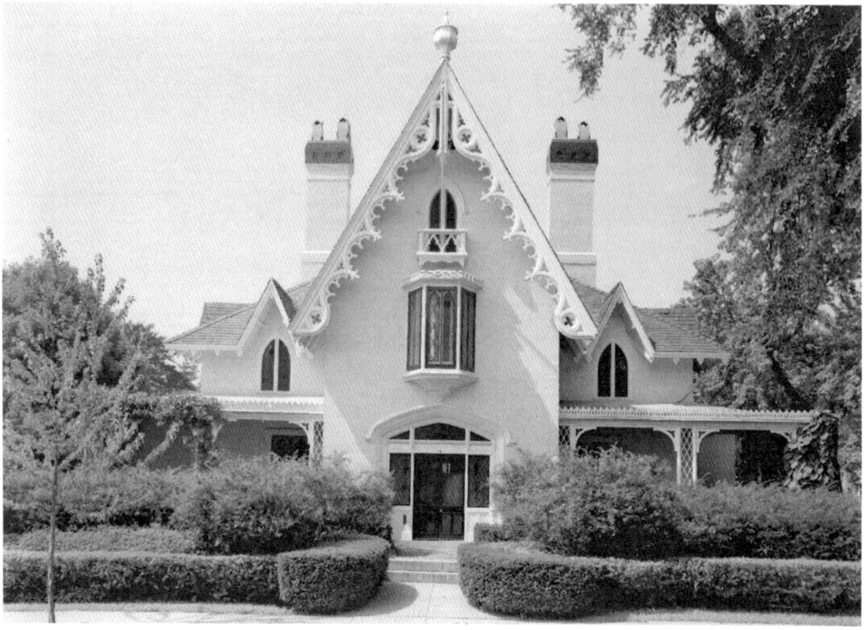

The William J. Rotch Cottage, 19 Irving Street, 1846. A.J. Davis, architect. *Library of Congress, Historic American Buildings Survey. Ned Goode, photographer.*

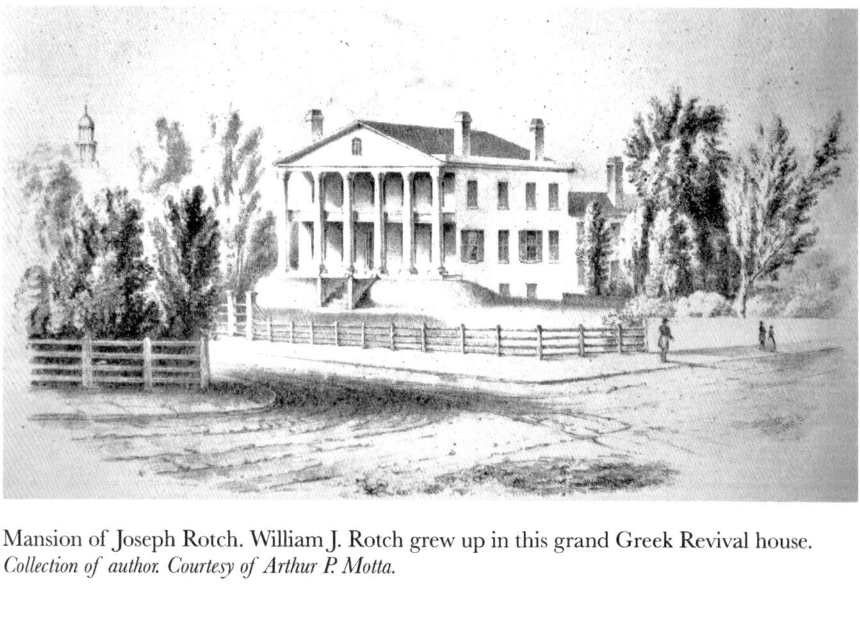

Mansion of Joseph Rotch. William J. Rotch grew up in this grand Greek Revival house. *Collection of author. Courtesy of Arthur P. Motta.*

marriage took place at a time when the rest of the family were becoming Unitarians. It may not have been a completely happy one.

Letters from William James Rotch to Anne while he was at Harvard University constantly remind her to rest and take care of her health. One letter of hers written on William's birthday speaks of wishing to live only for his sake.

William James, the third son in the family of four to survive childhood, was born on May 2, 1819. Anne Smith Rotch often went home to Philadelphia for long visits, taking some of the children and leaving one or two with Joseph in New Bedford. During one particularly long absence, Joseph built a family house and sent Anne a series of letters describing the construction. On August 15, 1821, he reminded her that it was time to come back to him:

> *My Dear Anna*
>
> *Last evenings mail brought me thy letter of the 8th—The plasters have yet both parlors and the front entry (downstairs) to finish all the rest is done & some of the doors are hung in the back buildings—Thou has not in thy letters said anything like a wish to return home, I presume thou doth not think of it, until our house is completed for thy reception—*
>
> *Kiss all the children for papa, who thinks of them almost every hour in the day who will come for them as soon as his business will with propriety allow. In fact of dear Anna I am almost tired of my Bacheloristic way of living—*
>
> *Affectionately*
> *Thy Joe.*

From this house, William and his brother, Benjamin, snuck out the back window to attend the dances that Anne Rotch hated. Later, like all good Rotches for generations to come, both boys went to Harvard.

On November 10, 1839, Joseph Rotch died at forty-nine. A few years later, Anne Rotch died on November 6, 1842, at forty-seven. William assumed responsibility for his younger sister, Joanna, who was then sixteen.

On May 24, 1841, Samuel Rodman, recorded a happier event: "Evening at the wedding of Charles Waln Morgan's of his daughter, Emily and William J. Rotch, where all of the family circle was generally collected in this place and vicinity. All went off well. The ceremony was performed by Mr. Peabody and no alcoholic liquors were exhibited." Later that year, Samuel,

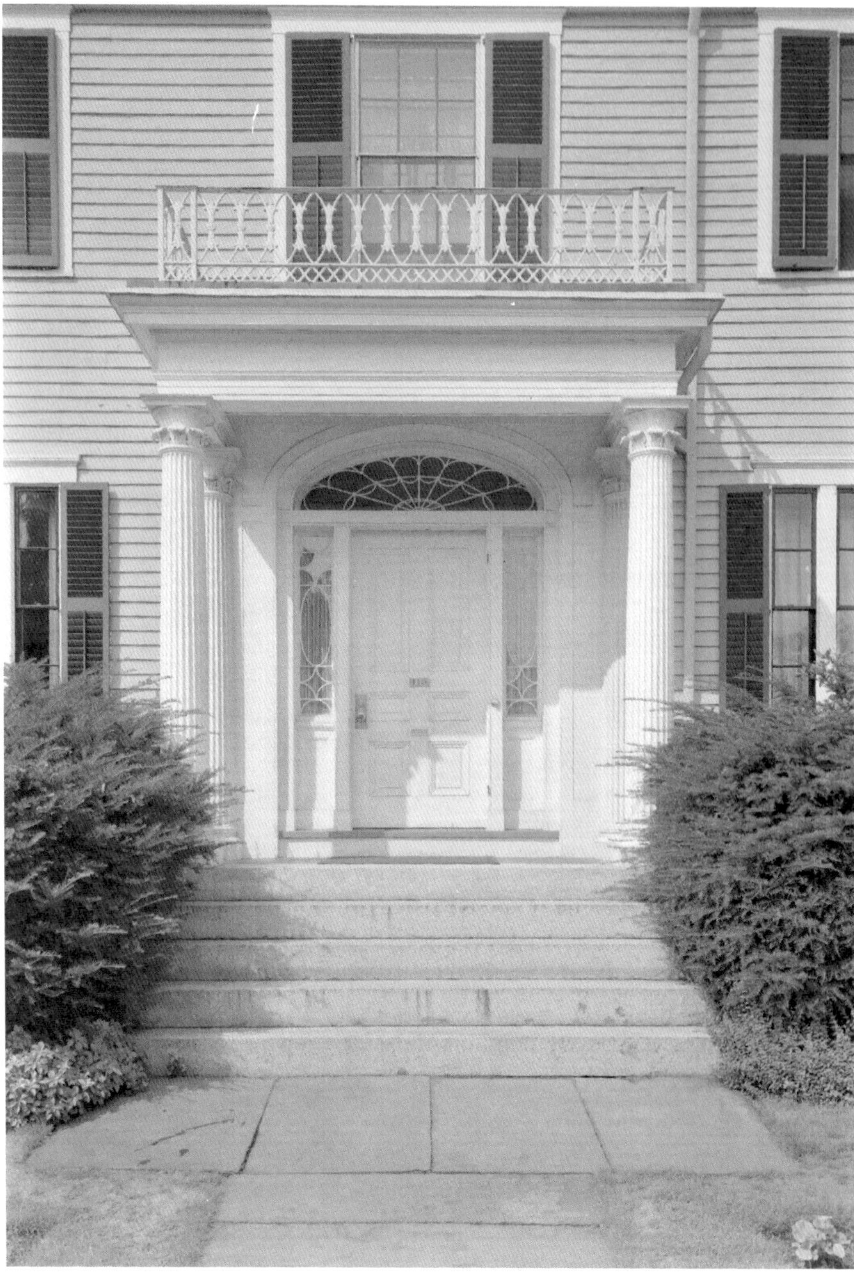

Henry Taber House, Orchard Street, entrance detail. One of many smaller houses just off County Street. *Library of Congress, Historic American Buildings Survey. Ned Goode, photographer, August 1961.*

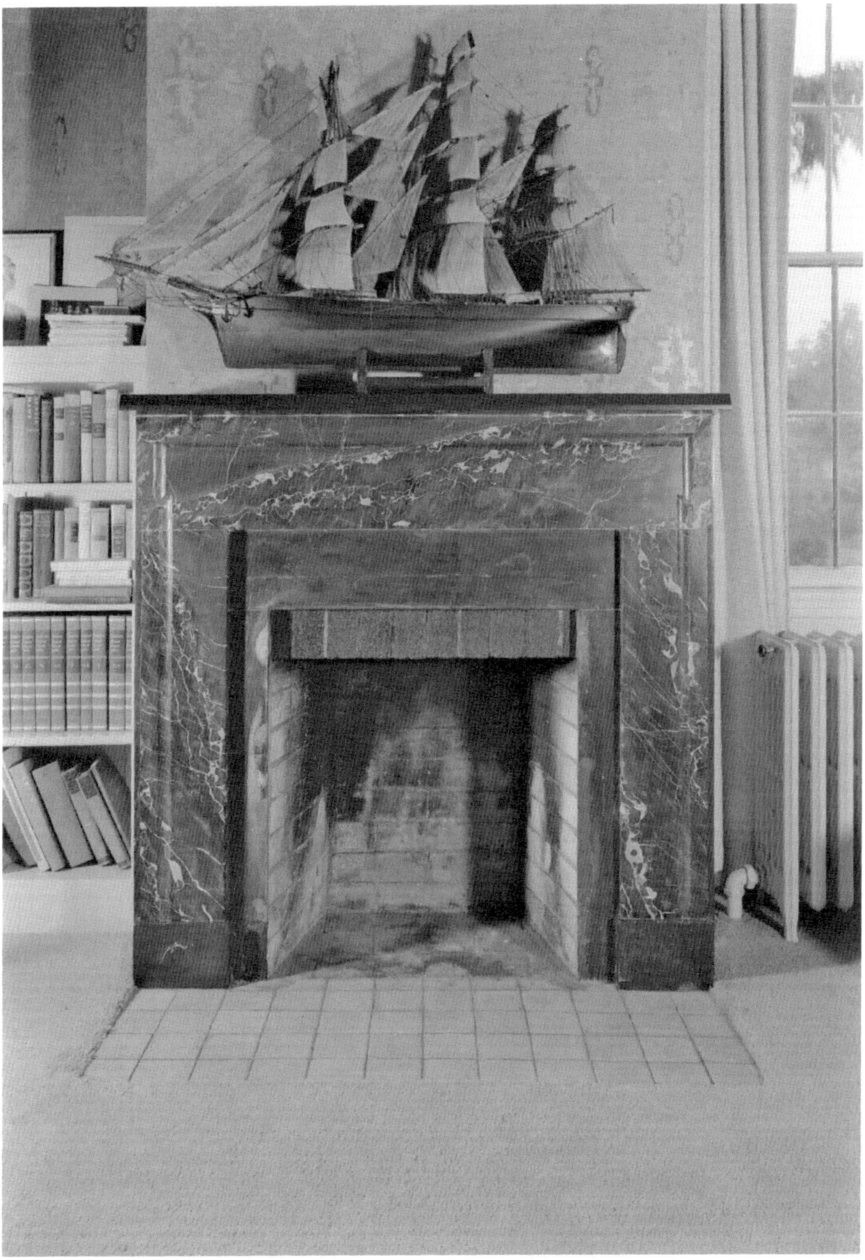

Henry Taber House, northeast parlor. *Library of Congress, Historic American Buildings Survey. Ned Goode, photographer.*

who disapproved of anything that smelled of social license, mentioned attending several parties in honor of Emily and William—where, again, no liquor was served or dancing permitted.

When William and Emily began planning for a house, they certainly didn't want another Rotch Rodman mansion exactly like all the others strung out along County Street. These were massive estates with grounds that each took in at least a modern city block. They were Russell Warren Greek temples. They didn't want to live in a temple. One supposes those temples were easier to admire than live in. In choosing Alexander Jackson Davis as his architect, William James Rotch chose a radically new architectural style that was intended to be the purely American style called for by tastemaker A.J. Downing. Rotch very probably met Davis in 1838 when he worked with Russell Warren on the new Gothic Unitarian Church for New Bedford or pored over the designs in Downing's *Rural Residences*.

William and Emily had seen Gothic houses on a honeymoon trip up the Hudson and had been enchanted. These houses were a total rejection of the Greek Revival style. Gothic Revival villas were elegant and spread horizontally on their sites. Instead of rearing up to massive

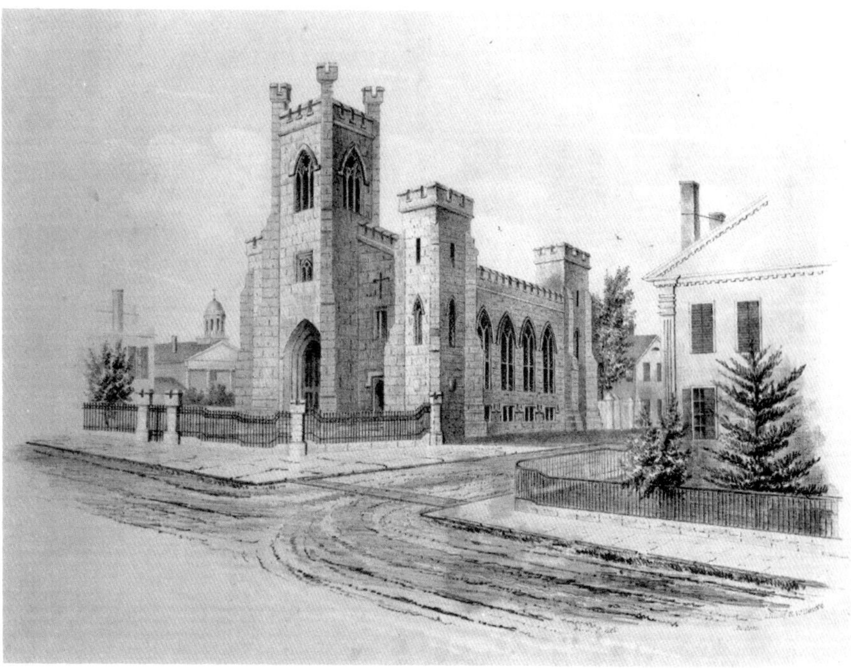

Unitarian Church, early lithograph. E.W. Bouve, Boston, lithographer. *Library of Congress, Historic American Buildings Survey. Ned Goode, photographer.*

porticos, these houses seemed taller because of gables embellished with lacy, hand-carved vergeboards and topped by finials shaped like flowers. Delicate cresting topped low-spread verandas, and Corinthian columns were nowhere in sight.

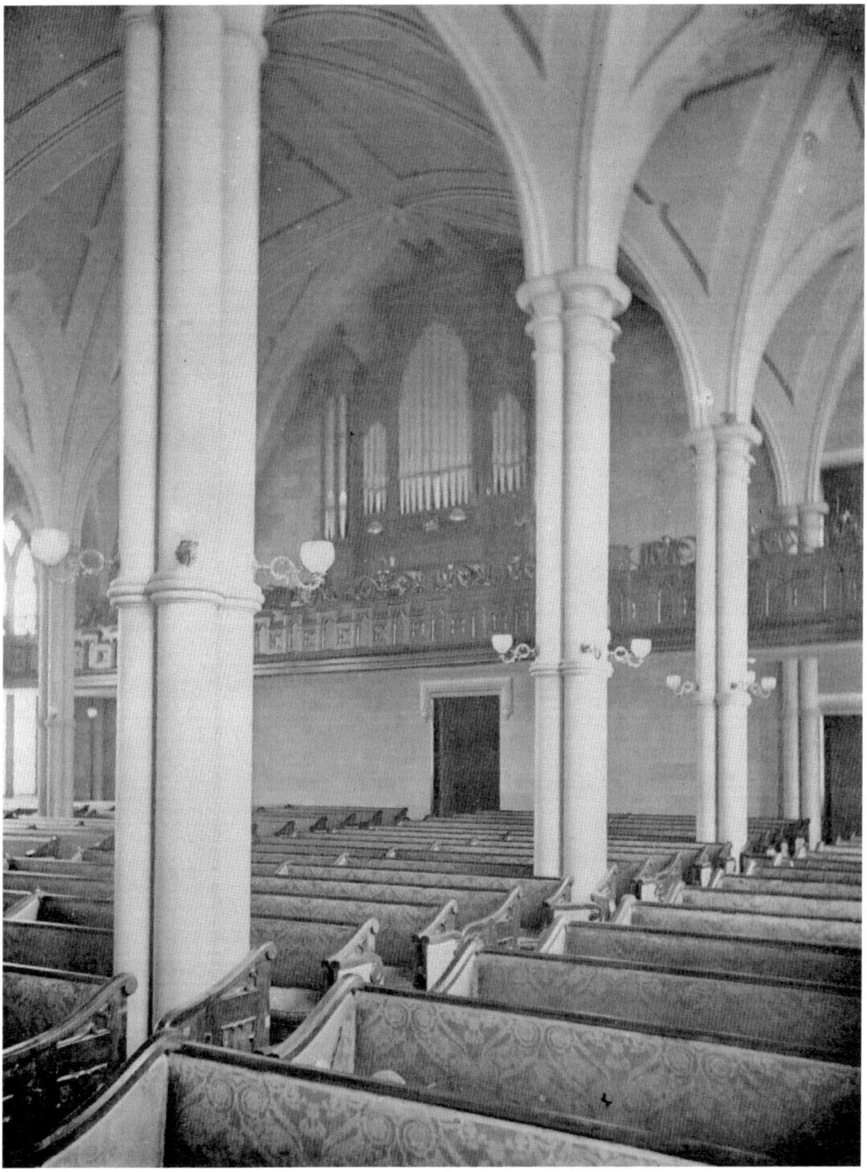

Unitarian Church, interior. *Library of Congress, Historic American Buildings Survey. Ned Goode, photographer.*

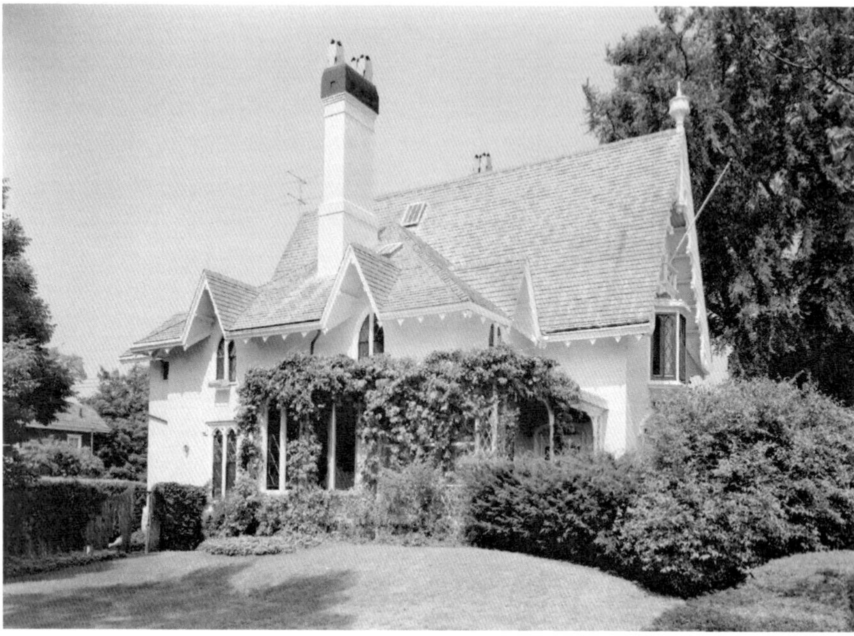

Rotch Cottage, south and east elevations. *Library of Congress, Historic American Buildings Survey. Ned Goode, photographer.*

William J. Rotch decided on a Gothic house, and in retaining Alexander Jackson Davis, he found the best architect working in America. Davis was forty-two in 1845 and at the height of his career. In April of that year, young Rotch wrote to New York, "I should like you to come on here as soon as you can conveniently do so and when you are on the spot we can decide upon the best place for a house." He added, "I like the Gothic Cottage style best and should like something of that kind very much."

Early in May, Davis did come to New Bedford and met with William and Emily at her father's home. Back in New York, Davis quickly drew up plans for the Rotch house. His diary on May 20, 1845, details his work:

> *Plans for Cottage for William J. Rotch, New Bedford, Massachusetts*
>
> *1. Plan Basement*
> *2. Principal floor*
> *3. 2 floor*
> *4. Attic*

5. Front Elevation
6. Rear west
7. South end
8. Section east and west
9. Section north and south
$100.00

Working Drawings
A. Cottage window, inch to foot scale A2
B. Plan elevation and section oriel window
C1 Bay window, plans and inside elements
C2 Section
D1 Doors, front door
D2 Folding and other door
Cornice Umbrage
F Tudor flower
G1 Sash full size at bottom
G2 Ditto
$50.00
Total $150.00

At the same time, William J. Rotch was legally acquiring the land to build the house. On May 28, 1845, his grandfather William Rotch Jr. deeded him "[f]or one dollar and love and good will to be paid a lot of land situated in New Bedford, South of Arnold Street and West of Orchard Street." The land, then well out in the country, was decidedly rural and seemed comfortably away from the family on County Street.

By May 31, the plans and drawings had arrived in New Bedford. William J. Rotch sent his immediate reaction to Davis:

> *I have reviewed the plans, drawings, etc., and they all seem perfect. I have seen some of our carpenters and they are to estimate upon the building. If it costs too much I shall let you know.*
>
> *In looking over the plans, it has occurred to me that the shutters to the windows cannot be closed when the windows are open. This is rather an objection in summer when you want your windows open and your shutters closed. I know that perfection is not always attainable in the world, but we like to get as near to it as possible particularly in our houses.... I like the look of the house very much and it has taken captive the hearts of all*

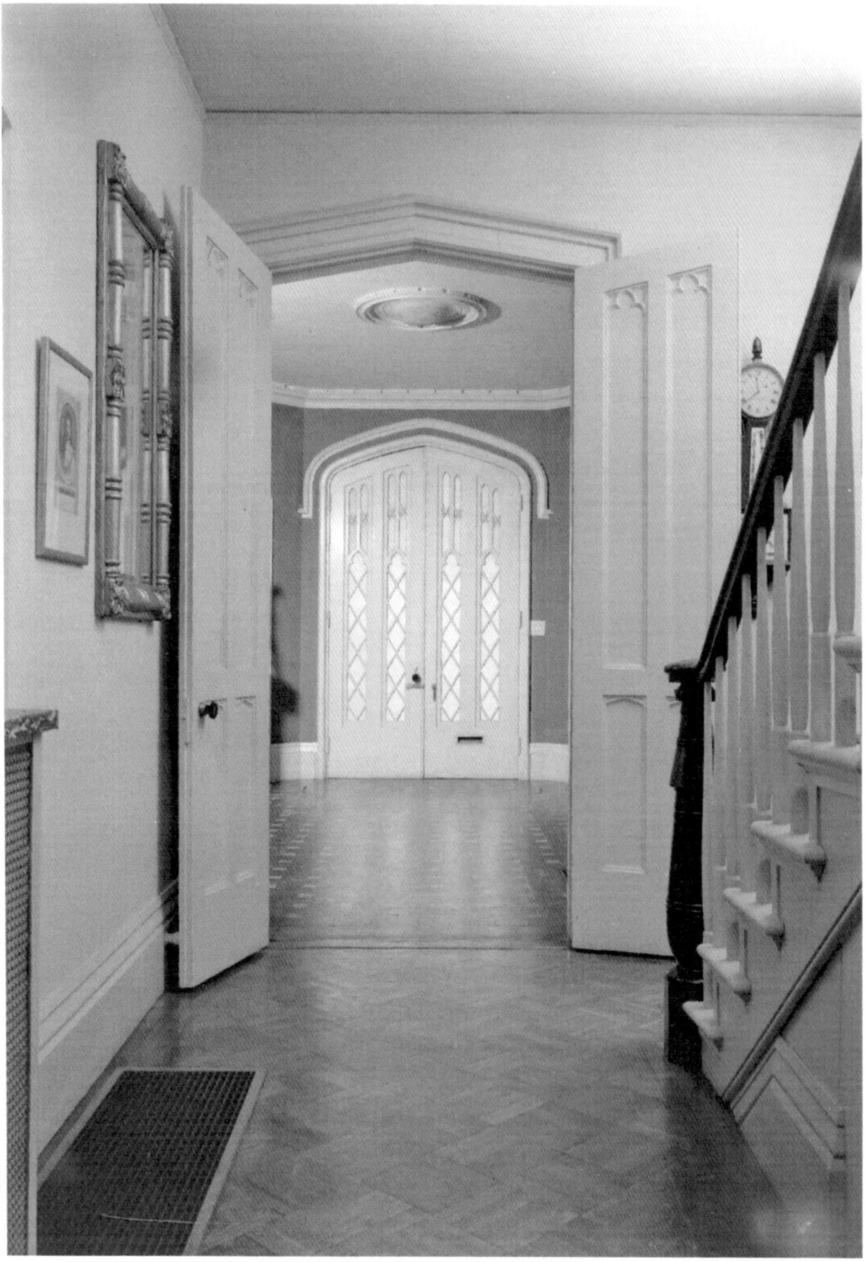

Rotch Cottage, interior entrance hall. *Library of Congress, Historic American Buildings Survey. Ned Goode, photographer.*

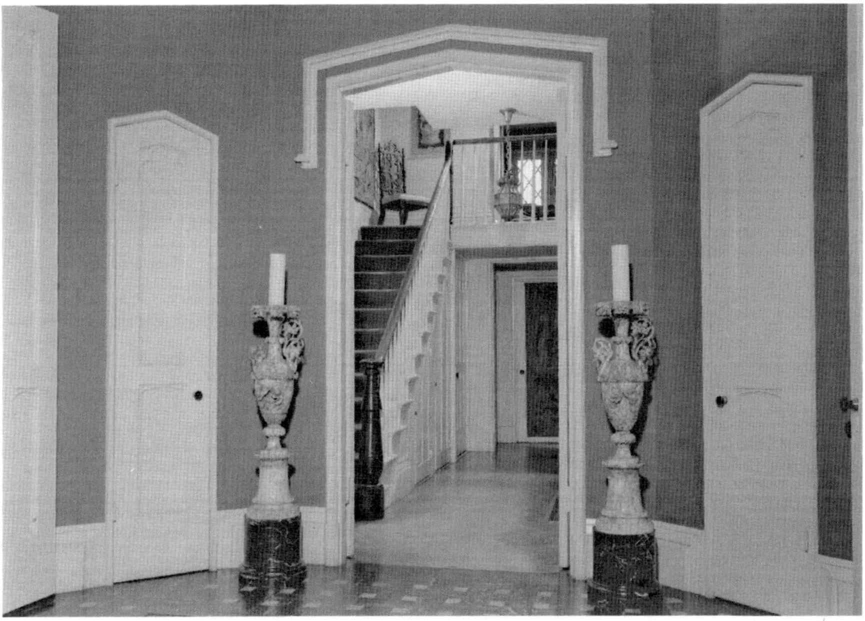

Entrance looking toward stairs. *Library of Congress, Historic American Buildings Survey. Ned Goode, photographer.*

> *beholders. If it looks as well when we get it up as it does neither you or I will be unwilling to look at it.*

Davis's interior plan has four major rooms on the ground floor. An octagonal entrance leads into the hall, with rooms leading directly off it. On the immediate left is the living room, with a conservatory bay. The library is directly behind the living room. The right side of the floor contains first the dining room then the kitchen. The second and third floors contain bedrooms. Although details changed during construction, the house built for William J. Rotch is, in essence, the house first sketched by Alexander Jackson Davis.

By the end of the summer of 1845, William J. Rotch had decided on workmen for the house. He kept meticulous accounts. The New Bedford Free Public Library owns several of his journal ledgers, beginning in 1846. By checking payments listed for the house, it is possible to determine with fair accuracy who had a hand in constructing the Rotch Cottage. The result is one of the most well-documented houses ever built anywhere in America.

William Rotch Jr. advanced his grandson the money to build the cottage. This was fully in the Rotch tradition of helping children and grandchildren

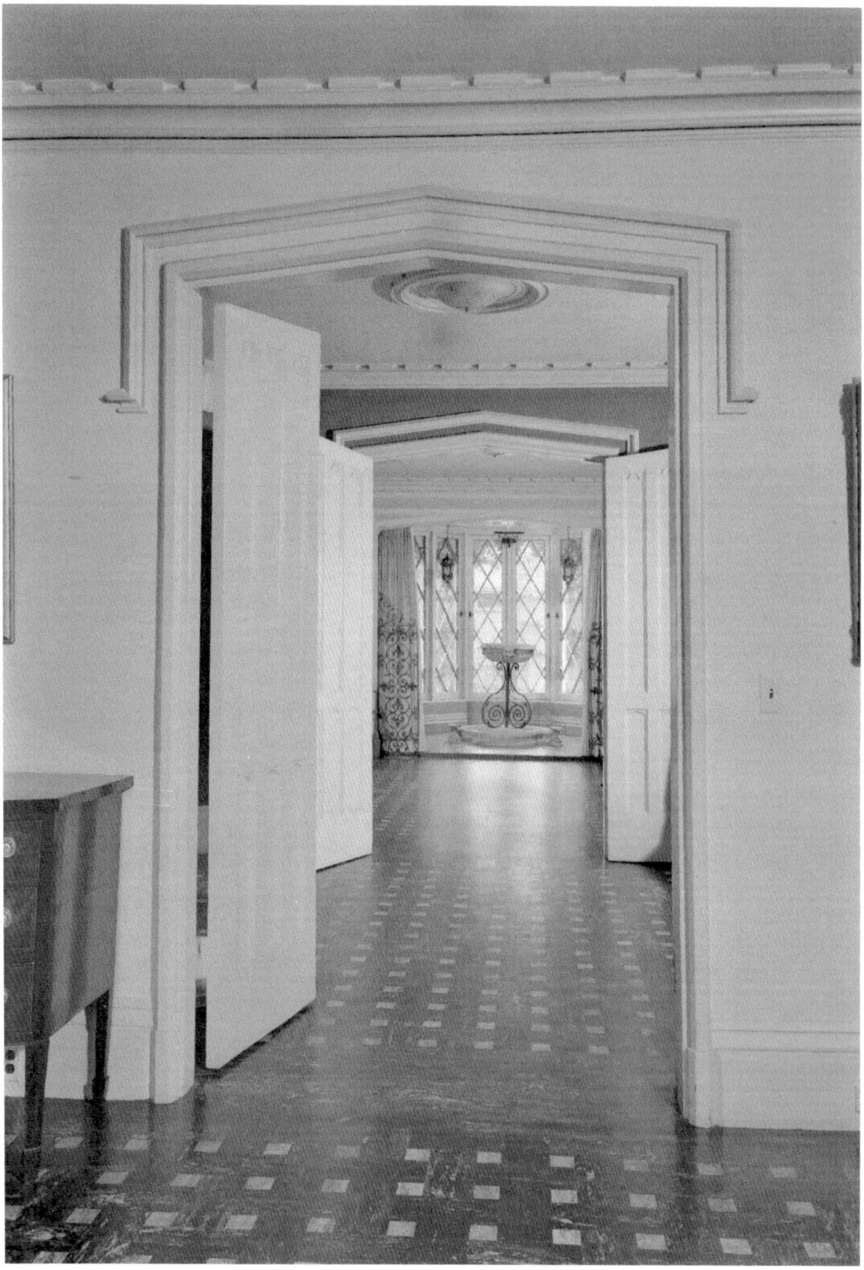

Rotch Cottage, entrance hall looking toward conservatory. *Library of Congress, Historic American Buildings Survey. Ned Goode, photographer.*

with finances. William J. Rotch, in turn, later built houses for his daughters when they married if he approved of the husband in question. He may have received the money as a gift rather than a proper loan.

A story often repeated and printed about the cottage is that William's father considered it unsightly. Since Joseph had died long before the house was built, the remark was possibly made by William Rotch Jr. As a result of his contribution to the financing, he probably felt free to comment on the result.

There are a few obvious differences between the house shown in the famous Davis watercolor (a Bullard family watercolor), now owned by the Metropolitan Museum of Art, and the house as actually built. Having copies of the Davis half of the Rotch-Davis correspondence would clear up questions about the order in which changes were made, at what stage in the construction and whether they were refinements of detail made by Davis or requested by Rotch. Although the Rotch Cottage is one of the best-documented houses ever built in New Bedford, there are still questions about it that cannot be answered.

The most obvious differences between design and execution are in material. The Davis rendering shows a stone or stucco house. William J. Rotch did not want to use stone and stated this clearly in two of his letters. This dislike of stone may have been because of added expense or it may have been an aesthetic decision. He won at any rate, and the cottage is clad in wood, with the boards laid horizontally and butted smoothly to form an unbroken surface.

At some point in 1846, Emily and William James Rotch moved into their house on Orchard Street. While the house was under construction, Emily had a third child, Helen, who was born in July 1846. The house was quickly filled with additional young Rotches.

New Bedford in general was endlessly fascinated by the Gothic cottage up on Orchard Street. In 1850, the house received a great deal of national attention when it was included in A.J. Downing's last book, *The Architecture of Country Houses*. Number 7 Orchard Street became "Design XXIV—A Cottage-Villa in the Rural Gothic Style." As a measure of the wealth of 1846 New Bedford, building costs were higher than in New York, and the Rotch Cottage is reported as running about $6,000 to build (about $153,500 in 2013 dollars).

Downing also edited the vastly influential magazine *The Horticulturist*, and a brief article featuring the cottage appeared in the November 1849 issue before the publication of *The Architecture of Country Houses*. A critique of the house by

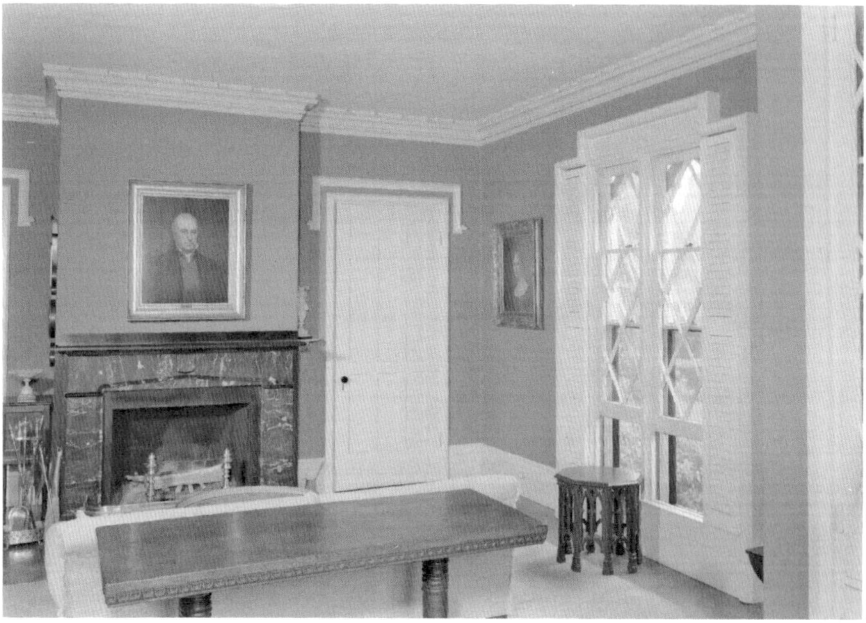

Rotch Cottage, library with portrait of William Rotch Jr. *Library of Congress, Historic American Buildings Survey. Ned Goode, photographer.*

a writer billed as "Jeffreys of New York" appeared. Jeffreys may have been Downing himself. On the whole, he approved: "Here is something that I like. A sensible house, and in very good taste: embodying in the main, the essentials of good house arrangement, as far as it goes, and adapted to the purposes for which it was intended an unpretending, quiet cottage of the first class."

During the late 1840s and early 1850s, while New Bedford finally became a city, William J. Rotch was busy fitting out whaling ships; running the New Bedford Cordage Company, which he also founded; and serving two terms in the Massachusetts General Court. Three additional children were born: Morgan in 1848, Isabel in 1850 and Sarah on 1854. In 1852, at the age of thirty-three, William became New Bedford's second mayor.

In 1861, Emily Morgan Rotch died shortly after the birth of her last child, daughter Anna, on April 30. With her death on June 13 at forty, William was left with seven children. Emily's father, the great Charles W. Morgan, had died on April 9 of the same year, and Rotch also became responsible for administering the estate and looking after the youngest Morgan child, Clara, who was then twenty-five. Five years later, on January 11, 1886, Clara Morgan married her brother-in-law, William James Rotch.

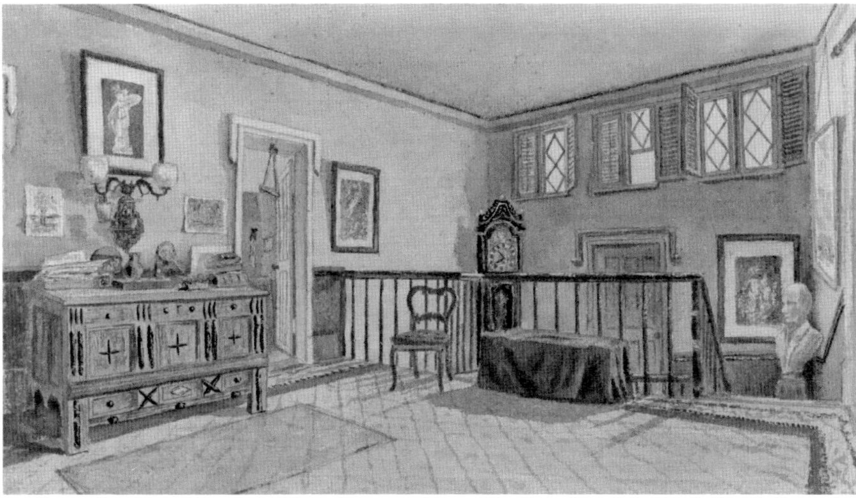

Rotch Cottage, photograph of watercolor by Henry H. Crapo II. Second-floor hall. *Library of Congress, Historic American Buildings Survey. Ned Goode, photographer.*

Even with an addition in the cottage (it eventually became a completely separate house and had not been designed by Davis), it was hopelessly cramped. When James Arnold died in 1868, William J. Rotch was his heir. The family moved into the Arnold mansion and rented the Gothic cottage. Congressman William Crapo and his family moved into the cottage and even asked to buy it. They were refused.

Although slightly outside the scope of this book, I can't resist quoting a letter about life in the house, especially because the Crapos did eventually own it. In a wonderful bit of historic serendipity, a Crapo-Rotch-Bullard marriage brought the house back to the Rotches:

> *When your grandfather lived in that house what fun I had when I visited there. The Christmas and Thanksgiving parties were so large the grownups were in one room and the young people in another...I think now of 1879 year. The dinners took time and when we children were restless we would sometimes go out into the hall between courses and take a peek into the grownups rooms.*
>
> *One Beau Brummel of the past had carried an opera hat and left it in the hall. That was a new one to us and afforded some amusement open and shutting. Fortunately the next course arrived and we scuttled back to our seats before harm was done.*

...The room was very large and had a lighted Christmas tree all decorated. Candles were mixed up with a few of my locks and someone thoughtfully put the fire out but the aromas was with me for a time.

...I think I must have been a pest in the early days for I sometimes offered advice when your grandmother and Uncle Henry then in college were talking and as it had not been asked I became aware I was a bit unpopular! I was more discreet after that.

...The back stairs oh!! The back stairs I wasn't supposed to patronize. They were wonderfully wide and were of dark wood. I wonder if I would see them now I would like to know how wide they are?

In my dreams I was continually flying down them just touching every other step. It was a most wonderful sensation and never a fall.

Number 19 Irving Street is a National Historic Landmark. It stayed in the family until recently. It remains the most perfect Gothic cottage in America.

Chapter 9

A Pack of Abolitionists, Artists and Transcendentalists

In 1845, Redwood Fisher discovered New Bedford. *Fisher's National Magazine and Industrial Record* gave the city a long and glowing profile:

> *There is scarcely a town in our country, of equal importance, about which so little has been said, by the book-makers, as New Bedford. From Peter Parley, upwards, through the whole catalogue of geographies, registers, gazetteers, encyclopedias, and histories, you shall look in vain for any thing approximating towards a decently truthful account of this flourishing town.*

The piece sets the stage for the greatest period of artistic and social growth New Bedford ever had:

> *Few strangers who visit New Bedford fail to be struck with the exceeding neatness and beauty of the dwellings in the more elevated portions of the town. Much of this attractiveness is owing to the circumstance, that they are nearly all surrounded by extensive and well cultivated gardens, and that the streets on which they are built are bordered with a beautiful growth and great variety of ornamental trees. County street, which runs the whole extent of the thickly settled part of the town, about two miles, upon the summit of the rising ground on which it is built, is allowed to be almost without a rival in this country for its various and attractive beauties.*

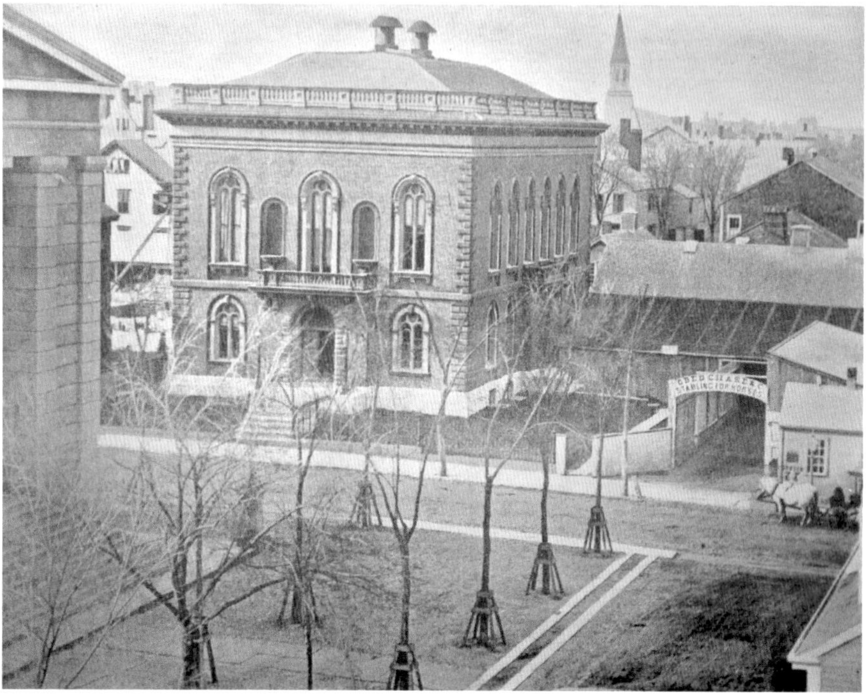

New Bedford Free Public Library (now New Bedford City Hall). *Collection of author. Courtesy of Arthur P. Motta.*

In the years before the Civil War, New Bedford became a city full of artists, abolitionists and writers. One of the city's gems was another Russell Warren classic. The town hall (then city hall and now the library) deserved showing off, and Fisher realized it:

> *The Town Hall is a magnificent structure. It is built of granite, and is one hundred feet long and sixty-one feet wide, and three stories in height. The lower story, or basement, is occupied as a public market. This room is spacious and convenient, and its stalls in good order, and all furnished with marble benches for the meats; and for the most part supplied with an abundance of those articles usually found in the public market.*
>
> *In the hall is suspended a full length portrait of Washington, painted by William A. Hall, a native artist, from Stuart's celebrated picture, and presented to the town by a small number of the citizens. It has been pronounced, by competent judges, to be well and faithfully executed; and while it reflects credit upon the artist, and upon the public spirit of the*

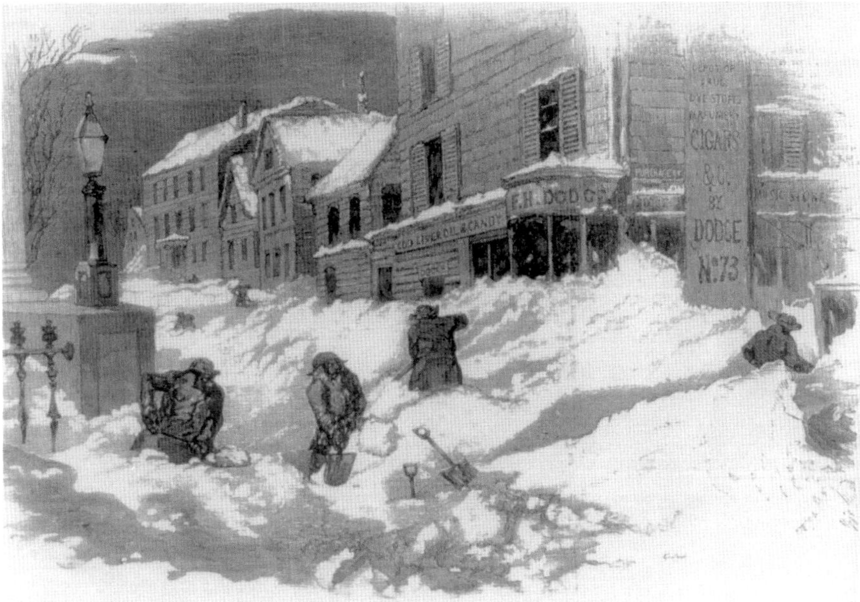

A recent deep snow in Massachusetts along a street in New Bedford, 1857. Wood engraving. *Library of Congress Prints & Photographs.*

> *individuals who caused it to be executed, it is highly ornamental to the beautiful hall.*
>
> *The edifice, which with the land beneath and around it, cost the town the sum of sixty thousand dollars, has been called by many, the handsomest building in New England devoted to civic purposes.*

John James Audubon loved New Bedford, and the city loved him in return. He called it his "beautiful New Bedford" and made extensive visits in 1805, 1839, 1840, 1842 and 1844. At one point, he seriously considered buying land and settling here. One of his closest friends, John Page, lived on South Sixth Street. Audubon knew all of the great families from Arnold to Howland to Robeson, and members of those families bought his great books and his less well-known oils.

James Arnold and Andrew Robeson gave the New Bedford Free Public Library two rare treasures: the Arnold "Double Elephant Folio" of *Birds of America* and the Robeson *Viviparous Quadrupeds of North America.*

Arnold, of course, had the means and leisure to create great gardens, host masques, collect art and travel in Europe. From Arnold's travel diary,

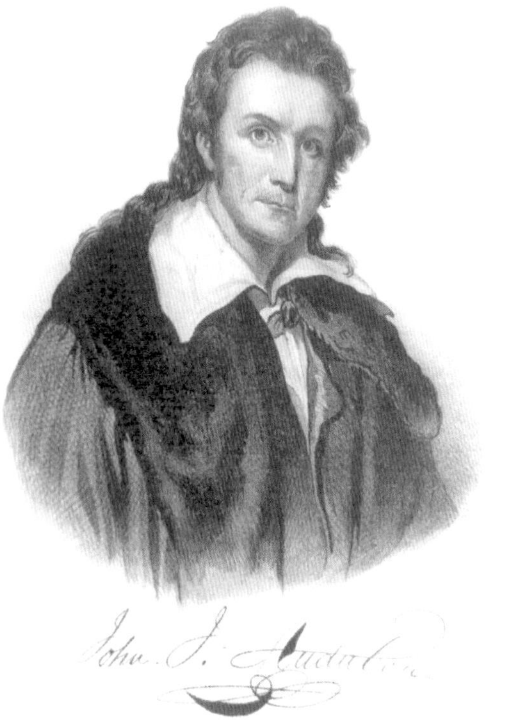

A young John J. Audubon as the English viewed him. The romantic from the wilderness. *Library of Congress Prints & Photographs.*

researched by historian Sally Sapienza, we know that during his European grand tour he visited Audubon in London. Audubon was preparing his masterpiece for publication. On September 1, 1837, the Arnolds drove to 4 Wimpole Street for what was probably their first face-to-face meeting.

According to Waldemar H. Fries's comprehensive book, *The Double Elephant Folio: The Story of Audubon's Birds of America*, James Arnold was the seventy-fourth of eighty-two American subscribers to Audubon's masterpiece. Originally the book cost $1,000 (about $21,560 in 2013 figures).

Audubon made sure that his subscribers completed their sets by rationing the most desirable birds. Each of the installments contained one of the most coveted large birds (for example, the eagle or snowy owls) and one medium-sized bird. Each of the four "Double Elephant Folio" volumes bound by the owner weighed sixty pounds.

Audubon however, already knew New Bedford. He arrived anonymously in 1805 at the age of twenty. He never expected to be here, though. Sailing on Isaac Howland's brig the *Hope*, he thought he was headed straight for France. Instead, as his journal noted:

> *We left the Hook under a very fair breeze, and proceeded at a good rate till we reached the latitude of New Bedford, in Massachusetts, when my captain came to me as if in despair, and said he must run into port, as the vessel was so leaky as to force him to have her unloaded and repaired before*

> *he proceeded across the Atlantic. Now this was only a trick; my captain was newly married, and was merely anxious to land at New Bedford to spend a few days with his bride, and had actually caused several holes to be bored below water-mark, which leaked enough to keep the men at the pumps. We came to anchor close to the town of New Bedford; the captain went on shore. Then and after a week, which I spent in being rowed about the beautiful harbor, we sailed for La Belle France.*

There he received his father's blessing to marry Lucy Bakewell. As an international sensation after the publication of *Birds of America*, Audubon returned regularly to New Bedford. A cosmopolitan, elegant city ready to lionize him, it was the perfect place to find subscribers. Audubon, a master showman and shrewd publisher, toured America selling subscriptions of a smaller, affordable version of *Birds of America* that became a massive success. After years of struggle, it brought his family financial security.

During his later visits to New Bedford, he found subscribers for the *Viviparous Quadrupeds of North America*. Audubon also sold a series of oil paintings based on his *Birds of America* images.

Our great guide to the period, Samuel Rodman Jr., wrote on December 19, 1839:

> *Mr. Audubon spent an hour with us but as our tea was late he excused himself on account of some engagements and necessity of retiring early as he leaves in the early stage for Boston tomorrow. He is an interesting old gentleman and is much pleased with New Bedford for the liberal manner in*

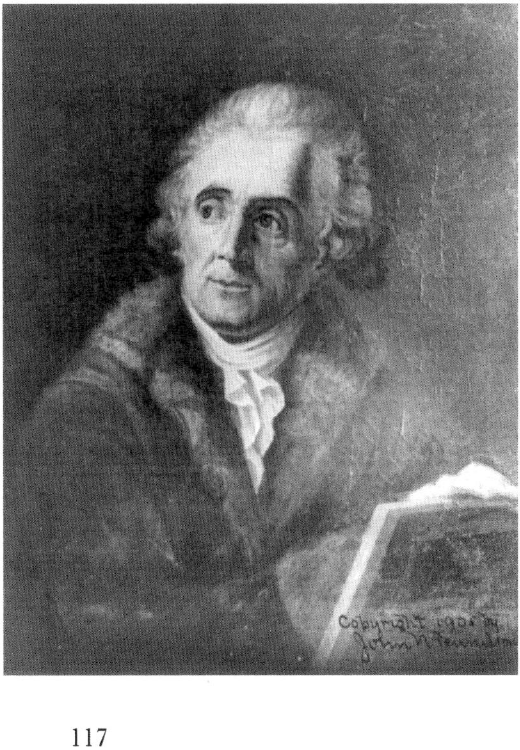

The Audubon who loved New Bedford. Photograph of portrait. *Library of Congress Prints & Photographs.*

which he has been patronized, having obtained subscribers for forty copies of the new edition of his ornithology. The old Gentleman was then fifty four.

Rodman even received a mention from Audubon in the fifth volume of the *Ornithological Bibliography* as a snipe donor. Audubon wrote, "Few individuals of this species are ever seen to the south of New York. Near Boston I procured several, and my learned friend Thomas Nuttall presented me with some that had been shot in the neighborhood of that city, as did Mr. John Bethune and Mr. Rodman of New Bedford." On August 1, 1840, Audubon wrote home from New Bedford:

As it is pouring rain this morning, I will give you an account of my proceedings since my last letter to you…

First add to the subscribers of this beautiful town, the name of J.H.W. Page. I delivered him up to No. 13 and he paid $24. The set I gave him was made up of Nos. 1, 2, 3, 4, 7, 8, 9, 10, 11, 12 and 13. Yesterday morning I sold 5 pictures as follows.

Mr. Geo. Howland Sr. 1 Bird of Washington $100. 2. Turtle Doves $75. 3 Red Shouldered Hawks $50 and I have received from him $225.

Mr. Morgan 1. White headed eagle $100. 2. Pheasants $75. Making $400

Mr. Morgan would not buy without my taking some sperm candles in part payment, and I thought it best to take 6 boxes.

Meanwhile John Page had been attempting to help his friend with finding painting specimens. It seems that Page had met Audubon in Boston, where they became close friends. Page introduced Audubon to his wife's family, the Almys. William Almy, living most of the year in the city, helped Audubon obtain subscribers and invited him to Thanksgiving dinner with the Page/Almy family:

October 21, 1841

My Dear Sir,
I hope you are alive, although I have had misgivings, as I have not heard from you since my last, which was a great while ago, but you are so busy with quadrupeds that you have no time to give to bipeds. In the first place, I have had D. Brigham and all the boys in the regions round about under

> *orders to catch a hare, but no have could be caught until yesterday. I have felt mortified that I could not* [obtain] *one before, but I used every means that I could devise to get one. But now I have a good looking fellow…and I have put him into a keg of rum and send him today.*

I'm quite fond of that hare and wondered if the rum was still drinkable. It is uncertain if a portrait of the hare actually made it into the Quads. There is a lovely swamp hare that I think is a definite possibility. In 1842, Audubon returned again:

> *New Bedford, August 15th—Here I am! At our Friends the Pages! I was up early but the weather was dry it has rained much in the night.—I sallied forth after breakfast.*
>
> *August 18th—Called on Mrs. Delano, James Arnold where I found a large party and declined going in—procured the subscription of William R. Rodman of this place…I felt well pleased and actually danced with Miss Dana* [a friend of the Pages].
>
> *August 19th—To my utter astonishment it was 20 minutes to 7 when I awoke this morning—Spent nearly 2 hours at James Arnold who did not subscribe.*

Arnold was famous for loving to keep friends talking for hours.

> *August 20th 1842*
> *In the afternoon I rode to Fairhaven with friend Page, and on our return stopped about an hour on the Bridge to see persons fishing. We ourselves tried but caught nothing. I saw a good-sized lobster actually taken by the Hook! It was given to us and has been demolished at our supper. Miss Dana and I called at James Arnold but the families were all out. We walked together admiring the moon now full. We enjoyed this superb evening, talking Dancing etc. until nearly 11 o'clock when I went to Bed… Mr. Jones gave me a remarkably Large sperm whale tooth. Rambling about the woods and fields until Dinner. Went to Mr. William Almy 12 miles with Friends Page, Lady & Miss Dana*

In December 1842, John Page celebrated the Audubons' first Christmas at their beloved Minnie's Land in New York City. Audubon died on June 27, 1851, and Page wrote immediately to the family:

We had already learned the fact of your dear father's decease, but were glad to hear from you. You cannot doubt of my entire sympathy with you all. I claim the bereavement as part my own. My acquaintance with your father commenced here about eleven years ago, perhaps twelve, and from that time I was honored by a close intimacy with him. He was many times an inmate of my house and always a most welcome and delightful guest. Of his varied talents and accomplishments, I could not speak in proper terms, and do not desire to speak. Of the man, the friend, the companion I could speak much. Suffice it to say, that he was one of the few men whom I had really loved and clasped to my heart, and in whom I could see no fault. I always enjoyed his society with my whole soul, and look back with delight upon every minute of my intercourse with him. Mary loved him as I did, and what great happiness to us both to believe that he loved us. It was a great grief to me that a dark veil should run over his beautiful and brilliant mind; but no man can choose the mode in which the sun shall go down either for himself or his friend.

Lucy Audubon tried to keep her family together at Minnie's Land. Despite all her efforts, the family became poverty stricken. In 1862, she wrote to John Page. The letter is owned by the Old Dartmouth Historical Society:

Washington Heights
June 25, 1862

My dear Sir,
It is long since we met and many are the sad changes to me, I am now in my seventy fourth year; without husband or child embarrassed with debts which before my dear heart broken John's death I knew not of. Pardon my giving you my trouble but as the adage says "a drowning man grasps at straws." I am in that unhappy position and no one to help me further than by kind words and advise, for which I am truly thankful but my case is desperate, and I write to beg you if you know of any monied person who would take my homestead for even two or three thousand dollars more than the mortgage of twelve thousand upon it, for I have no means of paying the interest by 20 half yearly. I teach a few pupils to pay my Board. There are also some debts that must be paid. I also wish you could sell my original drawings they number 420 for two or three thousand. My feelings now must confine themselves to the payment of the money my poor mistaken children left behind them. Your former interest in us has given my courage to address you.

If you cannot aid me at least be kind enough to write to me. With sincere regards to Mrs. Page. I am dear sir.

Yours truly
Lucy Audubon

It is not known if Page was able to help. Knowing the man, it is more than likely he did. Years later, a despondent John Page took his own life. Against his better judgment, he had left his law practice for business. The *Daily Evening Standard* reported on June 19, 1865:

Suicide of a Prominent Citizen—The body of Hon. J.H.W. Page, formerly of this city was found in the water at Breed's Island, Winthrop, on Saturday afternoon. His coat, hat and spectacles were found on the shore, and on the body, inside the vest and in the pockets were seventy pounds of stones. He has recently been subject to temporary fits of insanity, and had been missing three days.

There is, however, a lovely story mentioned in a New Bedford Whaling Museum sketch. It credits the elms that once lined Hawthorn Street to John Page: "The seedlings were obtained from John James Audubon, famous naturalist who visited this city on several occasions." If it isn't true, it should have been.

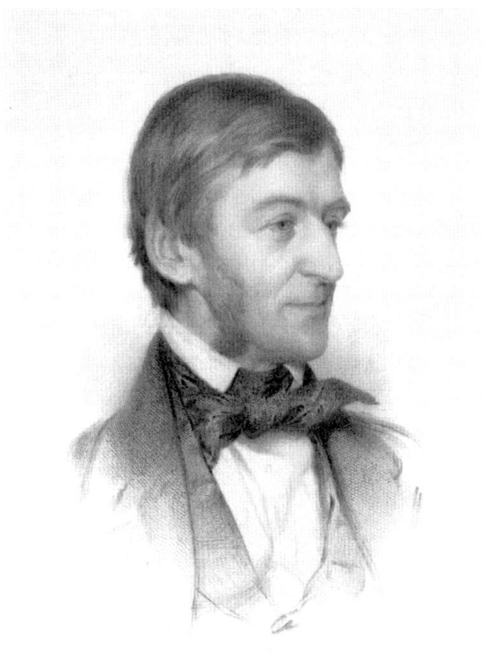

Ralph Waldo Emerson, the great friend of Aunt Mary Rotch and James Arnold. *Library of Congress Prints & Photographs Division.*

New Bedford can claim credit for convincing Ralph Waldo Emerson that he was not destined to be a minister. In 1830, the Unitarian Church sent him here as an interim minister. Already struggling with the question of what he truly believed, he learned about the Society of Friends from the extraordinary Mary Rotch, Sarah Arnold's own aunt. In his book *Liberal Pilgrims: Varieties of Liberal Religious Experience in New Bedford, Massachusetts* author Dan Harper, former minister of New Bedford's Unitarian Church, wrote of Mary Rotch and her impact on Emerson:

> *When Emerson came back to New Bedford in the winter and spring of 1833–1834, he got to know Mary Rotch better. At that time, Mary Rotch told the young Emerson something of the controversy between the New Lights and the Old Lights, and Emerson wrote in one of his notebooks that she had been "driven inward, driven home, to find an anchor, until she learned to have no choice, to acquiesce without understanding the reason when she found an obstruction to any particular course of action.*

Years later, Emerson quoted Mary Rotch in his essay titled "Greatness," expressing this same point in a different way:

> *I do not pretend to any commandment or large revelation, but if at any time I form some plan, propose a journey or a course of conduct, I perhaps find a silent obstacle in my mind that I cannot account for. Very well—I let it lie, thinking it may pass away, but if it do not pass away I yield to it, obey it. You ask me to describe it. I cannot describe it. It is not an oracle, nor an angel, nor a dream, nor a law; it is too simple to be described, it is but a grain of mustard-seed, but such as it is, it is something which the contradiction of all mankind could not shake, and which the consent of all mankind could not confirm.*

Emerson also became fond of James and Sarah Arnold. He took particular pleasure discussing the New Light/Old Light controversy with Arnold. In his journals, he wrote, "James Arnold said to me, Give this town of New Bedford to one man, say, an Irishman out of the street—tell him 'it is his, & he must manage it the best he can'—and you will find he will govern it better than it is governed now."

On March 12, 1852, Emerson wrote about arranging a visit to New Bedford:

> *My dear Mrs. Arnold,*
>
> *My wife begs me to reply to your kind note, as it found her, I am sorry to say, a little more invalid than usual. But I fancy the note was better than her drugs & set her upon her feet before sunset. At any rate, she charges*

> *me to thank you for your kind invitation, which she is bent on getting well enough to accept; and meantime charges me to write to Mr. Rodman, that I am to be released from all claims, in order to go with her to visit you. I shall immediately execute this command & put myself in your hospitality, confiding that Mrs. Emerson will accompany me.*
>
> *With respectful remembrance to Mr. Arnold & to Miss Arnold,*
> *Your affectionate servant…*

The second-floor guest bedroom the Emersons stayed in is still part of the remaining core of the Arnold Mansion.

I discovered Margaret Fuller in a college course on the American Renaissance. We were assigned Hawthorne's *Blithedale Romance*, and I loved it. During the discussion, my English professor, Dr. Marie Ahern, mentioned that the character Zenobia was based on Fuller, and that Hawthorne had very mixed feelings about her—a mix of fascination and complete male panic.

I filed that away along with an order that all of us go into New Bedford and actually look at the buildings that Melville had known. This was in 1969, long before the days of restoration. I remember being escorted out of a bar with boarded-up windows and guided out of what is now the national park. My friend and I were warned to *never* set foot in that bar again because someone had been stabbed the night before. It wasn't until I began researching Sarah and James Arnold that I discovered that Margaret Fuller had actually known New Bedford very well. She stayed with Sarah's aunt, Mary Rotch.

Emerson was one of Margaret Fuller's most adored friends and her true soul mate. She, of course, blazed across the country and, later, all of Europe. She was America's first great feminist writer, a teacher who led what she called "conversations" that set Boston on fire and a reporter for Horace Greeley in New York. From Italy, she sent back an account of the Italian revolution, lived through a siege of Rome, married an Italian count, had a son and then decided to come home. She drowned with her husband and baby off Fire Island within sight of land on July 19, 1850. Emerson sent Henry David Thoreau to the wreck sight to try to find her body. He was unable to find any of the bodies. Margaret Fuller was forty when she drowned.

Mary Rotch was introduced to Margaret by Eliza Rotch Farrar, her niece. Eliza had married a Harvard professor and taken young Margaret under

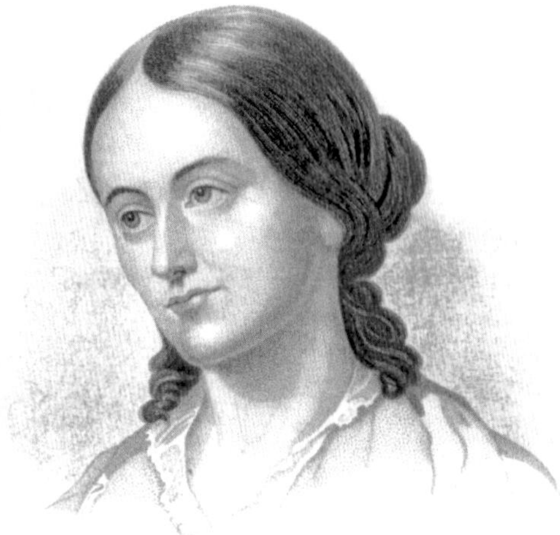

Margaret Fuller. Engraving. *Library of Congress Prints & Photographs Division.*

her wing. She wanted to make her a lady. In 1842, Margaret spent a week at Mary Rotch's home on South Sixth Street.

There are a number of letters from Margaret to "Aunt Mary," but my favorite is one from New Bedford to Emerson. Written on June 23, 1842, it begins:

> *Dear Waldo,*
>
> *I feel like writing to you, yet cannot perceive that there is much of a letter lying in my mind. It does not agree with my humor just now to be going about and seeing so many people, and I don't thrive under it. It is not Aunt Mary's fault, that I do exactly as I please, for she is a nonpariel of a hostess in her combination of quiet, courteous attention to the comfort of her guests, with the desire to be alone, whenever it is best…*

After discussion of plans and other friends, the letter ends, "Your Affectionate Margaret." There is also a famous postscript to the letter: "I like Aunt Mary's dry humor. Have you ever seen that?"

Madeleine Stern, in her wonderful *Life of Margaret Fuller*, wrote about what the friendship gave Margaret:

> *She could find even more relaxation at the New Bedford home of Mary Rotch, the Quaker. Had not Emerson suggested that it was the vision of Mary Rotch leaving church when the Last Supper was to be commemorated which first cast a blight upon that rite in his eyes? Even her humor was quiet, for she was ever listening to the voice within. Though Miss Rotch was entertaining other guests, Margaret could sit alone in her room several hours every day, and then converse with her "Aunt Mary" (it was pleasing to be allied with Emerson in the possession of an Aunt Mary) about the*

> *"leading oracles" at the latest meeting of Friends. It was new for Margaret, a stranger quiet than the howling of the wind.*

More frivolously, Aunt Mary gave her a black dress. Margaret never forgot her and continued to write to Mary Rotch from New York and even Europe.

New Bedford's greatest literary friendship was between Daniel Ricketson and Henry David Thoreau. It began on Christmas Day 1854, when Ricketson and his family received the gift of their lives. It was a visit from the man Ricketson worshipped as a hero and Louisa May Alcott knew and loved: Henry David Thoreau. It's best to let Ricketson remember it:

> *The season was winter, a snow had lately fallen, and I was engaged in shoveling the accumulated mass from the entrance to my house, when I perceived a man walking towards me bearing an umbrella in one hand and a leather travelling-bag in the other. So unlike my ideal Thoreau, whom I had fancied to be a man of unusual vigor and size…that I did not suspect…that the slight, quaint-looking person before me was the Walden philosopher.*
>
> *As he came near to me, I gave him the usual salutation, and supposing him to be either a peddler or some way-traveller, he at once remarked, "You don't know me." The truth flashed on my mind, and concealing my own surprise, I at once took him by the hand and led him to the room already prepared for him.*

Zephaniah W. Pease, in his *History of New Bedford*, quoted Ricketson's description of Thoreau that Christmas:

> *The most expressive feature of his face was his eye, blue in color and full of the greatest humanity and intelligence. His head was of medium size, the same as that of Emerson, and he wore a No. 7 hat. His arms were rather long, his legs short, and his hands and feet rather large. His sloping shoulders were a mark of observation. But when in usual health he was strong and vigorous, a remarkable pedestrian, tiring out nearly all his companions in his prolonged tramps through woods and marshes, when in pursuit of some rare plant. In Thoreau, as in other heroic men, it was the spirit more than the temple in which it dwelt, that made the man.*

Ricketson adored Thoreau. He loved their walks and evenings of talk in Ricketson's shanty. This tiny hut was his place away from the larger, more

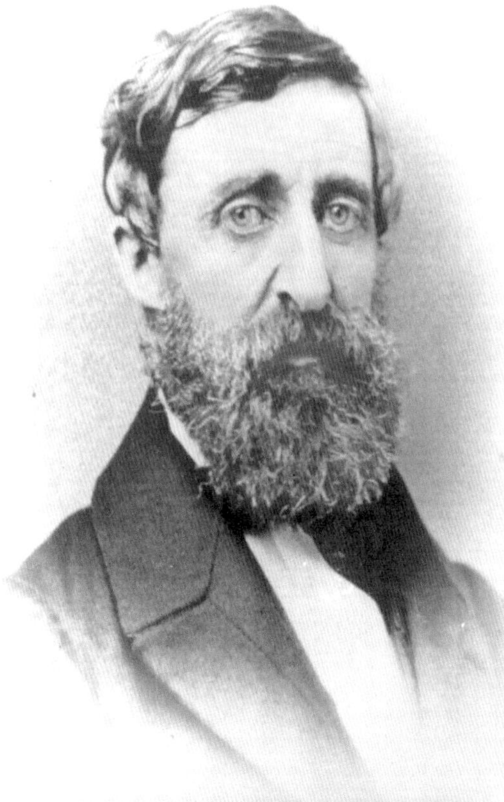

Daniel Ricketson's great friend Henry David Thoreau, circa 1879. *Library of Congress Prints & Photographs.*

formal home. For the rest of Thoreau's life, Ricketson was there writing letters, running errands and meeting him in Concord. He even helped to look after the impossible John Ellery Channing, Margaret Fuller's poetic, promising and ultimately awful brother-in-law. Channing, like Branson Alcott, felt that great men should not have to take jobs or support their families. Channing once attempted a real job in New Bedford editing the *Mercury*. Ricketson kept track of him.

One rambling, delightful errand took Ricketson to the Arnold gardens. Thoreau commissioned him to find specimens of autumn leaves. His spelling may have been off but he did know botany:

The Shanty, November 10th, 1858

Friend Thoreau—
Your very pleasant and encouraging letter reached me on Monday (the 8th).

This forenoon I made a visit to Arnold's garden, walking to and from through the woods and fields most of the way on the route by the upper road by which the wind-mill stands. In company with the gardener, rejoicing in the appropriate and symphonious name of Wellwood Young, whose broad Gaelic accent rendered an attentive ear necessary to catch the names. The following is the list I made in accordance with your request.

The Scotch larch, for instance, he said came from Norroway (Norway), the yellow fringes of which are still hanging on the branches.

I give the names without any order, just as we happened to meet the trees. Horse-chestnut, quite full of yellow and green foliage. English walnut, do. Beech, Linden, Hawthorn (nearly perfect in green foliage, only a little decayed at the top, but in a sheltered place), Silver Linden, Copper Beech, Elm, Weeping Ash, Weeping Willow, Scotch Larch, Euanimus European (Gardener's name), I suppose correct. These are all European or English, I believe. I give a few others not European, viz: Osage orange (or Maclura), Cornus Florida (handsome) Tulip, three-thorned Acacia, Mexican Cypress.

There were numerous shrubs in full leaf, among them the Gulder Rose, Vines, Bignonia radicans and Bignonia cuminata.

I send a few leaves. The largest green leaf is the American Linden—the smaller, the European copper leaved Beech. One English Elm (green), and the two smaller and narrower leaves, the Euanimus Europeus.

I am sorry the list is no fuller, but I think it includes all in these grounds. The location is quite sheltered. I could not ascertain from the gardener what trees exhibited particular brilliance of foliage, last month. I conclude however, that these I have named were quite fresh up to the last of October.

It is barely possible I may reach Concord on Saturday next and remain over Sunday, but hardly probable as they say.

Channing I understand has been to Concord since I wrote you last and is now here again. Is he not quite as much a "creature of moods" as old Sudbury Inn? But I am in poor mood for writing, and besides it is nearly dark (5 p.m.)

May I not hear from you again soon, and may I not expect a visit also ere long?

As this is only a business letter I trust you will excuse its dullness. Hoping I have supplied you (Channing has just come in) with what you wanted, I conclude. Yours faithfully,

D.R.

P.S. If I should not go to Concord I will endeavor to get one of my books to you soon.

The leaves survive at Harvard. If asked very nicely, they will show them. Channing outlived all of his contemporaries, wrote their biographies and was cared for by Ralph Waldo Emerson in a house just far enough away from Emerson's for comfort. Channing could be difficult company.

Thanks to Ricketson, who took careful notes at every meeting with Thoreau, we know about a most social and happy man:

> *While my wife was playing an air upon the piano Thoreau became very hilarious, sang "Tom Bowline," and finally entered upon an improvised dance. Not being able to stand what appeared to me at the time the somewhat ludicrous appearance of our Walden hermit, I retreated to my shanty* [Ricketson could be prickly at times] *while my older and more humor-loving friend, Alcott, remained and saw it through, much to his amusement.*

Thoreau actually became very fond of his prickly New Bedford friend: "He is the frankest man I know. He told me he sometimes thought he had all the infirmities of genius with-out the genius. He is wretched without a hair pillow."

On August 21, 1861, a desperately ill Thoreau visited New Bedford. Ricketson talked him into having his portrait made by Mr. Dunshee's studio. It was an ambrotype, one of only four photographs of Thoreau that exist. The last letter Thoreau wrote was to Daniel Ricketson, on October 14, 1861.

John James Audubon and Thoreau actually spent more time in New Bedford than Herman Melville ever did. The city clings to every shred of him, of course, because of *Moby Dick*. Without what many feel is the great American novel and whaling, the city would probably be lost to memory.

In January 1841, Melville sailed off on the *Acushnet* to learn the whaling trade. His second visit was in July 1852. He came with his father-in-law, the imposing Lemuel Shaw, chief justice of the Massachusetts Supreme Court. The pair were on a tour of southeastern Massachusetts. Shaw was the important member of the party. It was Shaw, not Melville, who described the visit to his son in a letter on July 20, 1852: "On Tuesday we left in the cars for New Bedford. Mr. Clifford meet us by appointment at the Cars and after riding about the town a little visiting Mr. Arnold's beautiful garden, we dined with Mr. Clifford."

John Henry Clifford was the only governor the city has ever produced. As a lover of the Arnolds, I'm delighted that they appreciated the garden. There was a third visit for what was remembered as an unsuccessful lecture on "Statuary in Rome" in February 1858. Melville did make fifty dollars, though.

That's it for documented appearances of Melville in New Bedford. For years there have been attempts to find more. Romantically, it has to be true because his sister, Catherine Melville Hoadley, did live in New Bedford from 1862 to 1866. With her husband, John, and their children, they lived at 100 Madison Street. He was an engineer who had come to run the New Bedford Copper Company. Hoadley and Melville were true friends. How could he not have visited them?

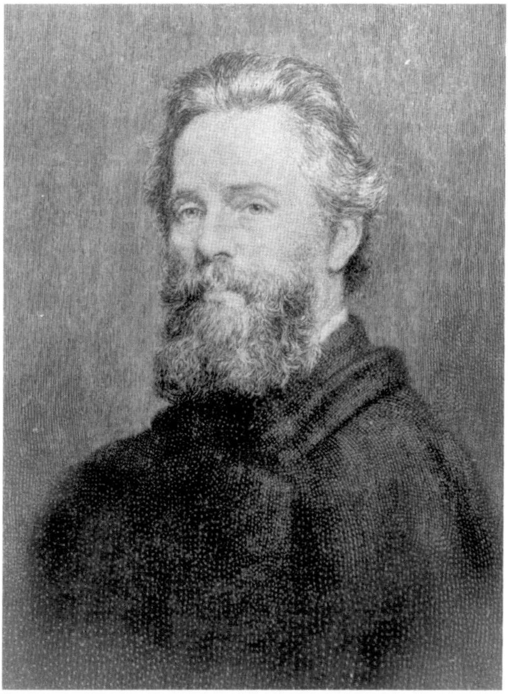

The classic image of Melville. *Library of Congress Prints & Photographs Division.*

Number 100 Madison Street was in the 1980s the library of the Swain School of Design. The school actually called it the Melville Hoadley Library and borrowed portraits of Catherine and John for a special exhibition. Unfortunately, there is no evidence that Melville ever visited the house. He may have, but proving it is another story. Jan Leyda's *Melville Log*, which has day-to-day documentation on where Melville was on every day of his life, never places him at the house. Newspaper accounts speculate endlessly, but that is not fact. Until a diary or letter turn up, all New Bedford has of Melville is that grand book and three visits.

The entire Bierstadt family, unlike Melville, did belong to New Bedford. Albert is the greatest artist New Bedford ever produced. He was *the* great painter of the West. His massive paintings demand single walls and are an astonishment. His brothers, Charles and Edward, were photographers, two of America's earliest and best. Eliza was the youngest Bierstadt child and the only one to be born in America, on August 3, 1833. Her family had arrived in New Bedford from Prussia the year before on August 22, 1832. They were said to be the first three German families in New Bedford. Eliza became the first woman in America to deal in art. She has been largely forgotten. She

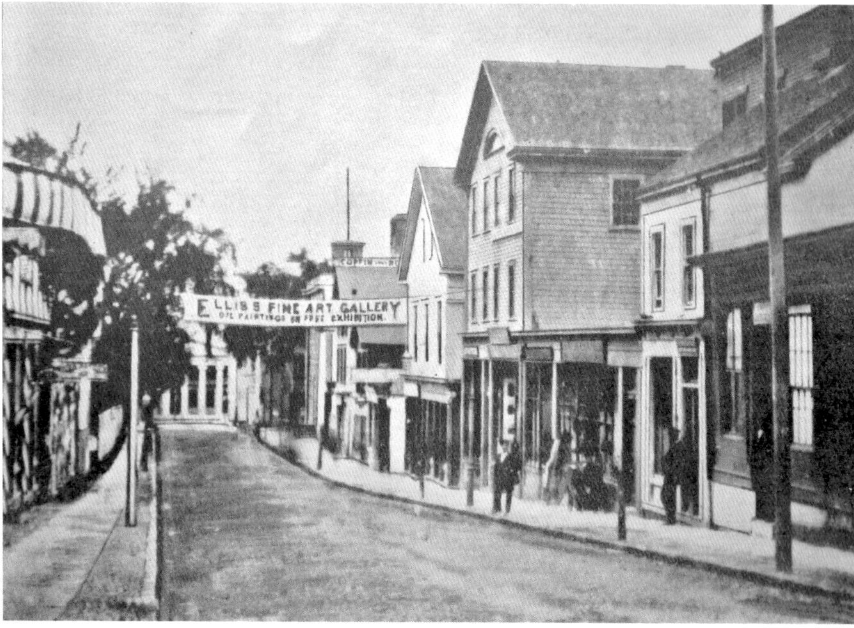

New Bedford's "Gallery Row." William Street, Ellis Art Gallery. *Collection of author. Courtesy of Arthur P. Motta.*

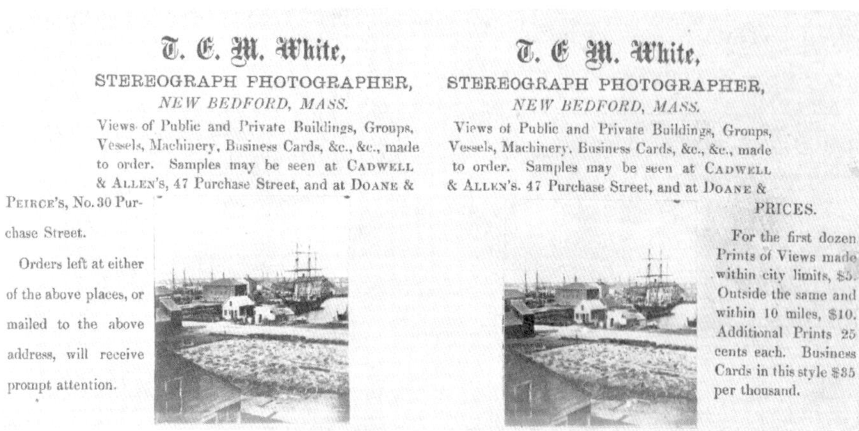

T. E. M. White,
STEREOGRAPH PHOTOGRAPHER,
NEW BEDFORD, MASS.
Views of Public and Private Buildings, Groups, Vessels, Machinery, Business Cards, &c., &c., made to order. Samples may be seen at CADWELL & ALLEN'S, 47 Purchase Street, and at DOANE & PEIRCE'S, No. 30 Purchase Street.
Orders left at either of the above places, or mailed to the above address, will receive prompt attention.

T. E. M. White,
STEREOGRAPH PHOTOGRAPHER,
NEW BEDFORD, MASS.
Views of Public and Private Buildings, Groups, Vessels, Machinery, Business Cards, &c., &c., made to order. Samples may be seen at CADWELL & ALLEN'S. 47 Purchase Street, and at DOANE &
PRICES.
For the first dozen Prints of Views made within city limits, $5. Outside the same and within 10 miles, $10. Additional Prints 25 cents each. Business Cards in this style $35 per thousand.

Stereograph business card of photographer T.E.M. White. *Library of Congress Prints & Photographs Division.*

grew up in a family of artists. It is natural that her brothers and their work led to her career.

She began dealing paintings at the Ellis Gallery on William Street (now the Bedford Merchant) and continued in Niagara Falls, New York. She sold not only Albert's paintings but also those of other Hudson River artists and New Bedford's Charles Henry Gifford. In late 1867, Charles, Edward, Eliza and Helen left New Bedford. Charles and Edward had established themselves as important early photographers, working as the "Bierstadt Brothers." It made sense for them to follow Albert to New York. Eliza owned the first Bierstadt masterpiece, *Sunlight & Shadow.*

Gordon Hendricks's book *Albert Bierstadt: Painter of the American West* includes a few intriguing glimpses of her life. Hendricks reported that in 1869, she went to Europe with Albert and his wife, Rosalie. In July, they were in London visiting the London Zoo and members of the aristocracy. Across the channel, the *Brooklyn Eagle* reported, "Bierstadt and his wife gave a magnificent soiree in Paris recently at which all the eminent artists there were present." Eliza was an enormous social success. The book continues: "In New York in October Dufferin had a 'great crow' to pluck with Bierstadt…Why did you not present me to your sister this morning according to your promise?" This was Eliza, "an unusually handsome young woman with marked individuality of character and distinction of manner." "Dufferin" turns out to be Lord Dufferin, then governor general of Canada.

Eliza learned to produce the famous Bierstadt butterflies—originally a party trick of Albert's. Taking paper and paints, he quickly sketched half a butterfly, folded the wet paper to produce the rest of the image and presented them with a flourish to female guests. The Winterthur Museum has an important of collection of Eliza's letters, scrapbooks and one of her own butterflies.

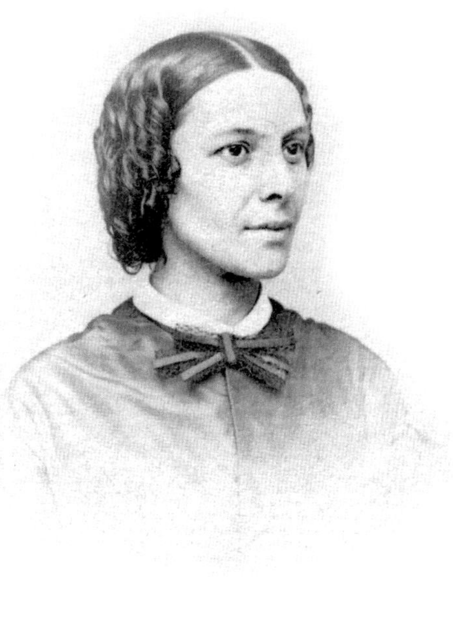

Eliza Bierstadt, Bierstadt Brothers. *Courtesy of the New Bedford Whaling Museum.*

Eliza lived most of her adult life in Niagara Falls

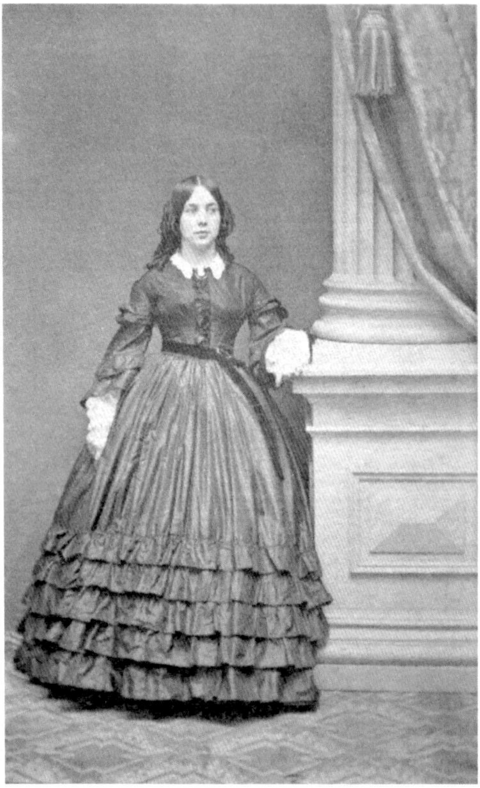

All that is known of this young woman is that she was beautiful and from a wealthy New Bedford family. Bierstadt Brothers. *Collection of author. Courtesy of Arthur P. Motta.*

with her brother Charles. She died at sixty-three on June 10, 1896. The *Niagara Courier* on June 13 wrote that she "will be sadly missed by a very wide circle of friends and acquaintances. Although a hopeless invalid with rheumatism being unable to walk for the last 15 years she retained her interest in outside affairs to a remarkable degree and her bright mind, keen sense of humor and retentive memory made her very attractive and companionable." In death Eliza Bierstadt returned to New Bedford and is buried in the Bierstadt plot at Rural Cemetery.

Charles and Edward, Albert's younger brothers, matter in their own right as artists. In 1857, they made their first appearance in the *New Bedford Mercury*:

> *TURNING AND SAWING*
> *The subscribers respectfully inform their friends and the public that they have taken the shop No. 147 North Water Street, for the purpose of carrying on the Turning & Sawing business. Having extra facilities we feel confident that we can accommodate all who may favor us in their patronage with every kind of Plain & Fancy Turning, large and small.*

In 1857, Charles and Edward were in their early thirties. They had been brought to New Bedford in their childhood by their parents, Henry and Christina. Henry worked for himself as a cooper from the shop behind the Bierstadt home. It is a safe assumption that their father taught them how to work wood.

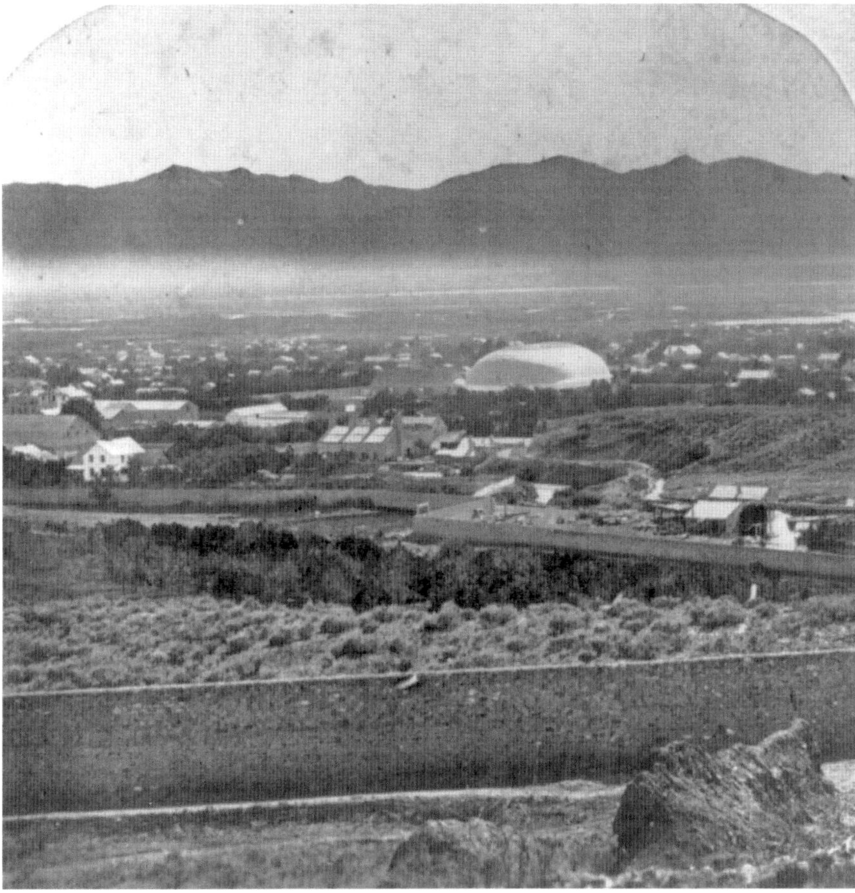

Salt Lake City, Utah. Bird's-eye view, with Mormon Temple in background. Bierstadt Brothers. *Library of Congress Prints & Photographs Division.*

If not for one of New Bedford's periodic "Great Fires" in 1859, Charles and Edward may never have been photographers. The first destroyed the shop. It had not been insured. They began again as Finnegan, Bierstadt Brothers Photographers with assistance from the already famous Albert. The most haunting images of New Bedford at this time were taken by Charles and Edward. By the outbreak of the Civil War, their work was becoming extravagantly admired: "Stereoscope Pictures—Bierstadt Brothers, China Hall, 89 Purchase Street, New Bedford, are earning a reputation as landscape photographers second to no other persons in the country and rivaling the best pictures by French artists." Not a bad

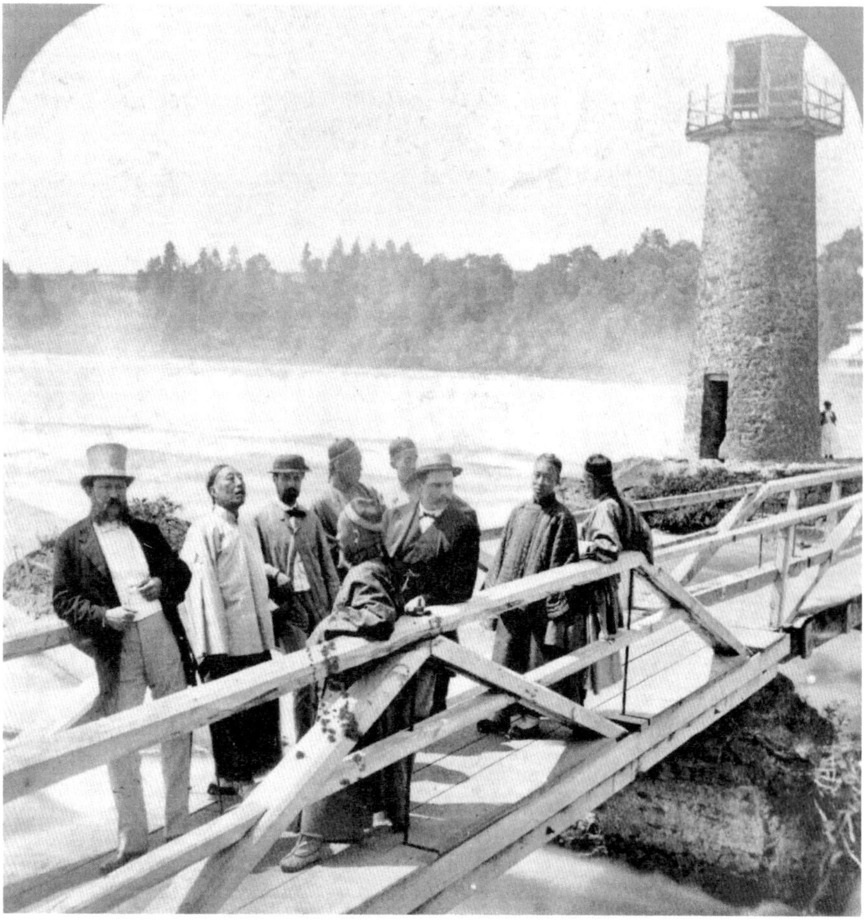

"Chinese and Others on Small Bridge." Niagara Falls Series, Charles Bierstadt, photographer. *Library of Congress Prints & Photographs Division.*

compliment given that the French had essentially invented photography. By that point, Charles and Edward had been working in both Washington and New York. Among their sitters was a very young John Hay, then Lincoln's secretary and future secretary of state.

The Bierstadt brothers photographed battles. They photographed landscapes. They photographed people. I own two of their New Bedford pieces of young unidentified women. They became major forces in their industry in two world-class cities, New York and Buffalo. Charles's most well-known photographs are of Niagara Falls. Edward in New York photographed Cleopatra's Needle when it arrived in the city and was

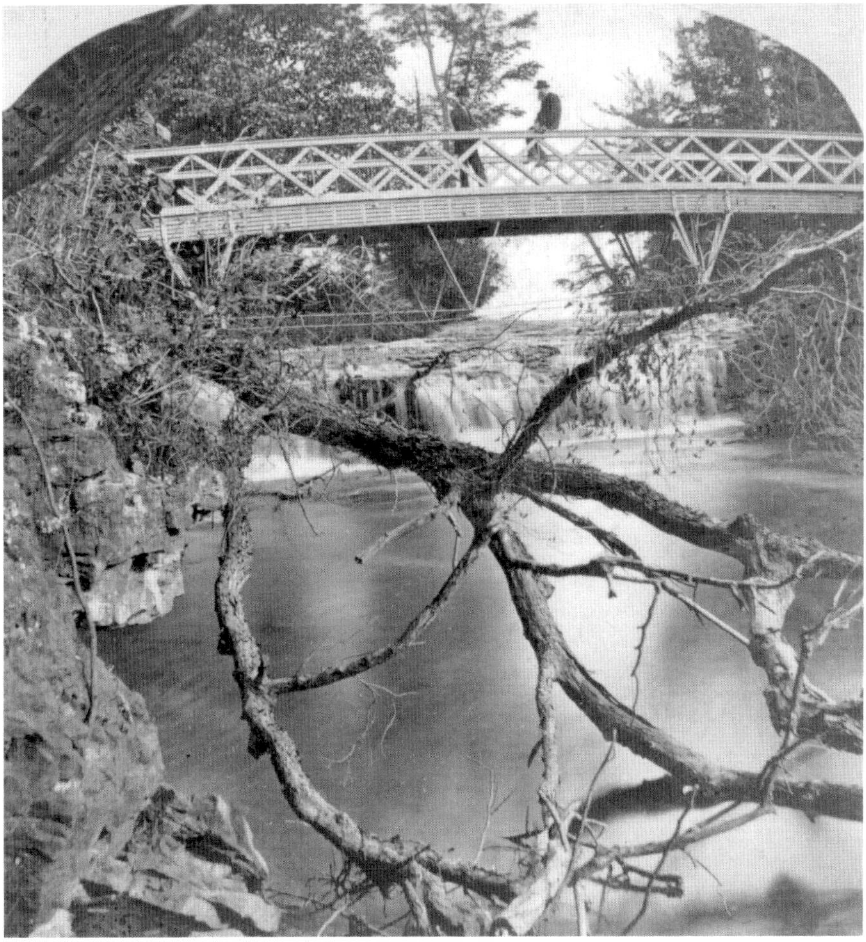

"Cave of the Winds." Niagara Falls Series, Charles Bierstadt, photographer. *Library of Congress Prints & Photographs Division.*

placed in Central Park. Later, Charles published books of his work. Albert, Eliza and Charles are all buried in New Bedford's Rural Cemetery. Their work survives.

Along with Boston, New Bedford was considered the home of a wild pack of abolitionists. Members of the Society of Friends abhorred slavery on principle. Frederick Douglass's first home out of slavery was in New Bedford. Liberty Hall was the moral compass, heart, soul and brain of New Bedford from 1842 until its demolition in 1893. It was a public space for abolitionists William Lloyd Garrison, Wendell Phillips and Douglass and also a theater playing *Uncle Tom's Cabin*.

More seriously, the Liberty Hall bell was rung in 1851 calling citizens to assemble. New Bedford was a proudly abolitionist city and had been since the late 1830s. L.B. Ellis, in his *History of New Bedford*, wrote:

> *The immediate cause for the alarm was that a strange vessel was reported to be in the bay, and on this account Rodney French ordered the bell to be rung. Some of our citizens will vividly remember the excitement that followed, for every one, especially the colored people, felt that real danger was at hand. No officers, however, made themselves known, and it is not certain whether they entered the city or not. One thing is sure, that the reported presence of the vessel was a mistake. The marshals would have assuredly met with a warm reception had they put in an appearance.*

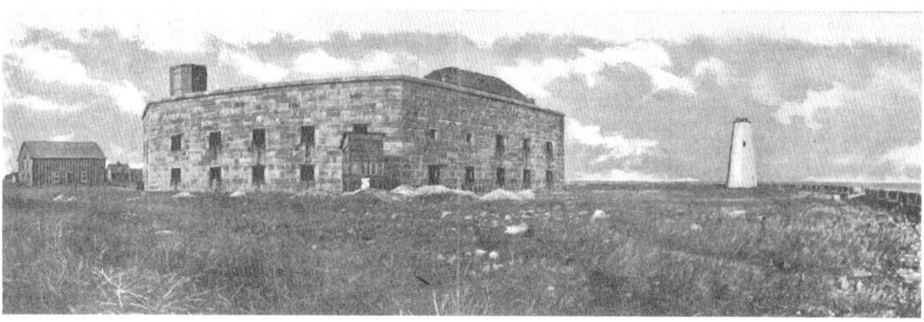

Fort Rodman with Clark's Point Lighthouse, 1906. Blanchard and Young panorama. *Library of Congress Prints & Photographs Division.*

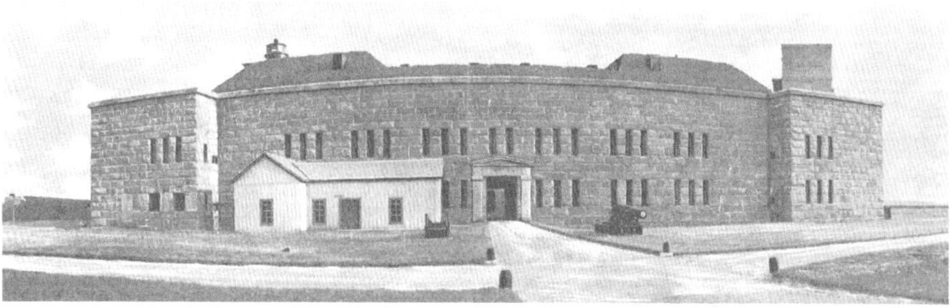

Fort Rodman entrance, 1906. Blanchard and Young panorama. *Library of Congress Prints & Photographs Division.*

On Christmas Day 1866, New Bedford welcomed home to a rebuilt Liberty Hall the man who had become a symbol of freedom. The *Mercury* reported on the twenty-eighth:

> *Frederick Douglass is at home in our city. It was to this place he came, when he escaped from slavery, and here he found a safe asylum. He became a servant but ceased to be a slave. He won respect by his upright conduct; but few dreamed then, that he would ever stand before such an audience, as flocked to hear him in Liberty Hall, on Tuesday evening and that he would hold his hearers as he did by the power of his reasoning and his eloquence. No public lecturer today, is better received than Mr. Douglass; and none is doing more to make healthy the tone of public sentiment.*

There are numerous accounts in New Bedford books about male abolitionists. Women, though, tended to be forgotten. Researching Sarah Arnold, I discovered the Weston sisters. On May 10, 1843, the *New Bedford Register* contained one of its most historically important advertisements: "School—The Misses Weston of Boston will commence a School for Young Ladies on Monday, May 21st in the building at the corner of Eighth Street and Mechanics Lane. Apply to John F. Emerson—Terms and Arrangements."

Actually, Deborah Weston had been teaching in New Bedford since the late 1830s. She came as a teacher but actually was in New Bedford to do abolition work. Her sister, Maria Weston Chapman, was one of the stars of the movement. She was a close friend of William Lloyd Garrison and on occasion edited the *Liberator* when he was away. Wendell Phillips was their cousin and close friend. Deborah, Anne and Caroline all taught in New Bedford at various times. Deborah was here the longest. In addition to their own Mechanics Lane school, they taught at Friends Academy and the "High School." Teaching was hard, unrelenting work. Deborah at one point had forty-four exhausting students. In early 1837, she wrote to Anne, "When Wendell Phillips left, I burst into tears, speaking metaphorically! Not from grief at his departure, but from desire to go with him."

Another letter to Anne displays her sense of humor:

> *Monday night we all received an invite to William Rodman's. I thought the anti-slavery prayer meeting would be held & concluded not to go, but on enquiry I found it was postponed.... So to the party I went. It was given in honour of a Miss Elliott from the District of Columbia, sister of him who said "that liar W.L. Garrison." She is a pretty little thing but a*

> *dreadful fool. In proof of which I will give evidence. I hear she said that last week she was in Boston & walking in Washington Street. She met nobody but ladies, ladies, but at last a gentleman came in sight & it was really refreshing to meet a pair of pantaloons.*
>
> *All New Bedford is ringing with this. The party was like all that are given here, only there was considerable dancing. The supper table was laid out beautifully. It is something new to set tables here. I talked with William Rodman some & what do you think upon? Why temperance.*

William R. Rodman, of course, had one of the grandest homes on County Street, served wine at evening parties and sheltered fugitives.

In addition to her teaching, Deborah went door to door across New Bedford gathering signatures for antislavery petitions and funds for abolitionist work. She argued with ministers who doubted the wisdom of abolition and boycotted the Lyceum when it refused to admit black members. She cheered lectures from Frederick Douglass, Garrison and Phillips. Her letters home give us a glimpse of a time when everything mattered and finding a friend for abolition was a victory. In another letter, she wrote, "I love Andrew Robeson." He spoke out often and bravely at antislavery meetings and gave funds without stinting. She made a life long friendship with Joseph Ricketson, who wrote to her throughout the Civil War.

In the turbulent years before the Civil War, the Arnolds continued to support abolition. Much of this work took place in silence, and it needs to be noted that New Bedford's primary newspaper, the *Mercury*, was not an abolitionist paper until the war broke out. At the time of John Brown's execution, the paper remained silent, while the *New York Times* reported that church bells had tolled throughout New Bedford. Most information regarding activities in the city needs to be traced through copies of the *Liberator*. Its report on August 14, 1851, specifically mentions the Arnolds as contributors.

In 1859, while John Brown's raid on Harper's Ferry was being planned and financed from Boston, Sarah Arnold was asked by her friend Maria Weston Chapman (Deborah's sister) to shelter Harriet Tubman. Both Tubman and Frederick Douglass knew of the planned raid, and John Brown expected both to participate. As Tubman's biographer, Jean M. Hunter, explained:

> *During her time in Boston Tubman also met Maria Weston Chapman, who was one of the original founders of the Boston Female Anti-Slavery Society, and a strong supporter of William Lloyd Garrison's philosophy and work.*

> *Chapman gave Tubman a letter of introduction to an antislavery friend in the seaport city of New Bedford, Massachusetts ("where many of her protégés are hiding), suggesting that she might be "the suitable person to undertake to bring off the children of Charles, about whom I had so fruitless a correspondence with the Philadelphia Vigilance Committee & other."*

The antislavery friend was Sarah Rotch Arnold.

> *When I wrote to you yesterday I had not learned what I have just heard—that Harriet Tubman our black heroine, is about to start for New Bedford where many of her protégés are in hiding.*
>
> *I venture to furnish her with a letter to you, in the hope that you may find a suitable person to undertake to bring off the children of Charles, about whom I had such a fruitless correspondence with the Philadelphia Vigilance Committee & others.*
>
> *There may be many persons of general humanity in New Bedford who would rejoice to aid this noble woman in her present purpose of securing a home for the parents she has rescued; and if your kind commendation of her to such, should prove the means of success to her, it will also be a real obligation to me, who would rejoice to aid this noble woman in her present purpose.*

The statement regarding Harriet being in New Bedford at the time of the raid is repeated in *Conductor on the Underground Railroad*, written by Ann Petry in 1955:

> *Harriet never heard from John Brown again, never saw him again. She was unaware of the fact that Brown and his assistants kept referring to her in the letters that they sent to the Boston Abolitionists who were helping to*

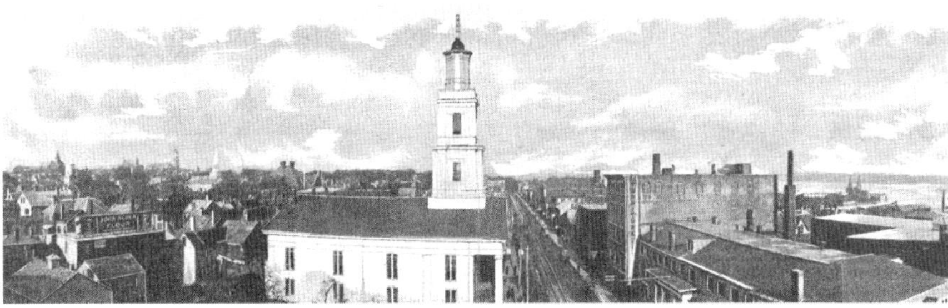

New Bedford, looking east, 1906. Blanchard and Young panorama. *Library of Congress Prints & Photographs Division.*

> *finance his project. "Harriet Tubman is probably in New Bedford, sick. She has staid in N.E.* [New England] *a long time. And been a kind of missionary"…"I have sent a note to Harriet requesting her to come to Boston"…"When Harriet comes…"*

Harriet Tubman did not go to Harper's Ferry. There is every reason to believe that Sarah Arnold did grant her friend's request.

Chapter 10

The Howlands

The Good and the Awful

New Bedford has had good Howlands, great Howlands and awful Howlands. One was the first mayor of the city. One became the richest woman in the world. At one point, the family owned the *Charles W. Morgan*. There are still Howlands in and around the city.

The Howlands began in whaling. When we talk about whale ships, no matter how beautiful, we are essentially discussing killing machines—the perfect factories designed to kill and process mammals. There was never any question that New Bedford's whaling merchants understood what they were doing. They were piling up great wealth while ironically bringing light to the world. As Peter Nichols wrote in *Final Voyage*, "Every man, woman and child in New Bedford knew that the whale was a divinely created oil reserve, placed floating in the sea by God so that his children might secure it for themselves."

Friends Here and Hereaway, written by Mary Jane Taber for an Old Dartmouth Historical sketch, captures the fierce attitude of one George Howland: "When told that if he and his contemporaries rushed around the globe killing whales at such a rate, the whales would be exterminated, and the world would sit in darkness, he replied very composedly: 'Let us make hay while the sun shines. Before the last whale is harpooned there will be a substance discovered which for light giving will far surpass whale oil lamps and spermaceti candles.'"

The conflict between truth to the inner light, blood and wealth were nearly irreconcilable. Rachel and Matthew Howland, in many ways, reconciled that conflict. Rachel Collins Smith was indisputably a great beauty. Peter Nichols called her a "trophy bride." She was much more than that. In 1842, she married Matthew Howland, the son of George and Susan Howland. Matthew's older half brother, George Howland Jr., tended to eat up the oxygen in any room and became the great public Howland of the time.

He seems to have gotten that confidence from his father. Mary Ellen Taber wrote, "George Howland, Sr., was by far the most original and picturesque member of the family. He perfectly idealized his daughter Elizabeth but for fear she might become vain, he constantly assured her that she was so 'humly' it was almost painful to look at her [and she believed him]." Let the fierce Quaker say what he would to his daughter, he was very susceptible to female loveliness. When his son, Matthew, brought the beautiful Rachel Collins Smith into the family, George beamed, "She was the sole human being who ever dared to cross words with him, and she always came off victorious."

The Howland family is vastly complicated without even including the singularly unpleasant Hetty Howland Robinson Green (and we will later). I will make no attempt to explain the brood other than discussing Matthew and, on the fringes, his brother, George Howland Jr. I do, however, think it's important to understand who Rachel Collins Smith was before she arrived in New Bedford.

Her family was a kind of royalty in the American Society of Friends. They were unfortunately poor for two generations. Rachel's father died young, and his father had also died too young. Rachel's daughter-in-law, Caroline T. Howland, explained in *Memories of My Childhood and Early Youth* how Rachel ended up marrying into New Bedford: "Rachel had been engaged to someone she loved desperately…Soon after their engagement, Mr. Jenkins visited Rachel's home and was taken seriously ill and died there very suddenly. I have been told that the shock of this tragedy for a short time unsettled Rachel's mind. Her father was not living at this time."

Heartbroken or not, Rachel was expected to prop up the family fortune. As Caroline Howland wrote, "Her mother was anxious for her to make a suitable marriage: and Matthew Howland of New Bedford, Mass was accepted as a promising suitor, and later they were married. And I, as Rachel's daughter-in-law, have always felt that her heart was not fully satisfied."

Thanks again to Samuel Rodman Jr. and his diary, we can trace Rachel from the moment she arrived in New Bedford:

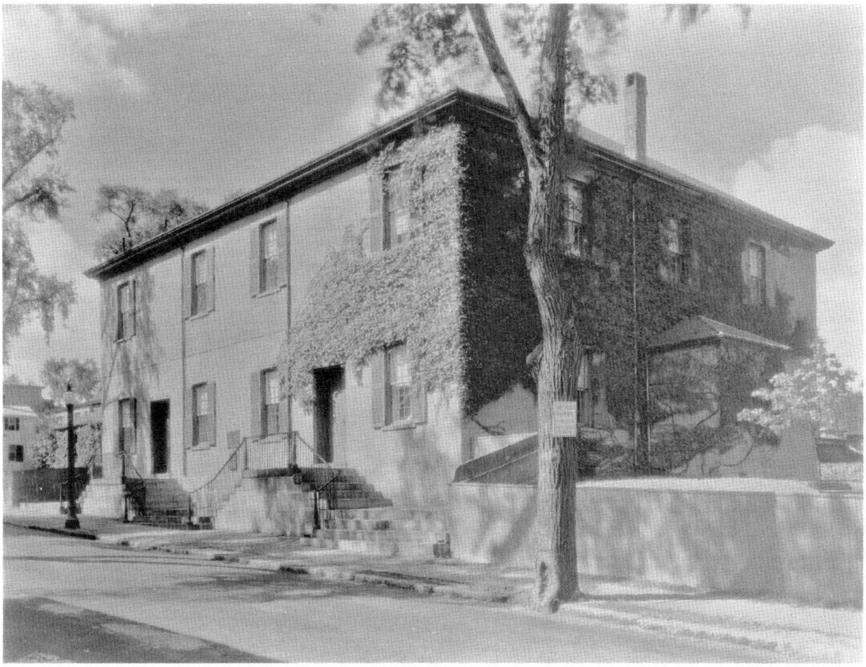

Rachel Howland's Friends Meeting House, Spring Street. *Library of Congress, Historic American Buildings Survey. Arthur C. Haskell, photographer.*

JANUARY 2, 1843
I might have mentioned in my note of yesterday that Matthew Howland's bride, Rachel Smith of Burlington, appeared in supplication in the morning meeting. I could hear indistinctly but what I did hear was of a sweet and interesting nature.

JANUARY 19, 1843
Returned from the counting house early to tea, we having a visit from Matthew and Rachel Howland... We had a pleasant visit. Rachel, to whom I was now first introduced, appears to be a lovely woman uniting a retiring modesty to her personal attractions and remarkable devotion to religious duty. Her style of dress is that of the English friends. Matthew may consider himself a very fortunate man in having been able to win the affections of so fine a woman, so intelligent, beautiful & good.

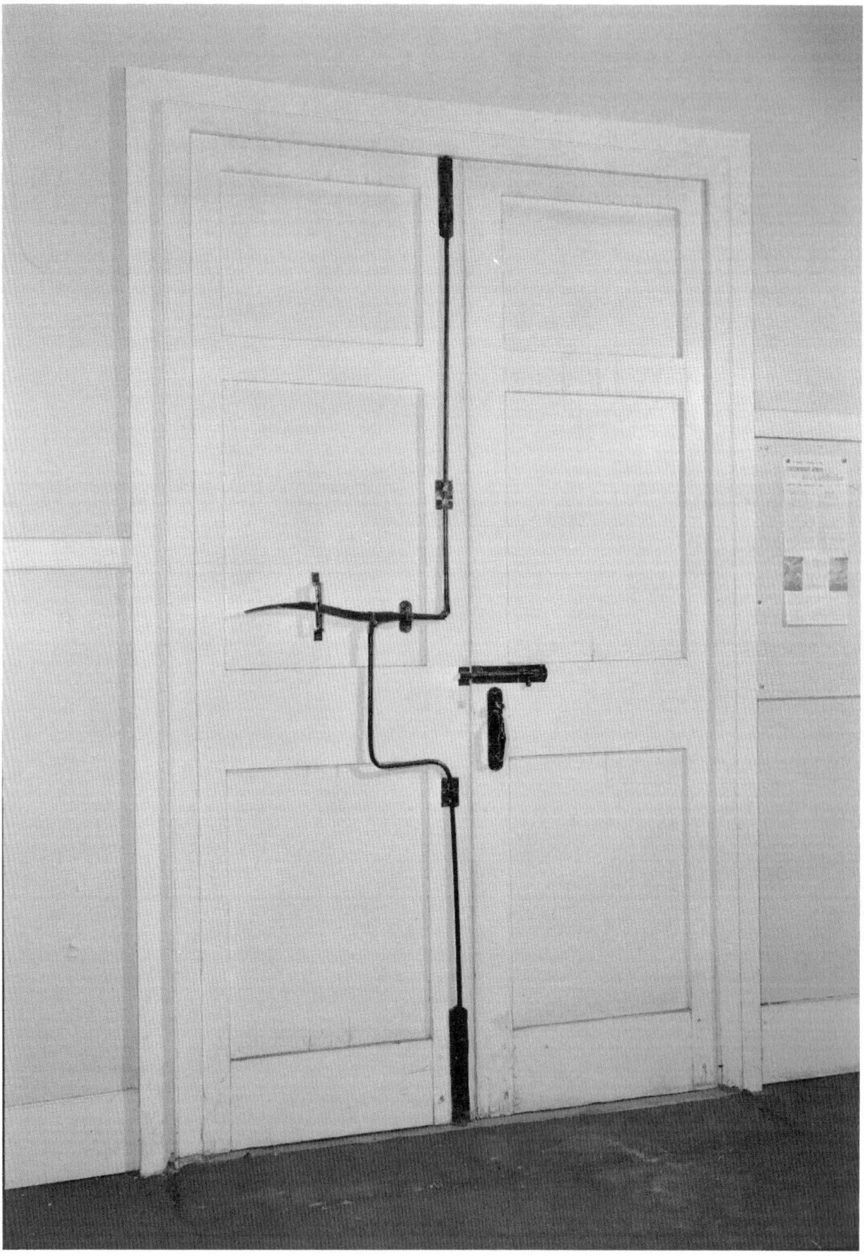

Friends Meeting House, south interior detail. *Library of Congress, Historic American Buildings Survey. Ned Goode, photographer.*

March 3, 1856
I should have mentioned last week that we have had a religious visit from Rachel Howland on 7th day meeting. She was accompanied by Sarah Anthony and William Penn Howland. She spoke interestingly and I hope profitably to us, all family being present. She has made a general visitation of families in this Preparation Meeting.

May 22, 1857
Attended meeting today was usual. Rachel Howland spoke at considerable length and very acceptably in exhortation in the forenoon. Daniel Ricketson was there, a very rare occurrence.

November 26, 1857
Rachel Howland laid before the assembly a concern which she has felt for years to hold a few meetings in Boston at Friends House there on several days and perhaps in one of two other points in that city…She was allowed and encouraged to go forward in the discharge of the apprehended duty.

August 16–30, 1858
On the 26th Rachel Howland returned her credentials for the missionary services which she engaged in some months since to several of the municipal and state reformatory institutions comprising several public religious meetings in Boston which services were performed to her own peace of mind.

Rachel Collins Smith was becoming a public figure with Matthew's full support and financial assistance. She was an early donor and trustee of Myrtilla Miner's school for free black children in Washington, D.C. She served with, among others, Harriet Beecher Stowe and her brother, Henry Ward Beecher. Myrtilla Miner was a woman of enormous principle and courage who dedicated her life to teaching. Even Frederick Douglass thought her plan for the school was far too dangerous. He was right to be concerned. George Washington Williams, in his second volume of *History of the Negro Race in America, 1619–1880*, wrote, "The house was set on fire in the spring of 1860 when Miss Miner was asleep in the second story alone in the night time but the smell of the smoke awakened her in time to save the building and herself from the flames which were extinguished."

Rachel Howland was a great friend of Harriet Beecher Stowe. Legend, of course, has it that Lincoln called Harriet "the little lady who started the war." Henry Ward Beecher, her brother, was called "the most famous man in America" by his biographer, Debby Applegate. He was an uncompromising abolitionist, speaker of brilliance and minister who held forth at Plymouth Church in Brooklyn. Beecher spoke at the New Bedford Lyceum, and the city never forgot. Harriet Beecher Stowe later summered at Westport Point.

In 1865, Mrs. Howland went to Washington. She was convinced that she had a calling, and she fulfilled it. The *Kennebec Journal*, on June 17, 1865, published a letter received from a Bostonian, Reverend Robert C. Waterston. He described Rachel's account of the journey:

> *Perhaps the charm of all was the presence of Rachel Howland, a leading member of the Society of Friends; with heavenly countenance and melodious voice she gave a deeply interesting account of a personal interview she had with the President—the good President, as she emphatically called him. It was at the White House, and they were by themselves and they united in prayer, both kneeling side by side. This account was given with such simple beauty and such deep spiritual feeling that all were melted to tears. The thought of the Quaker Lady with her delicate and celestial aspect, and the chosen head of a great nation, placed in his and responsible position by the voice of twenty millions of people, kneeling there in childlike faith before the Supreme Ruler of the Universe.*

Lincoln suffered from horrific depression, and there are hints that Matthew Howland did also. Rachel would have been perhaps all too familiar with comforting men in emotional pain. And what of Matthew? He had been twenty-eight when they married on September 8, 1842. He may have had epilepsy. Rachel was two years older, born in 1816.

Matthew was the private, responsible member of the Howland whaling firm. George was the vastly public man who could donate his salary as mayor to the public library. Matthew worked, managed and balanced books. He walked down to the counting house every morning from Hawthorne Street.

Everett S. Allen, in his classic book *Children of the Light*, wrote of Matthew, "The principal preoccupation for Matthew was the brothers' business, yet in noting this, one must avoid the simplistic error of assuming, as some do, that because a man spends his days with columns of figures, is shrewd to the penny and does things precisely the same each time—since that is his nature—nothing of other consequence, neither morning sky or bird song, nor the perennial plight of man invades his awareness."

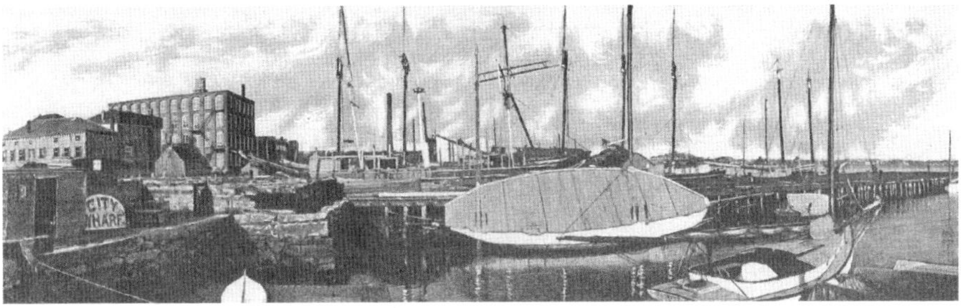

Dock scene, 1906. Blanchard and Young panorama. *Library of Congress Prints & Photographs Division.*

Matthew was much more than the Howland drudge. He gave back to his city. He remained a member of the Society of Friends when most of the others left. He stayed, and he believed in the light, although it was often hard to discover and often terrifyingly joyless. Allen wrote, "For some years Matthew had been a semi-invalid—Ricketson referred to the 'hard and unrelenting affliction against which he had to contend through life.'"

Depression is its own horror, but somehow Matthew forced himself on. He survived the Arctic whaling disaster of 1871 that took his newest, most lovely and elegant ship, the *Concordia*. The men got home, and whaling continued for a while longer.

Everett Allen also quoted one of Matthew's letters that could never have been written by a hard-bitten ship owner:

> *After tea we went down to the wharf and took Will's boat and went out on the river, sailing around the yachts, who began to send up fireworks about 8:30 p.m. till ten. There were about forty of them, and the river was all ablaze and looked as though it were on fire. It seemed like fairie land. The Yacht Club was brilliantly illuminated and the bridge and wharves were full of people and the city deserted. The night was perfect and the scene was brilliant, magnificent, granderous. I never witnessed such a sight before and never expect to again.*

This, too, was Matthew Howland.

Just after the Civil War, in 1866, Rachel Howland organized the Association for the Relief of Aged Women of New Bedford, perhaps her most enduring achievement. On May 7, 1869, the *New Bedford Mercury* reported on it:

> *A total of 59 women had been assisted...The largest sum given to any one person during the year is $52.70.... During the warm months a little money towards the rent enables many of our women to get along quite comfortably. And there are a few who do not call upon us for anything, at that time. To them summer comes as a kind friend, curing many ills and helping them to help themselves in many little ways. Of course the sick and the very aged need almost as much assistance in warm as in cold weather. As the winter approaches, the demands upon us increase rapidly, and so numerous were the calls during the month of December last, that it was found necessary to limit our contributions, even in the most urgent cases, to five dollars a month.*

What is most astonishing is that the Fund for Aged Women still exists in New Bedford, carrying out Rachel's plan.

Rachel never backed away from a proper fight, and it didn't matter a bit to her that George was mayor. New Bedford has never much liked strikes. This is a city that likes order. It likes workers who turn up on time. It doesn't like it when workers ask for more money. In 1867, workers at the Wamsutta Mill went on strike after Robert Bennett fired four operatives who protested what was in effect a cut in pay. The *Boston Journal* on February 18 reported:

> *WORKMAN'S STRIKE*
> *Saturday morning a large majority of the weavers, and spinners, about 900 in number left work. This caused an almost total suspension of operations, and at noon it was decided to stop the mills, entirely until the difficulties are adjusted. The strikers demand a guarantee of the ten hour system, and a return of the discharged men to their place. The full compliment of hands, employed at the mills is about 1,050.*

Mill owners were furious that the workers wanted a ten-hour day—a reduction in the eleven hours they already worked—and to top it all, they wanted the same pay for less work. *The Peacemaker* described a bit of what happened and Rachel's involvement:

> *An instance of her public spirit occurred in March of 1867 when she was instrumental in settling a strike at the Wamsutta mills. Some 1,000 employees demanded a 10 hour instead of an 11 hour day and went on a strike to enforce their demands. Neither side seemed disposed to give in. Mrs. Howland took the matter up and visited the directors and the*

> *operatives committee in an endeavor to effect a compromise. She succeeded in getting the consent of the directors to her proposal and the agent of the mills posted a notice that very day offering the operatives more liberal terms. At a meeting of the strikers it was stated by the chairman that no one else could have done what Mrs. Howland did and a vote of thanks to her was passed unanimously.*

The original fired workers were not taken back. George had threatened to call out the National Guard and give them live ammunition. Rachel and the Howland family earned the hatred of the mill owners. Much later, the hatred would haunt and ruin her son.

Rachel often was able to make a kind of peace more successfully. She cared passionately about public education and tried to bring often feuding teachers and administrators together. The *Massachusetts Teacher, a Journal of School and Home Education* reported on an 1874 meeting hosted by Rachel between teachers and a new school superintendent:

> *The gathering at the house of Matthew Howland of the Fifth Ward on Monday evening February was novel in its character but a more delightful one has not been found in the drawing rooms of wealthy fashion. Eighty four of the eighty nine teachers of the Public Schools Bedford were received and entertained by Mr. and Mrs. Howland at their beautiful home on Hawthorn street.*

It was a home they would soon be forced to leave:

> *The company with the exception of three or four of the school committee and a few of the neighbors was made up of the teachers, the family and the family circle. The extravagance and display of wealth and fashion were not there but in their place were found great satisfaction and exalted and rational enjoyment. Nowhere in our city could there be found drawing room and library better calculated to gratify and elevate the taste, no place of meeting more in harmony with the prominent idea that called the company together and pervaded the minds of those of whom it was composed.*

Sarah was determined to keep the evening calm. The way to peace can come with tea and talking:

> *With the exception of the half hour devoted to what may be called the business of the evening the time was spent in pleasant and elevated conversation in an examination of the pictures engravings illustrated books and the other attractive objects with which the rooms were filled and in the enjoyment of the creature comforts which had been most bountifully provided.*

Always ready to make her point in Weekly Meeting, the White House or her own home, Rachel pushed home the reason for the meeting:

> *The amiable and gifted hostess closed this simple but deeply interesting proceeding by a few words well chosen and beautifully spoken. She said it had been thought that as a majority of the company were females, there would be no impropriety in allowing one of their number to speak for them. It had seemed to her that there had been wanting a link to connect the people and the government with the teachers of the Public Schools and that this want been supplied by the arrangement which had given us a superintendent. She had felt great sympathy for those laborers of her own sex in the schools and could wish to encourage and to cheer them. She was glad to meet them, hoped they would be faithful in the discharge of duty and invoked upon them the blessing of the Great Teacher.*

Rachel's own children were not always joys to their parents. Their son Richard, in Peter Nichols's *Final Voyage*, wrote:

> *From my early childhood I always rebelled against some portions of the life on Hawthorn Street…Those grim Sundays and Quarterly Meets and travelling Friends, the whole horrible system of Quakerism, in its attempt to crush out all natural feeling…I don't want to be hard on Father and Mother…They thought they were acting for the best…But the theory was wrong and would have crushed me, if I had not struck out for myself.*

Richard, living and attempting to work in California, may not have understood the financial nightmare his parents were facing. Matthew and George had continued whaling after the first Arctic disaster, and whaling eventually ruined the firm and the families. Matthew became horribly ill. The decision was made to sell their home on Hawthorn Street. It had been expressly built for them in 1840.

In 1882, Rachel wrote to her son Morrie, then in New York:

> *I got the doctor here and he staid three or four hours trying to allay the pain, which he finally accomplished by several doses of morphine... William Crapo is still trying to get this place, but says he will not give over $30,000, while Father asks $40,000. What shall we do? I think Father is very poorly indeed and very low spirited. What shall we do with him or for him? Thee must come and see him...*
>
> *Crapo has not treated us handsomely...He seems to think he could just gobble us up and turn us out of house and home at his pleasure. And so the big fish eat up the little ones...Father has gone down to Meeting and I am alone.*

Matthew died soon after. When Rachel died in 1902, her cousin wrote her obituary for *The Peacemaker*: "I have known and loved her since I was seven or eight years old. She was the most beautiful woman I ever knew and passed through many afflictions which I trust she has left behind forever."

Rachel and Matthew have taken us slightly beyond the boxed compass of this book and beyond the Civil War. Rachel lived on, witnessing the brilliant and ultimately tragic career of her son William D. Howland. The fall of the Howland Mill in April 1897 damaged and changed New Bedford forever. Aggressive outside interests bought the fallen mills and from then on would determine the future of the city. Among those interests was the ultimate Howland: Hetty Howland Robinson Green. As a child, Hetty haunted the New Bedford docks, and as an

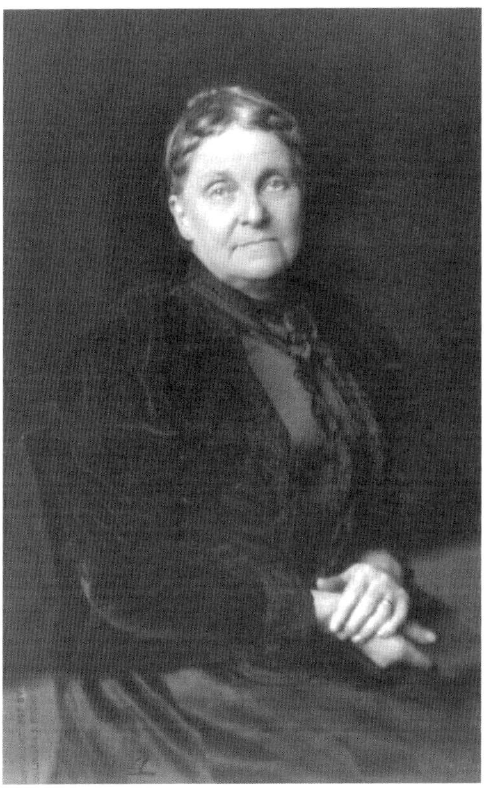

What Hetty Howland Robinson Green became. *Library of Congress Prints & Photographs.*

adult, she became the city's most famous, controversial and hated woman. She was her own force of nature, like a hurricane or blizzard.

The person she seems to have loved most was her father, the handsome, ruthless Black Hawk Robinson. Originally from Rhode Island, he married into the Isaac Howland & Company whaling firm. Abby Slocum Howland and her sister, Sylvia Ann, were heirs to the family fortune. Both were strict members of the Society of Friends. The pair were so straight-laced they would have felt Rachel Howland a loose woman because she loved music. In fact, the single memory that Abby left was a sour one. Hetty's grandfather, known in his city as "Uncle Gid," had allowed a piano into the house. Hetty loved it and invited a small friend, Mary, to try it out. According to Boyden Sparks and Samuel Taylor Moore in *The Witch of Wall Street—Hetty Green*, Abby Howland Robinson came home from Meeting and caught the two playing the infamous piano and singing:

The monkey married the baboon's sister
Smacked his lips and then he kissed her
Kissed her so hard he raised a blister.

Mary never forgot what Hetty's mother said. She remembered and told her son, William J. Swift, who remembered and told Sparks and Moore in the 1930s: "Mary, thee can take thy music, thy parasol, and thy furbelows and be gone, and when we next want music we will send for thee."

Edward Mott Robinson had great luck all his life. Two weeks after marrying Abby, her grandfather Isaac died. This left Abby and her sister Sylvia's father, Gideon, in charge of the firm. Robinson was his right-hand man. Most unusually, Sylvia was left in control of her share of the firm.

Henrietta Howland Robinson was born on November 21, 1835, a year after William Rotch Jr. built his County Street home. There was a baby brother who soon died. Abby was an invalid and, as we've seen, not a joy in the household at the best of times. Little Hetty took to following her father and grandfather around the waterfront docks, slipping onto Howland whale ships, their counting room and her uncle's whale oil factory. From all accounts, she acquired an astonishing vocabulary of shocking words. She certainly used them all later on Wall Street.

At ten she was sent off to a boarding school—a Quaker one and she hated it. In New Bedford she was a Howland princess. Here it was different. For one thing the food was awful:

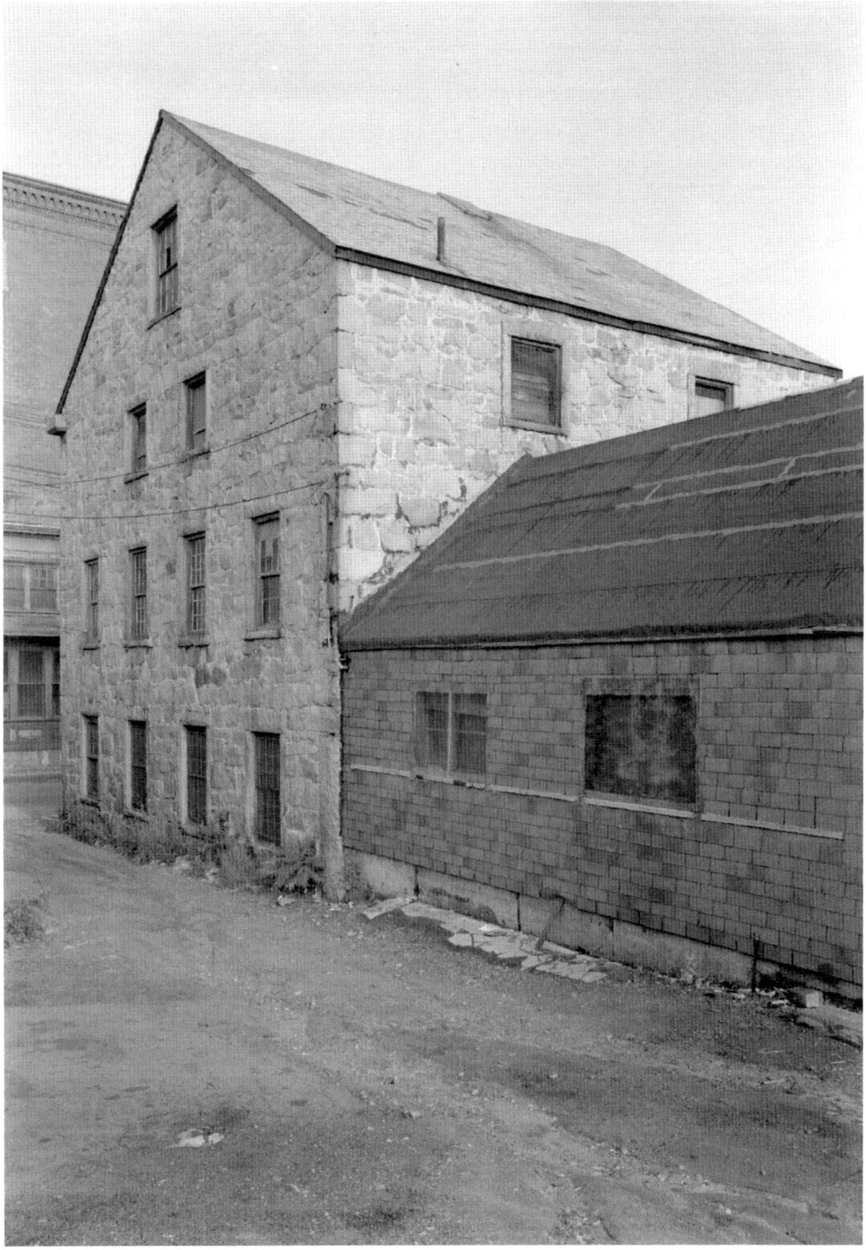

Hetty Howland outrageously roamed Rose Alley as a girl. *Library of Congress, Historic American Buildings Survey. Ned Goode, photographer.*

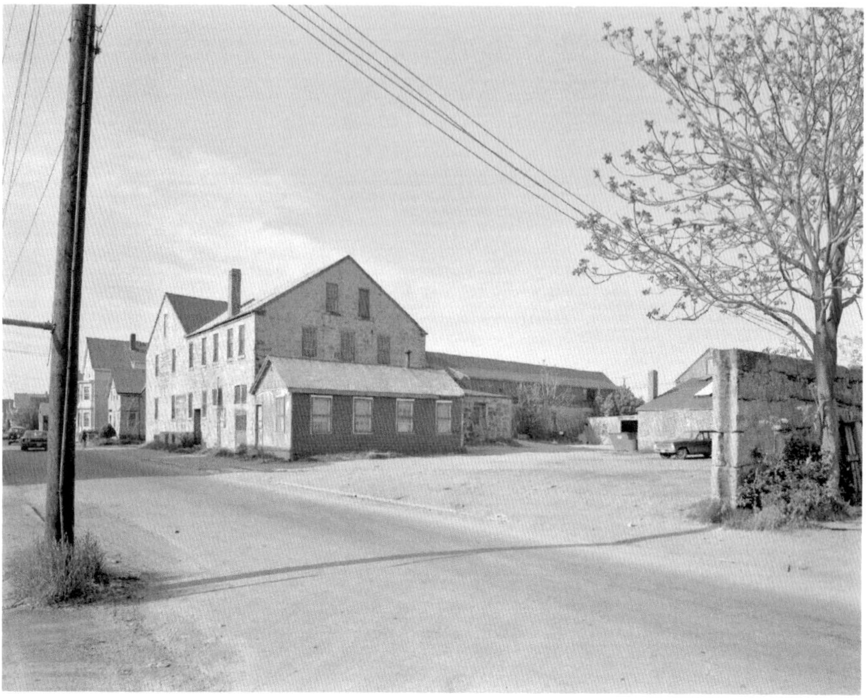

Another of Hetty's haunts—where the oil turned to money. George Delano Oil Works. *Library of Congress, Historic American Buildings Survey.*

> *Hetty said later, "Skinned milk when pitchers of cream were set on our table at home. I sent my plate away untasted. It was put aside and placed before me at supper, and my teacher informed me that I was expected to eat it. I was pretty hungry and managed to eat half. The next morning when the half-eaten meal made its third appearance, I made a desperate effort and finished the job. It taught me a good lesson."*

She did get to go home when Gideon Howland died. Hetty wasn't mentioned in the will; everything went to Abby and Sylvia Ann. Hetty was not pleased.

Back to school she went. Years later she told Dorothy Dix, one of America's great early journalists, about it. "I was forced into business, I was the only child of two rich families and I was taught from the time I was six years old that I would have to look after my property."

Hetty became brilliant at looking after money. At eleven she opened her own account at the old New Bedford Institution for Savings. She kept

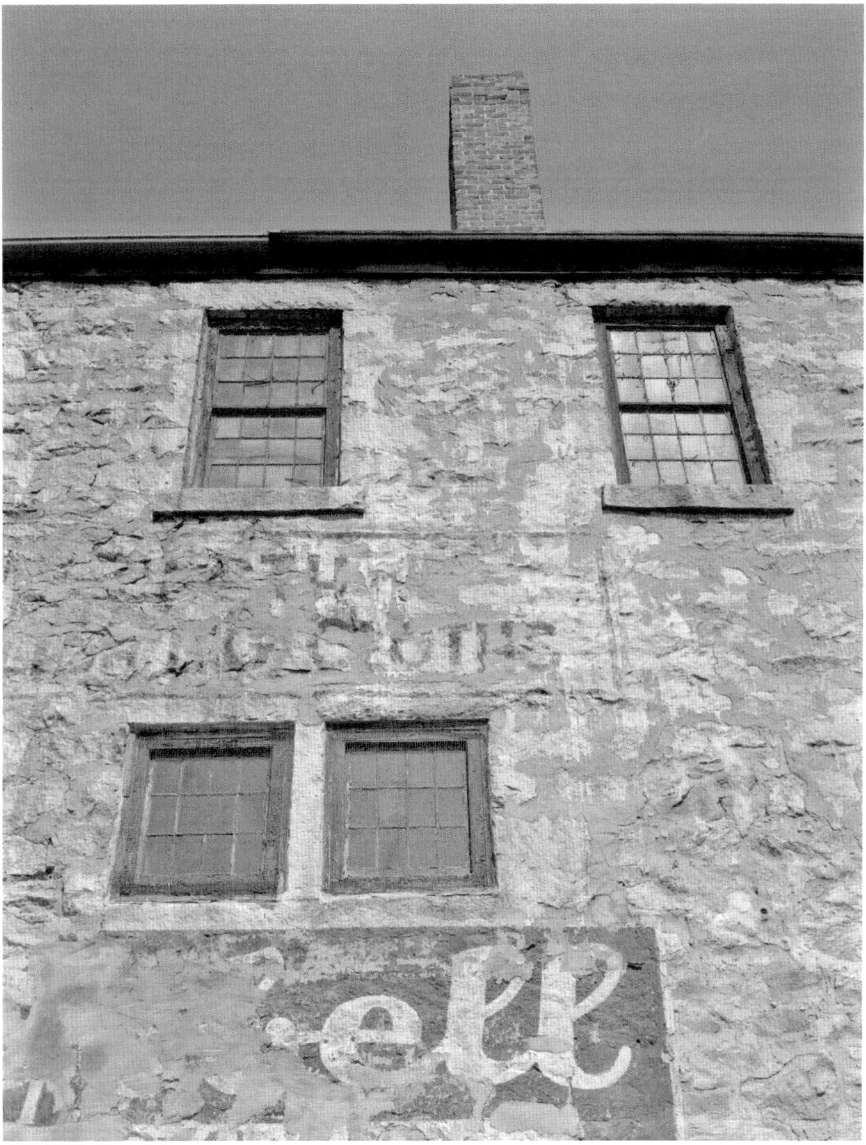

Delano Oil Works, west wall. *Library of Congress, Historic American Buildings Survey.*

right on following her father into the counting house and to lunch of hard crackers and cheese conveniently at the Central Union Store. Black Hawk owned a share in it. Years later Andrew Hathaway told Sparks and Moore about young Hetty: "What Andrew Hathaway remembered best was the

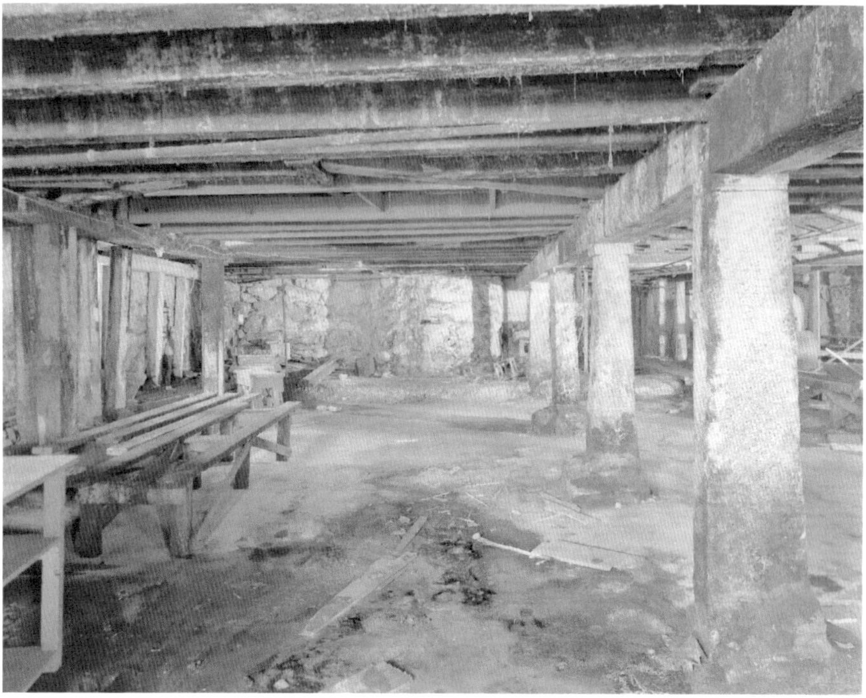

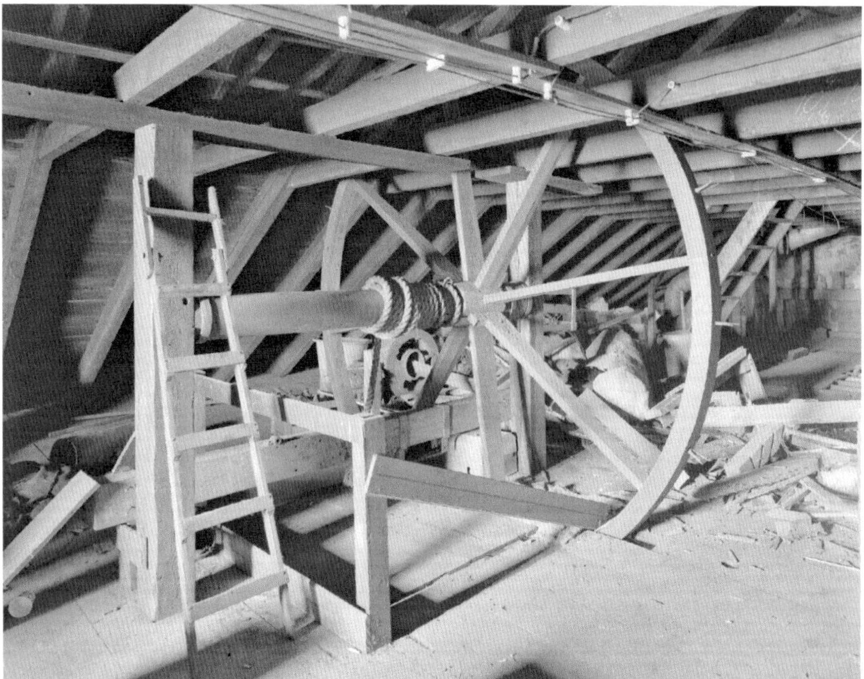

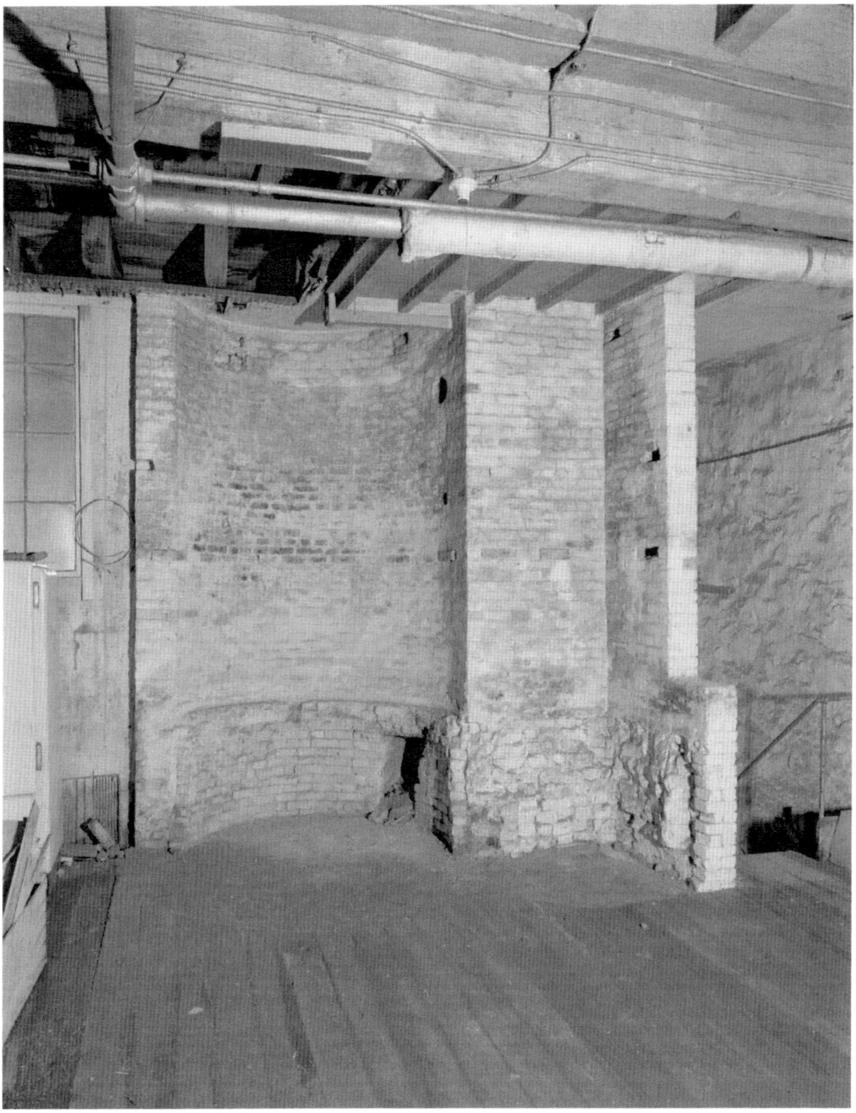

Delano Oil Works, bleaching tanks and skylights. *Library of Congress, Historic American Buildings Survey.*

Opposite, top: Delano Oil Works, interior basement. *Library of Congress, Historic American Buildings Survey.*

Opposite, bottom: Delano Oil Works, vat area. *Library of Congress, Historic American Buildings Survey.*

harsh parrot laugh of this girl…If a poor girl had acted as free and easy as Hetty Robinson, she would have been looked down on."

Instead, New Bedford gossips just whispered about her. Hetty Robinson wandered the city as she pleased dressed in ragged clothes. She made her own shoes. They thought she was more boy than girl. Her aunt Sylvia Ann was scandalized and insisted she be sent off to boarding school. Hetty went off to a proper Boston finishing school, made it through three years of a sort of polishing and then came home. Hetty did have a coming out party. She did dress up and seems to have cleaned up well as a Boston young lady. Hetty later talked about blowing out the spermaceti candles and selling the stubs the next day.

Both Abby and Sylvia were afraid of Black Hawk Robinson. Abby left the house and moved in with Sylvia Ann. Abby died in 1860. Soon Black Hawk decided that the days of whaling were numbered, pulled his money out and placed it into Chicago and New York investments. He was a natural financial genius.

Hetty followed her father to New York. She seems to have had no problem lacing into an evening gown and dancing at a ball with the Prince of Wales. Using her own charms, she managed to snare two dances with him. Hetty told him she was the "Princess of Whales." Victoria's son, the future Edward VIII, got the joke.

In between the balls, learning New York finance and how the stock market worked, Hetty was terrified of one possible event: Sylvia Ann Howland could die at any moment. Hetty knew very well that her aunt believed in public giving. Hetty was worried about where Sylvia Ann would leave the fortune that Hetty was positive belonged to her.

During the New York years, Hetty made flying visits to New Bedford and the Howland summer home at Round Hill in Dartmouth. During these

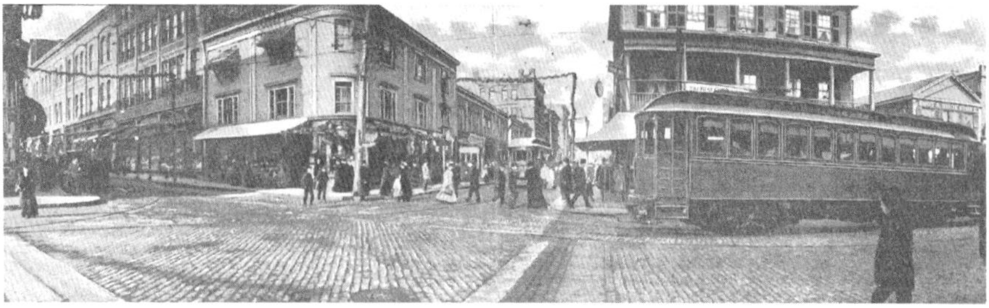

Hetty Howland never resembled any of these well-turned-out ladies. Blanchard and Young panorama. *Library of Congress Prints & Photographs.*

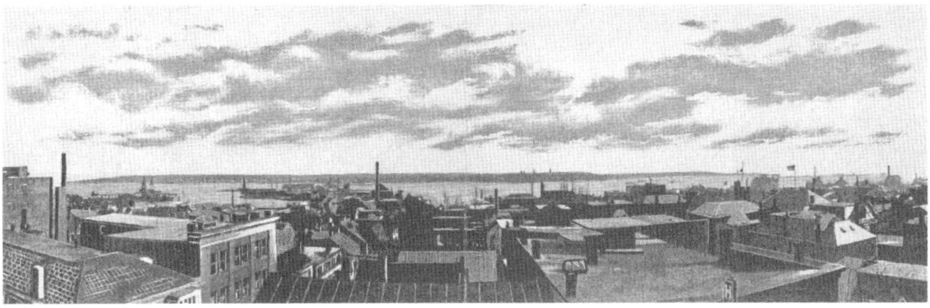

Looking east, 1906. Blanchard and Young panorama. *Library of Congress Prints & Photographs.*

visits, she screamed and bullied Sylvia Ann about the will. Servants, doctors and lawyers saw and remembered those visits. There was nothing pretty about those will sessions. Hetty latter claimed that she and Sylvia had made wills making each other their heirs.

In 1865, both her father and aunt died. Hetty received $5 million from her father. She invested the money in government bonds. Sylvia's will was a problem, however. One was produced that gave large sums to public charities and even the city government. The estate was $2 million. Hetty would receive the largest share after the gifts were made.

The *New York Times* reported on July 16, 1865:

> *SYLVIA ANN HOWLAND who died a short time since in New-Bedford, Mass., left an estate valued at two and a half millions. One million is bequeathed to public and private charities. The Mercury says: "The sum of $20,0000 is given to the Orphan's Home, and the further sum of $15,000, on the decease of three persons who are to receive the income during their lives.*
>
> *To the City of New-Bedford is given the sum of $100,000, to be expended under the direction of the City Government towards the introduction of pure water into the city and the encouragement of manufactures requiring steam power.*
>
> *To the City of New-Bedford is given a further sum of $100,000, to be invested by the City Government, and the income appropriated to the encouragement of liberal education here, and the enlargement of the free public library.*
>
> *To the trustees is given $50,000, to be invested by them, the income to be carefully divided among such aged and infirm females of this city as may need relief. The trustees under the will are George Howland, Jr. Dr.*

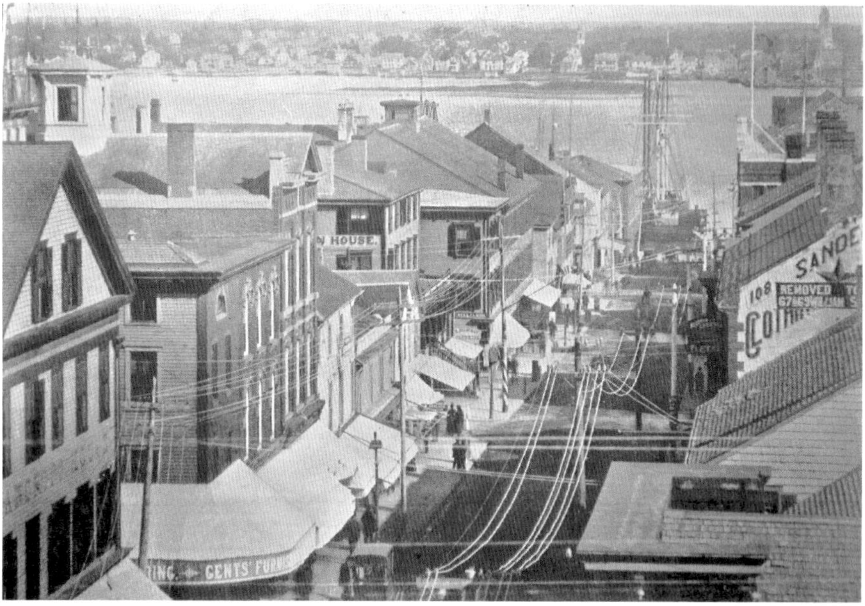

The city turning from whaling. Blanchard and Young panorama. *Library of Congress Prints & Photographs.*

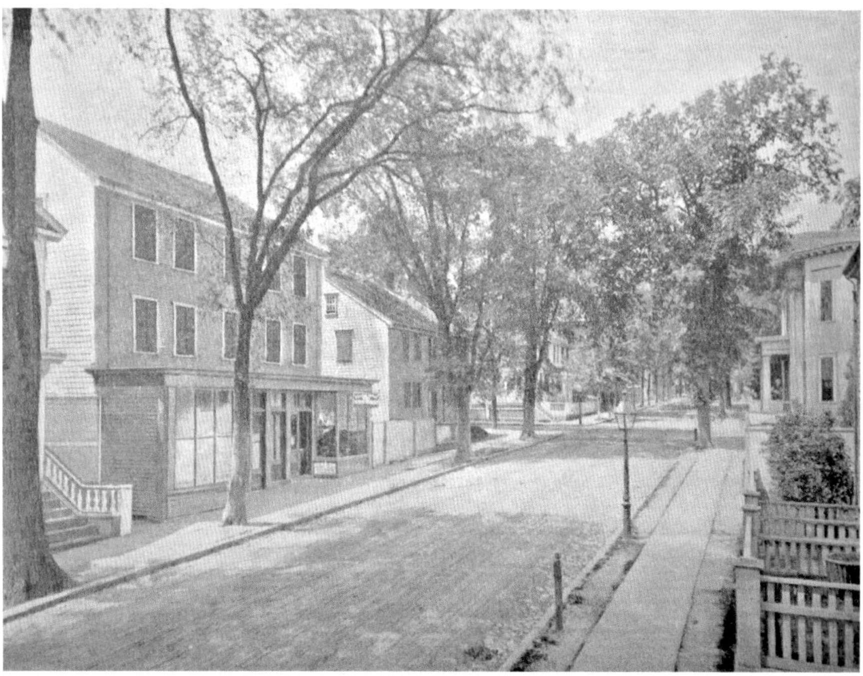

Union Street, 1880s. *Collection of author. Courtesy of Arthur P. Motta.*

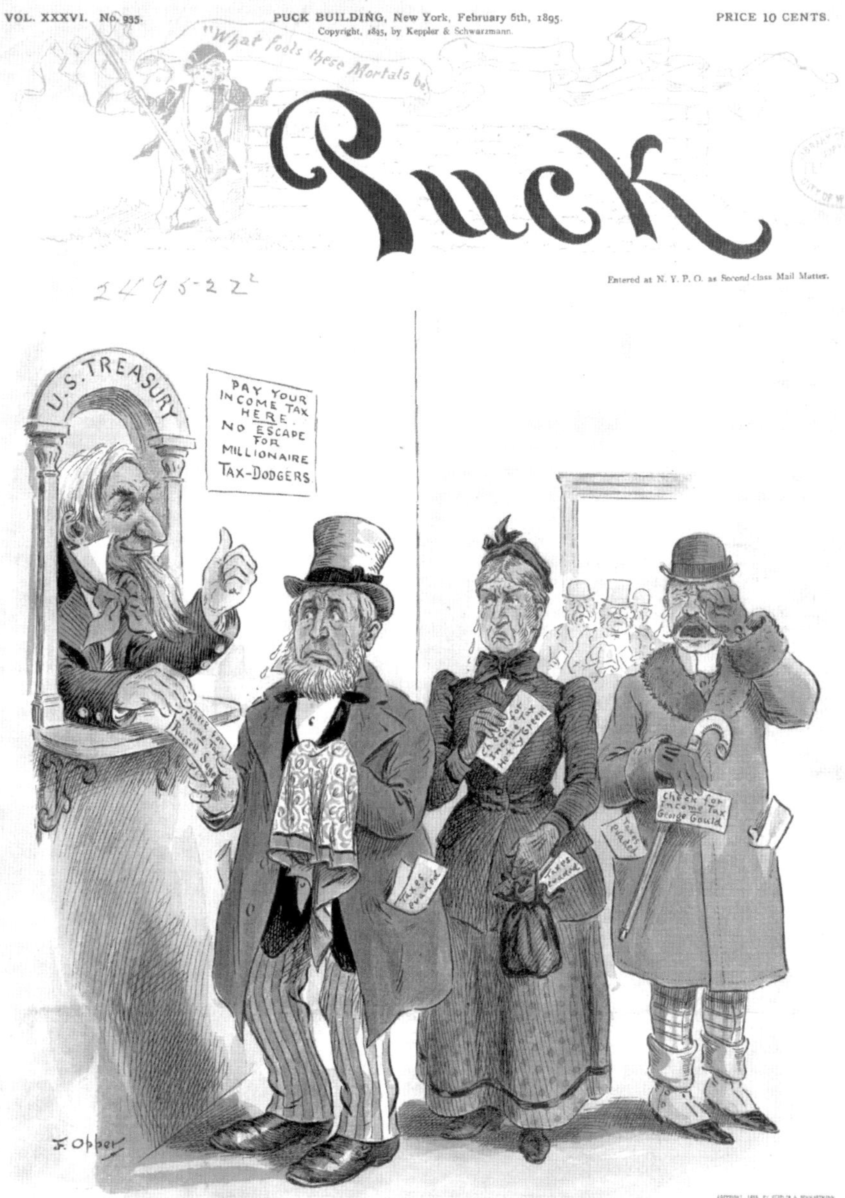

Hetty Howland Robinson Green as the "Witch of Wall Street," 1895. *Library of Congress Prints & Photographs.*

> *William A. Gordon and Edward D. Mandell, to each of which is given the sum of $50,000, and to Dr. Gordon, as a mark of the testatrix's personal esteem for his worth, a further sum of $50,000, Thomas Mandell is the sole executor of the will."*

Hetty, of course, produced another will that left all the money to her. There was a clause that made any other will invalid. Everyone and anyone who had been left money announced that the clause was a forgery and took to the courts. The trial became a classic and a circus. There were hundreds of witnesses—handwriting experts, lawyers, doctors, servants and more. Most announced out and out that Hetty had forged the will clause. For once in her life, Hetty Howland Robinson (soon to be Green) was frightened. To avoid jail, she fled to England and stayed there until the riot died down. Before leaving on July 11, 1867, she married Edward H. Green.

After years of lawyers and lawyers' fees, the City of New Bedford, the orphan's home and anyone who could trace their blood to Sylvia Ann received their money. A genealogist had to be hired to trace all of the heirs. Hetty stayed in London, and her two children, Edward and Sylvia Ann, were born there. When she returned in 1874, she was ready to become the "Witch of Wall Street."

Chapter 11

What Remains

New Bedford survived Hetty Green's childhood and the Civil War. Joseph Grinnell's Wamsutta Mills and the massive ones that followed, built like prison blocks, mushroomed. The mills made New Bedford for the second time the richest city per person in the world. Immigrants from Canada, England and Portugal flooded in to work those mills.

Mill owners became the new princes of the city, and they built their own palaces. They knew that they owned their workers, who lived in three-decker tenements. Even their children worked the mills and died of odd diseases like measles and typhoid fever. Child labor became a nightmare that brought Lewis Hine in 1914 to photograph. I have a photo of

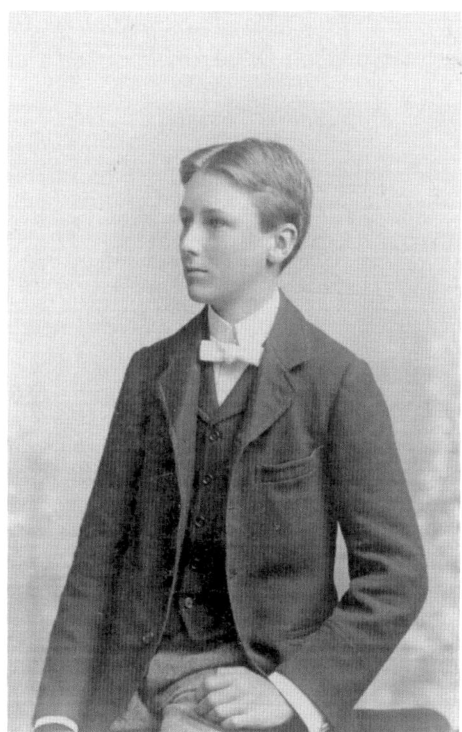

Young Franklin Delano Roosevelt in New Bedford. *Courtesy of Franklin D. Roosevelt Presidential Library.*

my uncle Louis Martin, a young mill rat who died at twelve of typhus. I found it sealed in a box after my mother's death.

George Delano's oil works became a boarded-up dinosaur, and whaling ended with the wreck of the *Wanderer* in 1924 in a storm just out of New Bedford harbor.

Artist and writer Clifford Ashley wrote that soon "there was not a single Yankee afloat on all the seven seas."

If anyone knew whaling, it was Clifford W. Ashley. His book, *The Yankee Whaler*, teaches in great style the history and mechanics of whaling. Ashley also was a New Bedford boy who saw the end of whaling:

> *The unpoliced ships and grass-grown wharves made a marvelous playground. We learned to swim from the bob-stays of the old hulks. We contrived to paddle and row on rafts fashioned of hatch covers, and used in boarding parties over side. We swarmed over the rigging and slid down the backstays, spun the wheels and on rainy days gathered in the cabins and played games and pretended one thing or another; and always it was something wonderful that smacked of the sea.*

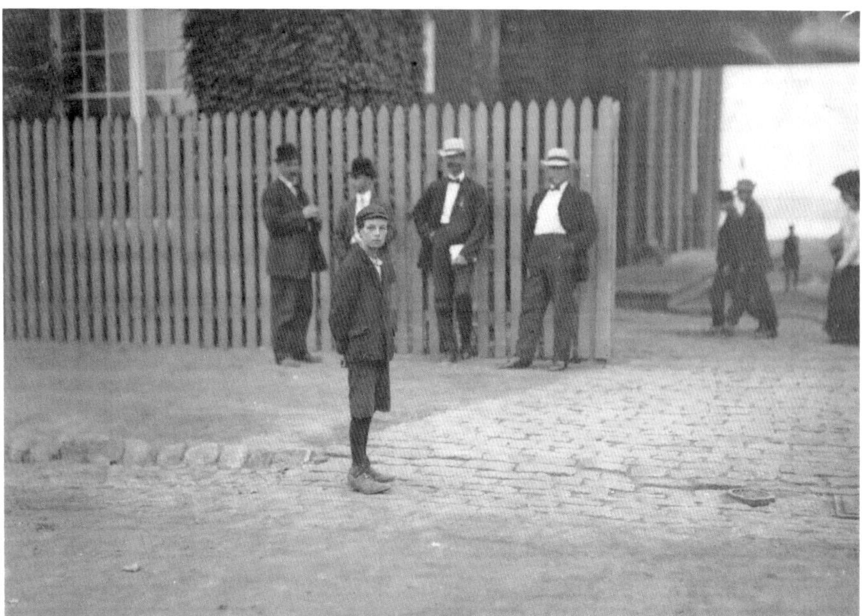

A New Bedford mill rat, 1911. *Library of Congress. Lewis Wickes Hine, photographer.*

In 1929, Franklin Delano Roosevelt was governor of New York. His mother, Sarah, had been a Fairhaven girl. In the fall of 1897, he visited his grandfather, Warren Delano II, in Fairhaven. He also went over to New Bedford and had photographs taken at the O'Neil Photographic Art Studio at 88 Purchase Street. FDR wrote an introduction for Clifford W. Ashley's *Whaleship of New Bedford.* It seems appropriate to end with his memories:

> *Forty years ago, a little boy sat on the old string-piece of grandfather's stone wharf at Fairhaven. Close by lay a whaleship, out in the stream another lay at anchor, and over on the New Bedford side shore…a dozen tall spars overtopped the granite warehouses. Even then, he felt that these great ships were but the survivors of a mightier age.*

The boy was Franklin Delano Roosevelt. He was right about New Bedford's mightier age.

Bibliography

Allen, Everett S. *Children of the Light: The Rise and Fall of New Bedford Whaling and the Death of the Arctic Fleet.* Boston: Little Brown and Company, 1971.

Anderson, Nancy K., and Linda S. Ferber. *Albert Bierstadt: Art & Enterprise.* New York: Hudson Press, in association with the Brooklyn Museum, 1990.

Anthony, Joseph. *Life in New Bedford One Hundred Years Ago.* Diary. New Bedford, MA: George H. Reynolds, Publisher, 1922.

Ashley, Clifford W. *The Yankee Whaler.* N.p.: Dover Publications Inc., 1966.

Atlas of Bristol County, Massachusetts. New York: F.W. Beers Company, 1871.

Atlas of the City of New Bedford, Massachusetts. Boston: Walker Lithograph & Publishing Company, 1911.

Audubon, John James. *Journal of John James Audubon Made While Obtaining Subscriptions to His "Birds of America," 1840–1843.* Cambridge, MA: Business Historical Society, 1929.

Blasdale, M.J. *Artists of New Bedford: A Biographical Dictionary.* New Bedford, MA: New Bedford Old Dartmouth Historical Society, 1990.

Bristol County Registry of Deeds, New Bedford, Massachusetts.

Bullard, Catherine. "Letter from 'Cousin Sarah,'" 1947. Crapo Family Papers. Privately owned.

Bullard, Catherine Crapo. Brief untitled history of 19 Irving Street. Three pages, typescript, with 1968 postscripts.

Bullard, John Morgan. *The Greens as I Knew Them.* New Bedford, MA: Reynolds De Walt, 1964.

———. *The Rotches.* Milford, NH: Cabinet Press, 1947.

Clayton, Barbara, and Kathleen Whitley. *Guide to New Bedford*. Globe Pequot Press, 1979.

Crapo, Henry Howland. *Certain Come Overers*. Vols. 1 and 2. New Bedford, MA: E. Anthony & Sons, 1912.

———. *The Story of Henry Howland Crapo, 1804–1869*. Boston: Thomas Todd Company, Printers, 1933.

———. *The Story of William Wallace Crapo 1830–1920*. Boston: Thomas Todd Company, Printers, 1942.

Davis, Alexander Jackson. *Day Book*. Vol. 1. A.J. Davis Papers. Manuscripts and Archives Division, New York Public Library.

———. *Rural Residence, Etc. Consisting of Designs, Original and Selected, for Cottages, Farm-houses, Villas, and Village Churches with Brief Explanations, Estimates, and a Specification of Materials, Construction, etc.* Watkins Glen, NY: Century House, 1967. Originally printed in 1842.

Delano, Sarah, and Julia Fifield. *Brave Houses and Flowery Gardens of New Bedford*. New Bedford, MA: published by the Garden Club of Buzzards Bay, printed by Reynolds DeWalt, 1976.

Dias, Earl J. "Daniel Ricketon and Henry Thoreau." *New England Quarterly* 26, no. 3 (1953).

Directory of American Biography. Vol. 3. New York: Scribners, 1959.

Donoghue, John. *Alexander Jackson Davis—Romantic Architect*. New York: Arno Press, 1982.

Downing, Andrew Jackson. *The Architecture of Country Houses*. New York, 1850.

Ellis, Leonard Bolles. *History of New Bedford and Its Vicinity, 1602–1892*. Syracuse, NY: D. Mason & Co., 1892.

Emery, William M. *Ancestry of the Grinnell Family*. N.p.: privately printed, 1931. New Bedford Free Public Library, Genealogy Room Collection.

Ferro, Maximilian L. *How to Love and Care for Your Old Building in New Bedford*. New Bedford, MA: City of New Bedford, Office of Historic Preservation, 1977.

Grieve, Robert, ed. *New Bedford Semi-Centennial Souvenir 1897*. Providence, RI: Journal of Commerce Company, 1897.

Harper, Dan. *Liberal Pilgrims: Varieties of Liberal Religious Experience in New Bedford, Massachusetts*. New Bedford, MA: Fish Island Books, 2009.

Heath, Kingston William. *The Patina of Place: The Cultural Weathering of a New England Industrial Landscape*. Knoxville: University of Tennessee Press, 2001.

Henricks, Gordon. *Albert Bierstadt: Painter of the American West*. New York: Harry N. Abrams Inc., in association with the Amon Carter Museum of Western Art, 1988.

Hodgin, Edwin Stanton. *One Hundred Years of Unitarianism in New Bedford, Massachusetts*. New Bedford, MA: First Congregational Society, 1924.

The Horticulturist and Journal of Rural Art and Rural Taste 4 (January 1850).

Hough, Henry Beetle. *Wamsutta of New Bedford, 1846–1946*. 1st ed. New Bedford, MA: Wamsutta Mills, 1946.

Hurd, D.H. *History of Bristol County, Massachusetts.* Philadelphia: J.H. Lewis & Company, 1883.

J.H. Beers & Co. *Representative Men and Old Families of Southeastern Massachusetts*. Chicago: J.H. Beers & Co., 1912.

Jones, Charles Henry. *Genealogy of the Rodman Family, 1620–1886.* N.p.: HardPress Publishing, n.d., print on demand.

Kugler, Richard C. *"New Bedford & Old Dartmouth: A Portrait of a Region's Past": A Bicentennial Exhibition of the Old Dartmouth Historical Society at the Whaling Museum in New Bedford, December 4, 1975–April 1976*. New Bedford, MA: Trustees of the Museum, 1975.

Lewis, Arthur H. *The Day They Shook the Plum Tree.* San Diego, CA: Harcourt, Brace & World, 1963.

McDevitt, Joseph Lawrence, Jr. "The House of Rotch Whaling Merchants of Massachusetts, 1734–1828." PhD diss., American University, 1978.

McKee, Harley J. Historic American Buildings Survey, 19 Irving Street. HABS No. Mass., 678, September 1961.

Medeiros, Peggi. "William J. Rotch Cottage." National Landmark Nomination Form. Available online.

Melville, Herman. *Moby Dick or The Whale.* New York: W.W. Norton & Co., 2002.

Morgan, Charles W. Unpublished diaries. Available online at Mystic Seaport.

Morning Mercury. New Bedford, Massachusetts, April 24, 1897, and November 2, 1908.

Old Dartmouth historical sketches. Available online at New Bedford Whaling Museum website.

Pease, Zephaniah W. *History of New Bedford.* Vols. 1, 2 and 3. New York: Lewis Historical Publishing Company, 1918.

Peck, Amelia, ed. *Alexander Jackson Davis: American Architect, 1803–1892*. New York: Rizzoli, 1992.

Puryear, Thomas W. *The Scholar Builders: Regional Architects of the American Renaissance, 1876–1913: An Exhibition*. North Dartmouth: University of Massachusetts at Dartmouth, 1987.

Representative Men of Old Families of Southeastern Massachusetts. Vol. 1. Chicago: J.H. Beers Company, 1912.

Ricketson, Daniel. *History of New Bedford, Bristol County, Massachusetts*. New Bedford, MA: published by the author, 1858.

———. *New Bedford of the Past*. Boston: Houghton Mifflin & Company, 1903.

Rodman, Samuel. *The Diary of Samuel Rodman: A New Bedford Chronicle of Thirty-Seven Years, 1821–1859*. Edited by Zephaniah W. Pease. New Bedford, MA: Reynolds de Walt, 1927.

Rotch, William James. Correspondence with Alexander Jackson Davis, April 16, 1845.

———. Correspondence with Alexander Jackson Davis, May 3, 1845, May 31, 1845, June 9, 1845, and June 12, 1845. A.J. Davis Papers, New York Historical Society.

Slack, Charles. *Hetty: The Genius and Madness of America's First Female Tycoon*. New York: HarperCollins Publishers, 2004.

Sparkes, Boyden, and Samuel Taylor Moore. *The Witch of Wall Street: Hetty Green*. Garden City, NY: Doubleday, Doran & Company Inc., 1935.

Topographical Atlas of Surveys Bristol County, Massachusetts. Philadelphia: Everts & Richards, 1895.

Unitarian Anniversaries 1708, 1795, 1808, 1838. First Congregational Society, New Bedford, Massachusetts. New Bedford Free Public Library, Genealogy Room Collections.

Whiffen, Marcus. *American Architecture Since 1780: A Guide to the Styles*. Cambridge: M.I.T. Press, Massachusetts Institute of Technology, 1969.

Whitman, Nicholas. *A Window Back: Photography in a Whaling Port*. N.p.: Spinner Publications Inc., 1994.

Worth, Henry B. *Ancient Landmarks of Old Dartmouth*. Manuscript in collection of the Old Dartmouth Historical Society.

———. "The Patrician Homes of New Bedford." *New Bedford Mercury One Hundredth Anniversary Supplement*, Wednesday, August 7, 1907.

Also studied were the photographs of Fred W. Palmer, New Bedford Free Public Library, Genealogy Room Collections.

NEWSPAPERS

Boston Cultivator. January 12, 1850.
Boston Daily Globe.
The Medley/New Bedford Marine Journal.
New Bedford Courier.
New Bedford Evening Journal.
(New Bedford) *Evening Standard.*
New Bedford Gazette.
New Bedford Mercury.
New Bedford Standard Times.
New York Times.
Whalemen's Shipping List New Bedford.

WEBSITES

Genealogy Bank. Historic Newspaper Collection. http://www.genealogybank.com/gbnk.

Massillon Memory, Rotch-Wales Collection, provides free online access to scanned images and transcriptions of significant materials from the history of Massillon, Ohio. It is primarily composed of the Thomas and Charity Rotch papers from the Massillon Public Library's Rotch-Wales Collection. http://massillonmemory.org/the-rotch-wales-papers.

New Bedford Whaling Museum. http://www.whalingmuseum.org.

Index

A

B

C

D

E

F

G

H

About the Author

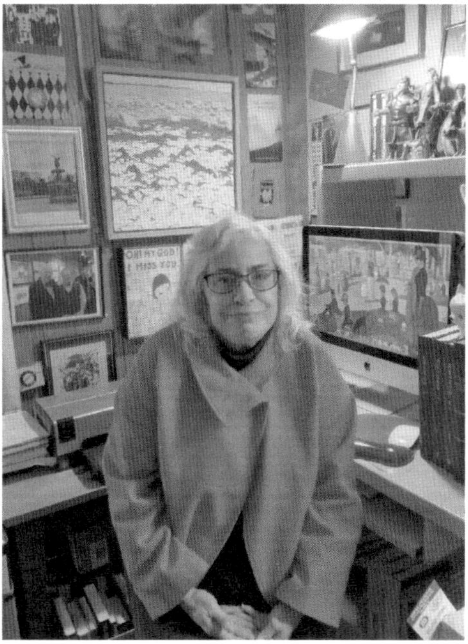

Peggi Medeiros. *Courtesy of Diane Gilbert, photographer.*

Peggi Medeiros is a research historian currently writing a column for the *New Bedford Standard Times* and blogging for the paper online. She was a contributing writer for *The* Charles W. Morgan *Returns to New Bedford* (produced by the *Standard-Times* in a magazine format; additional copies were distributed by the New Bedford Whaling Museum). She spoke at a special museum symposium as part of the *Morgan*'s return. In January 2014, Peggi presented a paper at the museum's The River and the Rail symposium. She is frequently a guest lecturer at the Rotch Jones House and Garden Museum and for the Dartmouth Historical Preservation Trust.

Peggi is a member of the New Bedford Whaling Museum and the clerk of the Dartmouth Historical Preservation Trust. As a historian, during the past thirty-eight years she has worked for the City of New Bedford, the Waterfront Historical Area League and the Swain School of Design and is currently the historian for the Wamsutta Club. She writes a monthly column on history for the club's members.